DIAMOND DUELS

DIAMOND DUELS
Baseball's Greatest Matchups

JOHN NOGOWSKI

LYONS
PRESS

Essex, Connecticut

An imprint of The Globe Pequot Publishing Group, Inc.
64 South Main St.
Essex, CT 06426
www.LyonsPress.com

Distributed by NATIONAL BOOK NETWORK

British Library Cataloguing in Publication Information available

Library of Congress Cataloging-in-Publication Data available

ISBN 978-1-4930-8482-1 (paper)
ISBN 978-1-4930-8483-8 (electronic)

CONTENTS

INTRODUCTION

A Closer Look at the Diamond's Most Historic Duels

OF ALL PROFESSIONAL SPORTS, BASEBALL REMAINS UNIQUE FOR ONE reason. The outcome of every single baseball game is determined by the results of a series of individual duels—at-bats—between a pitcher and a hitter over the course of nine innings. Sometimes, a few more innings, if necessary. We call these duels *matchups*.

Millions of words and thousands of books have been written about the grand old game and the sport's greatest players—including my own *Last Time Out*, my twice-revised book about the final major-league appearances of some of baseball's legends. But so far, there hasn't really been an up-close look at some of the game's greatest matchups, a deep examination of those dramatic pitcher-hitter battles that were played out on diamonds all over America throughout the years. If you're a baseball fan, you've already played them out in your mind.

How did Babe Ruth do against the fireballing Walter Johnson? What about his contemporary Ty Cobb? Who hit the most home runs off Nolan Ryan? (A: Will Clark, six.) Who gave up the most homers to Hank Aaron and Barry Bonds? How did Joe DiMaggio and Ted Williams fare against the best of their era? What middle-of-the-road pitchers were way too tough for some of the Hall of Fame's greatest hitters? What sorts of surprises will this up-close-and-personal look at these matchups reveal? What can we learn about the sport from taking a closer look at these historic duels on the diamond?

With the advent of the computer age and the modern technology that's infiltrated the game at levels you could not imagine, there isn't a manager in baseball who doesn't study these matchup numbers on a daily basis. We all know about them, too. That wasn't always the case.

Meet Ben Cantwell. A skinny right-handed junkballer from Milan, Tennessee, Cantwell had himself an 11-year major-league career (76–108). He's perhaps most noted for having one of the worst single-season won-lost records in history, posting a 4–25 record for the woeful (38–113) Boston Braves in 1935. Those Braves were also the team that saw Babe Ruth's final season. The Babe struggled through 28 games in the National League, hitting .181 with six homers, three of which came in a single game in Pittsburgh. Sadly, that was not his very last game like it should have been.

Cantwell wasn't always bad. Two years earlier, Cantwell was 20–10 with a 2.62 ERA for these same Boston Braves. But whether he was good or bad, despite what appears to be a pretty mediocre career, when it came to facing one of the greatest hitters in the history of the game, Cantwell was a combination of Christy Mathewson, Tom Seaver, and Sandy Koufax, without the strikeouts. When he matched up with the great Rogers Hornsby, to use the phrase coined by San Francisco Giants color man Duane Kuiper (or Mike Krukow, depends on who you ask), Cantwell had "ownage."

It's stunning. When you look at the career numbers of the great Hornsby, he of the .358 lifetime average and those seven batting titles, you can't help but notice his exceptional lifetime numbers against the top hurlers of his era. Facing the best in the game in his time, nobody could get Hornsby out. Look at these numbers against the top starters: Burleigh Grimes .343, Wilbur Cooper .391, Eppa Rixey .324, Grover Alexander .371, Rube Marquard .366, Guy Bush .442. Grimes, Rixey, Alexander, and Marquard were all Hall of Famers.

Though he only struck out more than 50 batters in a single season once (57 in 1933), with his assortment of curveballs, changeups, and

Rogers Hornsby vs. Ben Cantwell

Regular Season: 33 PA, .130/.333/.217, 0 HR, 1 K
Playoffs: 0 PA

Rogers Hornsby vs. Ben Cantwell: Batter vs. Pitcher

Rogers Hornsby vs. Ben Cantwell: Year-by-Year Totals E:

Rk	**Year**	**PA**	**AB**	**H**	**2B**	**3B**	**HR**	**RBI**	**BB**	**SO**	**BA**	**OBP**	**SLG**	**OPS**	**SH**	**SF**	**IBB**	**HBP**	**GIDP**
1	1928	5	3	1	1	0	0	0	2	0	.333	.600	.667	1.267	0	0	0	0	1
2	1929	23	15	2	1	0	0	2	5	0	.133	.348	.200	.548	0	2	1	1	1
3	1931	4	4	0	0	0	0	0	0	1	.000	.000	.000	.000	0	0	0	0	0
4	1933	1	1	0	0	0	0	0	0	0	.000	.000	.000	.000	0	0	0	0	0
	Totals	33	23	3	2	0	0	2	7	1	.130	.333	.217	.551	0	2	1	1	2

knuckleballs, Cantwell found a way to humble the great Hornsby, holding him to a stunning .130 batting average.

In 33 plate appearances, he surrendered only one extra-base hit to one of the game's greatest. The hit? A double to left in the third inning of a 9–2 loss at Wrigley Field near the end of Cantwell's career. That was it. And let's not forget that when Hornsby retired, he was fourth on the all-time home-run list behind Babe Ruth, Lou Gehrig, and Jimmie Foxx. By the way, Cantwell gave up 12 hits in that loss, which dropped his record that season to 4–11. Other guys didn't seem to have problems getting hits, but Hornsby couldn't hit him with a paddle. That's baseball.

Cantwell's "ownage" of Hornsby remains one of the fascinating elements of the sport. Regardless of how good a hitter a guy might be, there is always some pitcher out there who has his number. While to most of us, that particular pitcher might not have left his footprints on the sands of time, as A. J. Liebling might say, it doesn't matter. There is always somebody who can get you out, even if they tend to be very mortal among the regular players, guys who seemed to have no problem getting their raps.

Consider the case of St. Louis Cardinals Hall of Famer Stan "The Man" Musial. Over a remarkably consistent major-league baseball career, Musial was amazing. Why, the old guy got two hits in his big-league finale off one of the game's hardest throwers, Jim Maloney. By the way, those two hits gave Stan a perfect split on his hit totals home and away: 1,815 for each! It's clear that the great Cardinals outfielder seemed to be able to handle any pitcher's best stuff and did for a lot of years.

Like his fellow Cardinals great Hornsby, Musial's lifetime numbers against the cream of the National League starting pitching crop were remarkable: Facing Warren Spahn, Musial hit .321, Robin Roberts .384, Curt Simmons .364, Don Newcombe .349, and Carl Erskine .336. He even roughed up a couple of hard-throwing Dodgers Hall of Famers before he retired: Don Drysdale (.324) and a kid named Sandy Koufax (.342).

But when it came to Sam "Toothpick" Jones, a well-traveled former Negro Leagues right-handed hurler who went on to amass a

103–104 career mark for the Cardinals, Giants, Tigers, Indians, and Orioles, Musial might as well have given way to a pinch-hitter.

They dueled in National League parks for five years and Jones had "ownage" over the great Musial, holding the Hall of Famer to a paltry .122 batting average, some 209 points below his career mark of .331. Even the greats have an Achilles' heel.

The trouble with Jones started right away. Jones first faced Musial in 1955 holding him to 0-for-7 with two whiffs, then allowed a double in seven at-bats with two more Ks in '56. It got worse. He didn't face Stan for three years but didn't lose his mastery. He held Stan to a very sad 1-for-18 in 1959. In fact, Jones held him hitless for most of that 1959 season, allowing only a two-run, eighth-inning single in a 5–2 Cardinal loss very late in the year.

Over the next two years, Stan figured him out a little bit better, collecting four singles in 17 at-bats combined in 1960 and 1961 as both of their careers wound down. Still, looking at the overall picture, it's hard to imagine Stan Musial batting .122 against anybody.

There are times when these numbers tell you a lot about the development of a player. Kansas City's great Hall of Famer George Brett, for example, could not hit the flame-throwing Hall of Famer Nolan Ryan with a boat oar. At first.

As a rookie, Ryan made mincemeat of the sweet-swinging Brett, holding him 0-for-21 (with six strikeouts) in 1974, Brett's first full season. Brett managed a couple of hits in '75 and four more (in 15 at-bats) in 1976, then struggled to a 1-of-8 in 1977. Still pretty lousy for an eventual Hall of Famer.

Then it clicked. From 1978 until the end of his career, Brett batted .407 against the fireballing Ryan. While he never reached him for a homer, Brett did make consistent contact. After whiffing 13 times in his first 49 at-bats, Brett never struck out more than twice in a year in the next seven seasons against the game's great strikeout king. He had Nolan figured out. He learned how to prevail in the matchup.

Sometimes, one player's consistency seems off the charts. The great Ted Williams, for example, had a career batting average of .344 over his long career. Facing the dominant pitcher of his era, Bob Feller, Teddy

Ballgame managed to hit, you guessed it, exactly .344. But their matchup had some interesting shifts.

Feller pounced on the rookie in Williams's first season, holding him to 2-for-18 (both extra-base hits, a double and triple). From there, other than an unusual 0-for-8 in 1947, Williams figured out how to dominate the matchup, giving Feller all kinds of trouble, hitting almost .400 (.398) including five home runs and a double in his final 13 at-bats against the Cleveland ace. Imagine that, the final 13 times he faced the Hall of Famer, Williams touched him for five home runs and a double, getting his career mark up to his standard—.344.

The idea for a deeper look at these historic pitcher-hitter matchups came from a conversation I had with my favorite player, my son, John, who had made The Show as a first baseman with the St. Louis Cardinals in 2020 and 2021 and the Pittsburgh Pirates in 2021. John was playing winter ball in the Dominican Republic and happened to mention that the pitching coach for his team was former Dodgers reliever Phil Regan. Phil Regan! I knew that name. But wasn't he in his 80s?

After his remarkable 14–1 season in 1966, Regan earned the nickname "The Vulture" from Sandy Koufax for his knack for earning victories thanks to late-inning rallies by Dodgers hitters. So, the starter might work seven great innings, leave with the score tied or trailing, and the Dodgers would rally and give Regan the victory. All these years later, Regan was still in the game, working as a pitching coach for the Toros Del Este. He and John were to go play golf, so Dad did a little research to give John some conversational fodder.

In one start for the Detroit Tigers on August 28, 1960, pitching against the New York Yankees, Regan allowed four home runs (Dale Long, Johnny Blanchard, Mickey Mantle, Yogi Berra) in a 5–2 loss. Digging a little further, in Regan's matchups with Roberto Clemente, Roberto had "ownage" batting .533 with a home run, two doubles, and three triples. "I just couldn't get him out," he told John.

Researching all this, I wondered how some of the players I watched growing up did in these notable matchups. Boston's Carl Yastrzemski, my favorite player before John came along, was a left-handed hitter and as I watched his career progress, I could see Yaz struggled against some left-handed pitchers. Lots of lefties can't hit lefties. Seeing that ball breaking away from them is tough to handle. But you would figure that over time, you'd figure it out.

Not so. Yaz, who played for 23 seasons and had more big-league at-bats than just about everybody in the history of the game, never quite figured out how to hit left-handed pitching consistently. When I looked at his numbers, I was stunned. There were many lefties who "owned" him.

A fastball hitter, Yaz rocked Nolan Ryan's overpowering fastball to a .340 clip with four homers. Yaz also tattooed Blue Moon Odom for a .447 average and five home runs. He drilled veteran Robin Roberts for a .444 average, slammed six homers off Denny McLain (.291) and seven off Pat Dobson (.265), all righties. While he did hit seven homers off lefty Mickey Lolich, Yaz didn't hit much else (.226). That was a hint of what was to come.

Against some of the game's better pitchers, Yaz was pretty ordinary or worse. Gaylord Perry held him to .161 with no home runs. When facing Jim Palmer (.243, four homers), Catfish Hunter (.219, four homers), Sam McDowell (.191, one homer), or Vida Blue (.204, zero homers), he looked like just another guy. Like a lot of players did against the game's greatest.

So, if you're going to have a Hall of Fame career, you'd better murder the regular old pitchers. And Yaz did, for the most part. But when teams went to the bullpen for that lefty, sometimes Yaz was lost. One particular reliever had a special kind of "ownage" of Yastrzemski, so much so, you wondered if it was hard for Yaz to even walk up to the plate to face him.

Reliever Darold Knowles, who had a 16-year-career for the Washington Senators, Oakland A's, and other teams, posted a 66–74 mark with only eight starts, held the Hall of Famer to a brutal 2-for-26 (.077). The only two hits Yaz got off Knowles were an RBI single in 1969—after Knowles held him 0-for-6 with three whiffs. Yaz's only other hit came three years later after going 17 straight at-bats without a hit (eight whiffs, two game-enders!). Yaz dumped an opposite-field flare.

The question is, would Red Sox managers let Yaz face Knowles in a key situation late in a game now? They all have that information waiting for them every game, probably didn't then. Has it helped? How has the knowledge of these matchups changed baseball?

Carl Yastrzemski vs. Darold Knowles

Regular Season: 36 PA , .077/.222/.077, 0 HR, 11 K
Playoffs: 0 PA

Carl Yastrzemski vs. Darold Knowles: Batter vs. Pitcher

Carl Yastrzemski vs. Darold Knowles: Year-by-Year Totals

Regular Season																		
Rk	Year	PA	AB	H	2B	3B	HR	RBI	BB	SO	BA	OBP	SLG	OPS	SH	SF	IBB	HBP	GIDP
1	1965	1	1	0	0	0	0	0	0	0	.000	.000	.000	.000	0	0	0	0	0
2	1967	4	2	0	0	0	0	0	2	1	.000	.500	.000	.500	0	0	0	0	0
3	1968	2	1	0	0	0	0	1	0	1	.000	.000	.000	.000	0	1	0	0	0
4	1969	4	4	1	0	0	0	1	0	2	.250	.250	.250	.500	0	0	0	0	0
5	1970	6	6	0	0	0	0	0	0	3	.000	.000	.000	.000	0	0	0	0	0
6	1971	4	3	0	0	0	0	1	0	3	.000	.000	.000	.000	0	1	0	0	0
7	1972	4	1	0	0	0	0	2	2	0	.000	.500	.000	.500	0	1	0	0	0
8	1973	5	4	1	0	0	0	0	1	1	.250	.400	.250	.650	0	0	0	0	0
9	1974	3	2	0	0	0	0	0	1	0	.000	.333	.000	.333	0	0	0	0	0
10	1977	3	2	0	0	0	0	1	0	0	.000	.000	.000	.000	0	1	0	0	0
	Totals	36	26	2	0	0	0	6	6	11	.077	.222	.077	.299	0	4	0	0	0

In *Diamond Duels: Baseball's Greatest Matchups*, we'll take a close look at some of baseball's greatest hitters and the pitchers who gave them trouble, as well as some of the game's finest pitchers and the hitters they struggled with. We'll also examine how, for some of the game's best, their fortunes against certain pitchers—or hitters—changed over time. And finally, we'll examine how the game itself has changed. And it *has* changed—a lot.

There was a time, for example, when, as a hitter, you could count on seeing a starting pitcher for at least three at-bats per game. Over the course of a long career, there was a lot of history, a set of matchup experiences to draw on. It might not have been written down, but it ran through the hitter's mind. "He tries to get me out with his slider" or "He always goes to that pitch with two strikes." Nowadays, there are hard numbers for every manager (and pitcher!) to use to his advantage.

One of the biggest indications for me of how the game has changed was uncovering the matchup between two 20-year National League veterans, Stan Musial and Warren Spahn. Musial, a 22-year vet, faced off against the 21-year Hall of Famer a staggering 356 times! Imagine facing one hitter over 350 times.

Though facing a fellow lefty, Musial started his run with two straight hits off Spahn and seemed to have the upper hand for most of his long career, clubbing 15 homers off Spahn, the most he hit off any one pitcher.

Spahn did manage to equalize things down the stretch, holding Musial to just one homer over the final six years of their matchup. And there were a few years (four) he held Musial under .200. But Stan wound up hitting .321 against Spahnie, quite a number against a Hall of Famer.

When you contrast Stan's numbers with Derek Jeter, who started for the New York Yankees for 20 years, you see how the game has evolved. Even with his long American League career, Jeter had 100 or more at-bats against just three pitchers—the late Boston knuckleballer Tim Wakefield, the late Roy Halladay, and ex-Ray and Royal James Shields.

Unlike Musial, Ted Williams, Babe Ruth, and Joe DiMaggio, players from the earlier days, Jeter didn't get to see starters for that third or fourth at-bat. Modern-day hitters have to get used to seeing a lot of arms, each one often for just a single at-bat. And with the increasing emphasis on velocity or the focus on one unhittable pitch which the hurler might be called on to toss for a single inning, the old cat-and-mouse game between the hitter and pitcher has changed, maybe forever.

The more recent you go, the fewer at-bats players get against a particular hurler. Take a look at current players, like the Los Angeles Angels' Mike Trout. Trout had 88 plate appearances against Seattle ace Félix Hernández (.352, eight homers), but otherwise hasn't faced any pitcher more than 60 times. That's a lot less information than Stan Musial got to work with.

So, sit back and join me as we take a look through some of the most interesting matchups in the record books. Wandering through those long-ago box scores, there are some compelling stories. By the way, the stats collected here are courtesy of Stathead on the Baseball-Reference. com website. Enjoy the ride.

CHAPTER ONE

Stan Musial vs. Warren Spahn: An Epic Showdown

Warren Spahn (L) vs. Stan Musial (L)

CAREER MATCHUP: 1946–1963

Musial had 356 trips to the plate against Spahn.

Avg.-.321 (98-for-305), 6 2B, 3 3B, 15 HR, 47 RBIs, 48 BB, 30 K

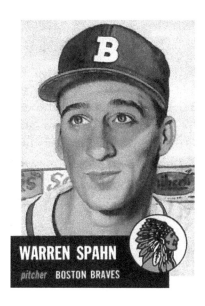

There might have been a chuckle on the St. Louis Cardinals bench when they saw the Boston Braves bring in a skinny left-hander for mop-up duty on a mid-June afternoon at Braves Field. The Cards were up 8–4. On that June afternoon, neither Stan Musial, kneeling in the on-deck circle nor the slender left-hander with the elaborate peacock's tail pitching delivery, arms and legs flying all over the place, could have imagined that each one would wind up as baseball immortals.

The 25-year-old Musial was on his way to an MVP season (.365, 50 doubles, 10 triples, 16 homers, 103 RBIs) while Braves manager Billy Southworth wanted to get a look at this 25-year-old lefty who'd spent the last three years in the 277th Engineer Combat Battalion, earning a Bronze Star for his efforts in the Battle of the Bulge.

Spahn's elegant windup—both arms swinging behind him, then up over his head, high leg kick, and an over-the-top delivery—was certainly stylish, but could he get guys out? He got Erv Dusak to bounce one to Billy Herman, but Herman threw the ball away. Next up, Stan Musial.

Hunched in the far corner of the left-hand batter's box, Musial looked a bit like a cat, all coiled to strike. Spahn fired and Musial spanked the ball into right field and Dusak scampered to third. Enos Slaughter lofted a sacrifice fly to center, but Spahn worked out of further trouble, getting Whitey Kurowski to pop out and Buster Adams to fly to right. He was in the big leagues now.

Spahn surrendered a single to Musial again in the eighth inning but allowed no more runs. Their diamond duel had begun. For the next 18 summers, they battled between the white lines, sometimes Stan getting the edge, Spahnie battling back.

Musial had the early edge. In '47, Stan hit a couple of homers and was walked seven times. He owned '48, ripping Spahn with a .526 average with two more homers, a double and triple.

Then Spahn took over and in '49, held Musial to a double in his first 14 at-bats, then allowed a ninth-inning home run on June 17, another homer on August 28, but for the year, he held him to .200, a win. In 1950, Spahn held Musial to .267 and allowed a single home run. Stan battled back and batted over .300 in three of the next four years against Spahn, including a sizzling 1954 (.444, three doubles, one triple, two home runs).

Spahn Speaks Up—and Regrets It

It might have been at that point that Spahn regretted his earlier indiscretion. Talking with the *New York Times*' Arthur Daley years later, he remembered hollering in to Musial from the mound in those early days.

"'Listen, son,' Spahn told him. 'You're never going to become a good hitter unless you change that silly-looking batting stance.' Musial laughed so hard he missed the next pitch."

Things seemed to change Spahn's way in 1956, when he was en route to his seventh 20-win season. He finally seemed to find a way to shut the Musial train down. Other than a harmless sixth-inning home run back in April, Spahn was finally getting him out. Stan was a rough 1-for-16 for the season heading into Spahn's final start of the season, on September 29.

Hooked up in a pitching duel with the Cardinals' Herm Wehmeier, the two hurlers battled into the 12th inning, unthinkable today. Starting the 12th, Spahn got Alvin Dark to bounce out and up came Musial, who was pretty much 0-for-the-year against him. Next thing you knew, Musial's bat flashed, there was a line shot down the right field line, and Stan had himself a double! The hit raised his season average against Spahn to .118. When Whitey Kurowski lashed a double to left, Musial came around to score, handing Spahn a 2–1 loss in his regular-season finale.

After they both had retired, Musial offered kind words about the lefty. "Facing Warren was the greatest challenge I knew because this man was a pitching scientist, an artist with imagination." Years later, Musial, working for Cardinals management, actually hired Spahn to manage the Cardinals' Triple-A team.

"Musial," Spahn said once, "was the hardest man to fool. He had an average of .321 against me, but I never brooded when Stan hit me. The time to worry was when some .250 hitter knocked my cap off with a line drive."

Spahn's wry remark on Musial's retirement had a little wrinkle to it. "I don't know how anyone can miss a toothache, but I'm going to miss you." Most of us thought Spahn's pain would have been located a little lower.

After that end-of-the-season loss and that Musial double, their duel reverted to the way it began. Musial ruled '57 (.438, four doubles, one homer) and '58 (.462). Over the next five seasons, Spahn faced Musial fewer than 10 times each season and Spahn had the edge in three out of five seasons (.167, .125, .143). In one bold moment in 1957, Spahn even had the last laugh.

In mid-August, Spahn found himself in a difficult situation. The Cardinals, losers of nine in a row, were desperate to stay in the pennant race while Spahn's Braves, winners of 10 straight, had a 7½-game lead.

Two days after Spahn had pitched a complete game win over Cincinnati, Braves manager Fred Haney brought the lefty on in relief in the ninth with the score tied 3–3 to face left-handed hitter Wally Moon. Reds manager Fred Hutchinson, seeing Spahn come in, made his own

Stan Musial vs. Warren Spahn: Batter vs. Pitcher

Stan Musial vs. Warren Spahn: Year-by-Year Totals   Export Data

Regular Season

Rk	Year	PA	AB	H	2B	3B	HR	RBI	BB	SO	BA	OBP	SLG	OPS	SH	SF	IBB	HBP	GIDP
1	1946	8	7	3	0	0	0	1	1	1	.429	.500	.429	.929	0	0	0	0	0
2	1947	24	17	5	0	0	2	3	7	1	.294	.500	.647	1.147	0	0	0	0	0
3	1948	23	19	10	1	1	2	4	4	1	.526	.609	1.000	1.609	0	0	0	0	0
4	1949	26	25	5	2	0	2	5	1	1	.200	.231	.520	.751	0	0	0	0	1
5	1950	17	15	4	0	1	1	3	2	2	.267	.353	.600	.953	0	0	0	0	1
6	1951	28	22	8	0	1	1	4	6	2	.364	.500	.591	1.091	0	0	0	0	0
7	1952	30	27	9	1	0	2	5	3	3	.333	.400	.593	.993	0	0	0	0	0
8	1953	29	27	7	1	1	0	1	2	2	.259	.310	.370	.681	0	0	0	0	0
9	1954	32	27	12	3	1	2	4	5	3	.444	.531	.852	1.383	0	0	0	0	0
10	1955	25	21	7	2	0	0	1	3	4	.333	.417	.429	.845	1	0	0	0	0
11	1956	20	17	2	1	0	1	4	3	3	.118	.250	.353	.603	0	0	0	0	0
12	1957	21	16	7	4	0	1	4	4	2	.438	.571	.875	1.446	0	0	0	1	1
13	1958	16	13	6	2	0	0	1	3	0	.462	.563	.615	1.178	0	0	0	0	0
14	1959	8	6	1	0	0	0	0	2	0	.167	.375	.167	.542	0	0	0	0	0
15	1960	26	23	7	3	0	1	6	2	3	.304	.385	.565	.950	0	0	0	1	0
16	1961	8	8	1	0	1	0	0	0	0	.125	.125	.375	.500	0	0	0	0	0
17	1962	7	7	1	0	0	0	0	0	2	.143	.143	.143	.286	0	0	0	0	0
18	1963	8	8	3	1	0	0	1	0	0	.375	.375	.500	.875	0	0	0	0	0
	Totals	356	305	98	21	6	15	47	48	30	.321	.417	.577	.994	1	0	0	2	3

countermove, sending up Del Ennis. To the surprise of everyone, including Ennis, Spahn called for an intentional walk. He wanted to face the next guy. Yes, Stan Musial.

Sure enough, Spahn knew what he was doing. He got Musial to rap into a double play and the Braves went on to win in 11 innings.

In their swan song year of 1963, Musial managed a pair of hits in Spahn's 3–1 loss to Lew Burdette on a Thursday afternoon in July. He only had one last at-bat against the lefty on a Friday night in September in Busch Stadium.

And Spahn, a 20-game winner for the final time that season, didn't have it on this night and got bombed. In the first, Musial doubled, and a Ken Boyer homer staked the Cards to a 2–0 lead. And the hits kept on coming and Spahn couldn't get out of the second. When opposing pitcher Curt Simmons reached him for a double, he got the hook.

History does not record Spahn's reaction to that last double by the opposing pitcher. But it might have been this: *At least it wasn't that damn Musial.*

CHAPTER TWO

The Big Train Faces Ty and The Babe

Walter Johnson (R) vs. Ty Cobb (L) and Babe Ruth (L)

CAREER MATCHUP: COBB and RUTH vs. WALTER JOHNSON

COBB (1917 to 1926) 92 trips to the plate: .398 (33-for-83), 7 2B, 3 3B, 0 HR, 14 RBIs, 9 BB, 5 K

RUTH (1915 to 1927) 128 trips to the plate:.280 (38-for-102), 8 2B, 2 3B, 7 HR, 20 RBIs, 19 BB, 25 K

THEY WERE THE YIN AND YANG OF THE AMERICAN LEAGUE IN THE early days of major-league baseball. Tyrus Raymond Cobb, the firebrand hands-apart batting wizard who wound up with the game's highest lifetime average of .366 and George Herman Ruth, the ultimate swing-from-the-heels natural home run king who transformed the sport and caught the imagination of the nation, two players who were complete opposites in every way.

For a good chunk of their careers, they shared the national baseball stage with the greatest pitcher of their time, the Washington Senators' whip-armed Walter Johnson. There wasn't quite anyone like Johnson, firing unhittable fastballs for 20 seasons, winning 417 games for a not-very strong franchise, amassing a still-record 110 shutouts, nine times recording an ERA under 2.00, twice fanning over 300 men in a season in a time when that just wasn't done.

Walter Johnson

Looking back, much has been made of Cobb's impressive .398 average against the great Johnson and those numbers are undeniable. But a closer look shows that that career mark was largely built on a couple of sensational seasons—1921 and 1922—when Johnson, then 33, was starting to feel the effects of all those innings and all those seasons. In 1921, Johnson was coming off his worst season (8–10, 3.13 ERA, only 143.2 innings) and went 17–14 with a then-career high 3.51 ERA, having allowed 265 hits in 264 innings, a long way from his usual standard. He slipped a little more in 1922, falling to 15–16, 2.99 ERA, 283 hits allowed in 280 innings. Not the usual numbers.

With that as context, seeing Cobb collect 11 hits in 15 at-bats in 1921 (.733 with one double and one triple) wasn't all that surprising. When you look closer at those 15 at-bats, the shine comes off that achievement even more.

In order, here's Cobb's 15 at-bats that season: pop fly single to short right field, walk, pop fly to deep third base, groundout, infield hit to first base, triple to right field, single to left field, walk, infield hit to second base, bunt single, groundball single to center, double to right-center, ground single to right, groundout, single to right, groundout, flyout. What is it? Pesky.

Yeah, he drove in six runs, but Johnson won three times against the Tigers, lost four.

The next season, it was more of the same, seven hits in 12 at-bats, two doubles, one triple, four RBIs as Johnson went 1–3 vs. the Tigers. So, if you take away that remarkable two-season run (18-for-27, .667), Cobb's numbers in the other seven seasons he faced Johnson were just okay—15-for-56, .268. Nothing to brag about.

For Ruth, who began as a pitcher-hitter for the Boston Red Sox, his first full season as a regular player was 1919 and he did well against Johnson, with a .400 mark, adding a double and triple. Dealt to the Yankees in 1920, Ruth swatted 54 homers but none against Johnson, who held him to a pair of doubles and a .429 average that season. The Yankees beat Johnson three of the four times they faced him.

It wasn't until 1921 that Ruth connected for his first home run off Johnson in his first at-bat against him on April 25, then another on May 7, and a third on June 25. Ruth hit .389 with four RBIs and five walks, making his mark in the American League. Johnson went 3–2 against the Yanks that year and Ruth went on to clobber 59 home runs, then an American League record.

In Ruth's star-crossed 1922 season, Johnson was able to toy with him, holding him to .182 (4-for-24) with a lone homer, a solo shot on August 29, a 3–1 Yankee win. That was the year Ruth was suspended six weeks for barnstorming in the offseason, losing his World Series share ($3,500). He also got suspended twice more for arguing with umpires and throwing dirt on them.

Ruth rebounded over the next two seasons (1923 and 1924) against the fading Senators star, going 10-for-19 (.526) with a couple more homers, three doubles, and a triple. And they shared a historic moment in 1925, the year of "The Bellyache Heard 'Round the World" when Ruth was out for two months with an abscess and wasn't able to return to the lineup until June 1. And who did he end up facing? Walter Johnson.

Johnson's Senators, who had shocked the world by winning the 1924 World Series, thanks in part to Johnson's dramatic relief appearance in Game 7, were playing quite well. They began the month of June in second place while the struggling Yankees were trying to adjust to life without Ruth in the lineup. As a result, Yankee fans weren't exactly enthused about their team and only about 10,000 fans showed up for the Monday afternoon showdown, even though it was advertised that The Babe was returning to the lineup.

Ruth came up against Johnson in the second inning and nubbed a weak grounder back to him. Later, he ripped a long foul to right field, then walked. Further on into the game, after being thrown out at the plate trying to score on a Bob Meusel double following that walk, Ruth fell down in right field while snagging a Joe Judge liner, and manager Miller Huggins took him out of the game. Johnson went on to win, 5–3.

In 1926, Ruth turned it up against the fading Johnson with three doubles, a homer, and a .462 average. Johnson bowed out after the 1927 season. He fanned Ruth one more time that year, then surrendered a single to him, working four innings in relief in a 12–1 Senators loss in June. But he had one more connection to The Babe.

It was September 30, the next-to-last game of the regular season. Johnson's days as a starter were gone, like his arm. He was seated on the bench as young lefty Tom Zachary stood on the hill at Yankee Stadium, facing the formidable Yankees featuring Ruth and Lou Gehrig, one of the mighty teams in baseball history, who were on their way to winning 110 games. Zachary had a goal. Ruth had swatted 59 homers, matching his record 1921 total and with two games to go, he wanted to get to 60.

Zachary was just as determined not to let that happen. He walked Ruth in the first, surrendered a ground single to right field in the fourth, and another ground single in the sixth. The fans were loud when Ruth

	Babe Ruth	Ty Cobb	Walter Johnson
Overall Stats			
WAR	**182.6**	151.5	165.1
G	2503	**3034**	802
PA	10627	**13103**	2533
H	2873	**4189**	547
HR	**714**	117	24
RBI	**2214**	1944	255
SB	123	**897**	13
BA	.342	**.366**	.235
OBP	**.474**	.433	.274
SLG	**.690**	.512	.342
OPS	**1.164**	.944	.616
OPS+	**206**	168	76
Awards & Honors			
Hall of Fame	✓	✓	✓
Championships	7		1
All-Star	2		
MVP	1	1	2
Batting Title	1	12	
ERA Title	1		5
Triple Crown		1	3

came up for the last time in the eighth, the score tied 2–2, Mark Koenig on third after he had hit a triple.

Zachary fired a fastball low and away and Ruth picked it off his shoe tops and launched it into the right field seats for number 60 and a 4–2 Yankee lead. Ruth had his 60th and the New York crowd went wild. When it came to the top of the ninth, who did fate have due to come up? Young Tom Zachary. So, Senators manager Bucky Harris had pity for the young hurler and called on a future Hall of Famer, a guy who had actually been used a pinch-hitter several times throughout his career.

Walter Johnson stepped up for the final time he was on a major-league field and lifted a flyball that had to go to only one guy. Sure enough, Babe Ruth reached up and caught it to end the game and the great career of Walter Johnson.

Chapter Three

Whitey Ford: Handle with Care

Whitey Ford was not only the New York Yankees' winningest pitcher of all time, he was one of the few that was actually homegrown. As the game's wealthiest franchise, the Yankees have always been a team well known for renting some of the game's great pitchers, hurlers who may have cut their teeth with other organizations and then came to the Yankees to cash in.

The list of Yankee mercenary hurlers is a long and distinguished one—Catfish Hunter, Roger Clemens, Randy Johnson, CC Sabathia, Mike Mussina, Luis Tiant, Mike Torrez, Goose Gossage, David Wells, David Cone, and Sparky Lyle among others.

You could even include Babe Ruth on that list. You don't hear much about it, but Ruth actually did pitch for the Yankees—twice in 1921, once in 1930 and once more in 1933, winning four games in all. He even struck out Ty Cobb.

Ford, on the other hand, started his career and ended it as a Yankee. His arm ailing, he threw just one inning of his final start in Detroit on May 21, 1967 in the first game of a doubleheader. Ford walked into the dugout, told Yankee manager Ralph Houk he was done, and flew back home to New York. That was that.

It was a great career, certainly. Ford's lifetime mark of 236–106 got him into baseball's Hall of Fame with no questions asked. His Yankees appeared in 11 World Series over his career, and his 22 World Series starts, 10 Series victories, and 94 strikeouts in 146 Series innings are totals that will never be challenged.

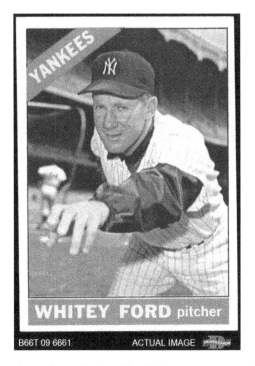

WHITEY FORD pitcher

B66T 09 6661   ACTUAL IMAGE

When you take a closer look at Ford's long career, you find some surprises. It's not hard to find former Yankees who'll say "if you had to win one game, Whitey Ford is the guy." But how does Whitey Ford match up *with history?* Was that actually the case? No!

Despite many opportunities, he *never* was the guy to pitch the deciding game of any one of those many World Series—with the "what-the-hell" exception of Game 4 of the 1950 World Series against Philadelphia in Ford's rookie year.

In that case, the Yankees were up, 3–0, and knew the Phillies were overmatched. That ended up being Whitey's only deciding-game performance. And looking back, he had several other opportunities. It is surprising to see that, considering Ford is someone who holds so many World Series records.

Now, Yankee manager Casey Stengel *did* have him warm up in the first inning of Game 7 against the Brooklyn Dodgers in 1956 when surprise starter Johnny Kucks gave up a walk and a first-inning single at

Ebbets Field. Stengel *did* have Ford trot down to the bullpen and warm up during the seventh inning of Game 7 against the Pittsburgh Pirates four years later, even though he pitched a complete game the day before. He sat him down after a few throws, and two innings later, Bill Mazeroski's homer off Ralph Terry gave the Pirates the World Series title. But he never came in either game.

For a large part of his career while Casey Stengel was his manager, who Ford started against and where he pitched was carefully and sometimes, curiously managed. And nobody ever says much about it.

Whitey Ford was a most effective starting pitcher for the New York Yankees from 1953 through 1965. He pitched parts of two more seasons but was just 4–9 in his final two seasons.

When you look at his career numbers, it's the Casey Stengel years—1953 to 1960—that make you stop and look. Ford's starts were so carefully managed, you had to wonder. What was Casey afraid of?

Looking back, Ford had just a dozen starts at Boston's Fenway Park across his career, posting an ERA of 6.16. Under Stengel, he faced Boston 17 times, but almost always in New York. Casey had him pitch just five times at Fenway Park. He had just 42 starts against Boston for his whole career with almost twice as many against the White Sox, starting 73 games. Think about that; 73 against the White Sox, 42 against the Red Sox. That's a big difference, isn't it?

Those career starts are revealing. Whitey had 64 starts against the Orioles, 57 against the Twins and Indians, but just 47 against the Tigers.

Year-By-Year: BOS-Fenway Pk   Permanent Link   Click Year to see all of year's splits

I Year	W	L	W-L%	ERA	G	GS	GF	CG	SHO	SV	IP	H	R	ER	HR	BB	IBB	SO	HBP	BK	WP	BF	WHIP	SO9	SO/W
1950	0	0		10.38	3	0	2	0	0	0	8.2	16	12	10	1	8	0	6	0	0		50	2.769	6.2	0.75
1953	1	0	1.000	11.81	1	1	0	0	0	0	5.1	9	7	7	0	6	0	1	0	0		30	2.813	1.7	0.17
1954	0	1	.000	6.75	1	0	1	0	0	0	2.2	2	2	2	0	3	0	5	0	0		13	1.875	16.9	1.67
1955	0	0		3.38	1	0	1	0	0	1	2.2	1	1	1	1	1	0	3	0	0		9	0.750	10.1	3.00
1956	2	0	1.000	2.00	2	2	0	2	0	0	18.0	14	4	4	1	5	0	9	0	0		69	1.056	4.5	1.80
1957	0	1	.000	27.00	1	1	0	0	0	0	1.0	3	3	3	0	2	1	0	0	0		8	5.000	0.0	0.00
1959	1	1	.500	4.50	2	1	1	0	0	0	6.0	10	5	3	0	2	1	5	0	0		30	2.000	7.5	2.50
1960	0	0		7.36	1	0	0	0	0	0	3.2	3	3	3	1	3	1	2	0	0		17	1.636	4.9	0.67
1961	1	1	.500	6.48	3	3	0	0	0	0	16.2	20	12	12	3	12	1	15	0	0		76	1.920	8.1	1.25
1962	0	1	.000	4.50	1	1	0	0	0	0	6.0	9	3	3	0	4	0	3	0	0		32	2.167	4.5	0.75
1963	1	0	1.000	6.00	1	1	0	0	0	0	6.0	8	4	4	1	1	0	1	0	0		24	1.500	1.5	1.00
1965	1	1	.500	6.55	2	2	0	0	0	0	11.0	15	9	8	2	5	0	5	0	0		52	1.818	4.1	1.00
Career	7	6	.538	6.16	19	12	5	2	0	1	87.2	110	65	60	10	52	4	55	0	0		410	1.848	5.6	1.06

Just 42 vs. archrival Boston? Only 47 vs. the Tigers? Why the difference? He was pitching for the mighty Yankees, after all. It wasn't like they weren't going to give him some runs. Does this make us reassess Ford's career?

Stengel was convinced that Ford would only pitch against the Red Sox at spacious Yankee Stadium. In fact, Boston's great star Ted Williams, who hit .378 lifetime against Ford, managed only one career home run off him, that a pinch-hit job on September 27, 1957, a game at Yankee Stadium where Ford was up 7–0 in the ninth inning.

Though statistical breakdowns against a particular pitcher weren't common in those days, Stengel and later Ralph Houk must have known some of Boston's other top hitters—Jackie Jensen (.321), Carl Yastrzemski (.296), Eddie Bressoud (.368), Ken Harrelson (.391), Tony Conigliaro (.364), and Vern Stephens (.450)—had great numbers against the crafty lefty. So, for the most part, Stengel kept him from the Fenway mound.

As noted, the team Casey *would* let Ford pitch against was the Chicago White Sox. Since Ford had 73 lifetime starts against the ChiSox, it's not surprising that when you run down the list of how American League batters fared against #16 over his long career, those players with the most at-bats against him are almost all former White Sox. Here's the top of his list: Nellie Fox (201 plate appearances, .268); Luis Aparicio (178, .234); Minnie Minoso (169, .262); Al Smith (169, .262); Sherm Lollar (125, .269); Jim Landis (119, .229); Chico Carrasquel (114, .255).

Whether it was to control their running game, or Stengel's insistence in pitching him in a big ballpark, Stengel started Ford vs. the White Sox 49 times over those seven years he ran the club, way more than against any other team.

Let's look at Ford's starts under Stengel. In the 1957 season, for example, Ford started seven games against the White Sox, five against the Senators, five against the Orioles, one against Kansas City, two against the Tribe, and only four against Boston, three of those at Yankee Stadium.

When he did get a start at Fenway on August 14, he couldn't get through the second inning, giving Ted Williams an intentional walk in the first inning! He went 11–5 that season.

The 1958 season was similar; Ford had just one start against the archrival Red Sox at Yankee Stadium on August 8, a 2–0 shutout. That season, he had six starts against the White Sox including a game where he struck out six hitters in a row, five starts against the Tribe, five against Kansas City, four against the Senators, and four against the Orioles. Just one against the Tigers, one againsBoston en route to a 14–7 record. Interesting, isn't it? If you're the team's ace, you only face the Red Sox once? In an entire season?

Playing for such a dynamic, high-scoring team, you would have expected more decisions from him, wouldn't you? Maybe that was good managing; the Yankees sure did win a lot of games. But when you think of an ace, you don't expect a manager to say, "Naw, we'll pitch you Tuesday in Chicago instead of Sunday in Boston."

WORLD SERIES WONDER?

While Ford's World Series numbers are extraordinary and likely will never be approached, what remains surprising is when it came to selecting a pitcher for what should have been the decisive game of those Series, Casey Stengel and later, Ralph Houk always seemed to pick someone else. Normally, when you have an ace, you usually give him the start in Game 1 of the World Series, figuring that he can likely come back at least once more and maybe even be around for a Game 7.

As baseball fans know, pitchers like Bob Gibson, Lew Burdette, Mickey Lolich, Christy Mathewson, and Randy Johnson have been able to win three games in a single World Series. Neither Stengel nor Ralph Houk ever gave Whitey Ford that chance—even with all the World Series opportunities he had.

Stengel's decision in 1960 to start Art Ditmar in Game 1 instead of Ford ended up costing the Yankees another title in the minds of many. Ditmar was routed in his two starts, while Ford threw a pair of shutouts against the Pirates.

"That was the only time I was mad at Casey," Ford told Fay Vincent in his book *We Would Have Played for Nothing*. "I didn't let him know I was mad but I was really annoyed that he did that . . . you know I would have had a chance to pitch three games."

"There never had been a Series as wacky as this one," teammate Bobby Richardson told the *New York Times* after the Yankees' stunning defeat. "It also left Casey's decision to hold back Ford even more open to second-guessing. And with leads of 10 and 12 runs, he let Whitey pitch complete games, eliminating the chance that he might have been available for a batter or two in relief in the seventh game."

Much of Ford's cache comes from his World Series numbers. Thanks to the Yankee dynasty, Ford got the chance to pitch in 11 different Series and amass those amazing numbers. But never a Game 7. Surprising, isn't it?

WHITEY IN THE SERIES

Whitey's first World Series start was terrific. Stengel let the rookie start Game 4 of the Yankees' four-game sweep of the Philadelphia Phillies in 1950 and the rookie went into the ninth with a shutout. But when left fielder Gene Woodling dropped a flyball, ruining his shutout, Stengel brought in Allie Reynolds to get the last out for Ford. The Yankee crowd booed and Ford, at first, thought they were booing him. Turns out they were booing Stengel.

Afterwards, Ford also found out firsthand about the New York media and its impact—good and bad. *New York Times* columnist Arthur Daley shared a story of ex-Cardinal great Dizzy Dean complimenting Ford on his Game 4 win.

"It wasn't anything," Ford told Diz, according to Daley. "No wonder you became a thirty-game winner in that crummy National League. I would win forty myself."

After some years in the service, Ford returned to the Yankees and pitched twice in both the 1953 and 1955 Series, taking the Game 1 loss in 1953 after the Dodgers nailed him for a three-run first but rebounded by throwing seven strong innings in Game 6, leaving with a 3–1 lead. But when Allie Reynolds gave up a two-run homer to Carl Furillo in the ninth to tie it, there went Whitey's win. The Yanks won it in the bottom of the inning on Billy Martin's single, but again, no win for Whitey.

In 1955, the Yanks finally lost a Series to the Dodgers and Ford was again on his game, winning Games 1 and 6. But when it came to Game

7, it was Tommy Byrne who Stengel gave the ball. Could he have saved Ford for that one and flipflopped with Byrne? Maybe.

In the 1956 World Series rematch with the Dodgers, Ford did get the start for Game 1 but couldn't get out of the third inning at tiny Ebbets Field. He gave up home runs to Jackie Robinson and Gil Hodges and was drubbed.

When the Dodgers grabbed Game 2 to take a 2–0 Series lead and started talk of a Dodgers' repeat, Stengel panicked and sent Ford back out with just two days' rest. The game was, of course, at friendly Yankee Stadium and Ford came through with a complete-game effort and a 5–3 win.

When the Yankees won the next two, Don Larsen throwing his perfect game in Game 5 to give New York a 3–2 Series edge, it was all set for Stengel to come back with Ford to wrap it up? He didn't get the chance.

Instead, it was Bullet Bob Turley, who hadn't started a game since early August, who ended up getting the nod in Game 6. Turley ended up a hard-luck loser, falling 1–0 on Jackie Robinson's 10th-inning game-winning hit, a sharp response to Stengel intentionally walking Duke Snider again ahead of Jackie. Casey did it earlier in the game and had gotten Jackie to pop out.

So . . . a rested Ford *could* have taken the hill for Game 7 back in Ebbets Field. But Stengel evidently remembered how Ford struggled in Game 1 against the Dodgers' right-handed power bats (Gil Hodges, Roy Campanella, Jackie Robinson). The start instead went to young sinkerballer Johnny Kucks against Cy Young Award winner Don Newcombe, and Casey's move worked out. Though Stengel had Ford and right-hander Tom Sturdivant warming up throughout the first inning just in case, Stengel stayed with Kucks. When Yogi Berra hit a pair of homers and Elston Howard hit one, the Yanks chased Newcombe in the third and rolled to a 9–0 win. Kucks's only strikeout of the game was the game's final batter—Jackie Robinson, an out that ended his career.

Stengel let Ford open the 1957 Series and he did outduel Warren Spahn (3–1). But Ford was a hard-luck loser in Game 5 when, in the sixth inning of a scoreless game, Eddie Mathews reached on an infield hit, Hank Aaron singled, and Joe Adcock singled Mathews home for the game's only run.

Stengel turned to Bob Turley in Game 6 (a 3–1 win) and instead of turning to Whitey with two days' rest for Game 7, which he had done before, Stengel started Don Larsen, who got bombed. The Braves' Lew Burdette, the Series MVP with three wins, ended up beating the Yanks, 5–0.

The two teams met again in the 1958 Series and in Game 1, Ford was leading Spahn in the eighth, 3–2. But Mathews drew a walk leading off the inning and Aaron doubled him home, tying the game. Stengel went to Ryne Duren who worked into the 10th but there, surrendered singles to Del Crandall and Adcock before Bill Bruton's walkoff single for a 4–3 Braves win. In Game 4, Spahn outpitched Ford to win, 3–0.

Three days later, Stengel let Ford start Game 6 but the lefty lasted just 10 batters, giving way to Art Ditmar, who did well in relief. The Yankees came back to win that game and clinched the Series in Game 7 with a four-run eighth-inning rally off 1957 nemesis Lew Burdette. So while we might think Whitey Ford pitching in a World Series is an automatic win, that wasn't the case, even with the mighty Yankees lineup behind him.

Ford, who ended up breaking Babe Ruth's long-standing World Series scoreless inning mark during that stretch of Yankee dominance, earned a pair of wins over Cincinnati in 1961, getting a win and a loss against the San Francisco Giants in 1962, suffering two losses to the Dodgers in 1963, and then absorbing a final loss in 1964 to the St. Louis Cardinals.

The extra workload seemed to take a toll on Ford as his career continued. He won 16 in 1965 but that was his last double-figure win season. He was just 2–5 in 1966 and battling arm problems, Ford played on into the first couple months of 1967 and was on the other end of a memorable Red Sox–Yankees game in the third game of the 1967 season at Yankee Stadium as Red Sox rookie Billy Rohr tossed a one-hitter to beat him, 3–0. It was the last time he pitched against the Boston Red Sox. And of course, it happened where he felt most comfortable—at Yankee Stadium.

A 300-Game Winner?

Seeing how Ford's career changed once Stengel was fired after the 1960 season, you wonder if Whitey might have been a 300-game winner had he been in a regular pitching rotation instead of Stengel's move to have him pitching against the White Sox until further notice. Looking back, it does make you wonder. After all, it wasn't like he was going to be lacking in run support from these dominant Yankees teams.

Once Houk took over, things did change. Instead of picking and choosing his starts, Houk decided to pitch Ford every fourth day, starting in 1961.

With one of the strongest lineups in baseball history, there was no reason not to. By late July, Walter Bingham's *Sports Illustrated* story explained how well Houk's change was working out. At 16–2 in mid-July, Ford was well on his way to his first 20-game winning season—finally. There was even talk about him winning 30.

"In the 10 years that he has been pitching for the New York Yankees, Ford has compiled the highest-winning percentage of any pitcher in history, .710," Bingham wrote. "His lifetime earned-run average of 2.73 is lower than that of any active pitcher. But, in spite of this, Ford has never been able to achieve what baseball regards as the symbol of pitching success, 20 victories in one season. He won 19 games once, 18 games twice and 16 games twice, but never 20. 'I never minded too much at first,' says Ford, "but people kept bugging me every spring. 'When you going to win 20, when you going to win 20?' It began to get me down.'"

Bingham went on to explain that "several things have contributed to Ford's success this year, but undoubtedly the most important was Manager Ralph Houk's decision to start him every four days during the first half of the season. Casey Stengel, who referred to Ford as 'my professional,' used to rest him generously between pitching assignments. Often, Ford was held out of pitching rotation so that he would be ready for an important series. As a result, Ford just didn't pitch often enough to get a fair chance at 20 victories. In 1956, for instance, the year he won 19 games, Ford started only 30 times. This year, through the All-Star Game (in which he pitched three innings, giving up one run), Ford had 21 starts. In June alone, he started eight games and won them all, something no American

Leaguer has ever done before. Opponents are watching skeptically—and hopefully—for some sign that he has been overworked, but Ford says he has never felt better. Now, with the hottest summer weeks coming up, Manager Houk has announced Ford will start every five days, but even so, Ford will be pitching far more than in past years."

Except for certain ballparks. Which is the mysterious part of this story and something that most baseball fans don't ever talk about. For the great Whitey Ford didn't have a single start in Fenway Park in 1958, 1964, and 1966 and only one in 1953, '55, '57, '60, '62, and '63. That's picking your spots, isn't it?

Whenever Houk decided to have him pitch against the Red Sox, it was almost always in the cavernous Yankee Stadium, where it was 471 feet to dead center. Whitey gave his outfielders plenty of work.

There was a double-edged sword to Houk giving Ford more starts. It did result in a couple of fabulous seasons—25–4 in 1961, the year Roger Maris and Mickey Mantle challenged Babe Ruth's single-season home-run record, and a 24–7 record in 1963.

But all those additional innings—never less than 244 and as many as 283 in 1961—took a toll on Ford's arm. He was essentially done as a starter by age 36 in 1965.

WOULD KNOWING HIS NUMBERS HAVE CHANGED THINGS?

As we take a statistical look back at Ford's career numbers, his starts against certain teams, how he did against particular hitters, it's important to keep in mind that in those days, that really wasn't part of the game.

Frank Robinson explained that to former baseball commissioner Fay Vincent in Vincent's *We Would Have Played For Nothing*.

"I used to get up in the mornings and I couldn't wait to get the newspaper to see who was pitching, because we weren't given all this advance information you get today," Robinson said. "Now you know who's pitching against you two weeks in advance because the PR guys get it out and everybody wants to know.

"We didn't know who was pitching the following day because the managers wouldn't tell you until you read the paper the next day or got to the ballpark."

For example, Yankees hurler Johnny Kucks didn't even know he was starting Game 7 of the 1956 World Series until he saw the ball resting in his cleat before the game. Kind of an important assignment.

Now, when you think of an intelligent hitter like Ted Williams, remembering he was always pumping the umpires, chatting with other players, trying to get as much information as he could, what would Ted have done with all this advance information? It's worth thinking about.

The same goes for the pitchers. While they certainly had an idea what players hit them and who didn't, having the actual numbers before them might have changed things. Both for them and for management.

Was Stengel right to not let Ford pitch against Boston, particularly at Fenway? Would managers have reworked their lineups if they knew what their numbers were? Does it make us look at Ford's career a bit differently? I think perhaps it should.

When you think about the ace of a staff, a guy who's out there every fourth day whether you're on the road or at home, whether the team you're facing is in a hot stretch or struggling, your ace, your bell cow is the guy you're counting on to end a losing streak or start a winning one. Did Walter Johnson or Tom Seaver or Bob Gibson or Sandy Koufax have managers who cherrypicked their starts?

While sportswriters of the day did note that Ford always seemed to be pitching against the White Sox or Indians and not Boston or Detroit, they never really made an issue of it. And neither did he.

In today's game, with agents and the media and the open questioning of managerial decisions in the newspaper, on the radio and TV, Stengel might not have been able to get away with that strategy, especially with the relentless New York media these days.

Back in that time, with the Yankees winning so often, there wasn't much reason for the media to ever get in management's face. Take a spin sometime through the coverage of those Yankees teams. You won't find a lot of criticism. And in those days, the players, generally, went along with whatever the boss said. That has certainly changed.

Some will ask, would Ford have been successful in today's game? He wasn't a hard thrower, really. But he was smart, had outstanding control, fielded his position well, and had always been a winner.

"He threw a two-seam fast ball, a four-seam fastball and a slider," his former catcher Jake Gibbs said, looking back at his years catching the crafty lefty. "You see those big strapping guys today throwing 95 and 99 miles per hour. Whitey was 5-foot-10, tops, and he probably threw 87–88 mph, but he knew where that ball was going. I'd put my mitt down about two inches off the corner on a right-handed batter. He'd hit the mitt right there, and I never moved the mitt. Nine times out of 10, it was a strike."

Ford was also not above pulling a few tricks, loading the ball with saliva or mud—or nicking it with his ring—for a crucial pitch. "If there was a nick or a spot on the ball, Whitey could make that thing talk," Gibbs said. "He could make it drop out of sight." Would today's umpires have permitted that? Good question.

One thing is for sure—he would not have had trouble with a pitch clock. Whitey Ford pitched to contact and worked quickly.

"In '65, I caught one of Whitey's games that we won one to nothing," Gibbs said. "The entire game lasted an hour and a half. Can you believe that? Ninety minutes."

WHITEY FORD'S LAST 11 GAMES AT FENWAY PARK
1957
August 14—Boston 6, New York 4: Ford was taken out two batters into the second inning. After surrendering a single to Gene Mauch, Ford intentionally walked Ted Williams, then gave up a single to Dick Gernert for a 1–0 Boston lead. After allowing a Billy Consolo walk and a Sammy White single, Stengel pulled him for Don Larsen. Larsen later gave up Ted Williams's 31st home run of the season. Larsen did hit two doubles off Red Sox starter Tom Brewer, who allowed 15 hits.

1959
July 10—Boston 8, New York 5: After three scoreless innings, Ford fell apart in the fourth. Bobby Avila singled, Ford made a bad throw to second on Jackie Jensen's comebacker, Ted Williams singled to left, Frank Malzone hit a two-run single, and after an intentional walk to Sammy White to load the bases, pitcher Tom Brewer singled to right to score two

more runs. Boston went on to score a fifth run later in the inning on an error by second baseman Bobby Richardson. Eli Grba took over in the fifth. Ford's record fell to 8–6.

August 10—New York 7, Boston 4: Coming on in relief in the ninth inning of a 4–4 tie, Ford allowed a one-out single to Jackie Jensen and a walk to Frank Malzone. Ted Williams came up as a pinch-hitter and Ford got him to hit into a double play. After a three-run New York 10th, Ford allowed singles to Sammy White, Pumpsie Green, and Pete Runnels but a double play bailed him out. Gary Geiger grounded out to end it.

1960
July 10—Boston 9, New York 5: Coming on in relief of starter Ralph Terry, Ford went 3 2/3 innings, allowing three hits and three runs, including a grand slam to Vic Wertz.

1961
May 29—Boston 2, New York 1: Boston's Ike Delock outdueled Ford, who worked the first seven innings, allowing a second-inning homer to Jackie Jensen, then a Vic Wertz RBI single in the seventh after he'd walked Jensen and Jim Pagliaroni.

July 21—New York 11, Boston 8: Ford pitched the first 4 2/3 innings, allowing seven runs and hits, including doubles to Jackie Jensen, Don Buddin, and Chuck Schilling but the Yankees prevailed, pounding Bill Monbouquette and two relievers thanks to home runs by Mickey Mantle, Roger Maris, Yogi Berra, and Johnny Blanchard.

September 23—New York 8, Boston 3: Ford won his 25th game, throwing five innings, allowing nine hits, including a pair of home runs, Don Gile's only home run of the '61 season in the second inning and Carl Yastrzemski's 11th in the fourth. Mickey Mantle hit his 54th off Don Schwall in the first.

1962

September 16—Boston 4, New York 3: After RBI singles by Roger Maris and Mickey Mantle off Boston starter Gene Conley staked Ford to a 2–0 lead, the Red Sox rallied on an RBI single by Carl Yastrzemski, a Lu Clinton RBI triple, a Frank Malzone RBI single, and a Clinton RBI single, dropping Ford's record to 16–8.

1963

June 22—New York 6, Boston 5: In the first game of a doubleheader at Fenway, Ford threw the first six innings to raise his record to 10–3, allowing eight hits and four runs. Frank Malzone hit a home run and Bob Tillman hit an RBI single.

1965

May 13—Boston 4, New York 1: Ford went four innings, allowing four runs, dropping his record to 2–4. He allowed a Carl Yastrzemski sac fly and a bases loaded triple by Felix Mantilla.

October 3—New York 11, Boston 5: Ford raised his record to 16–13, allowing 11 hits and four runs in seven innings, handing Boston its 100th loss of the season. Ford allowed home runs to Jim Gosger, his ninth, in the second, Carl Yastrzemski's 20th in the third, and Yaz's 45th double.

Top Hitters vs. Whitey Ford

Frank Bolling .444 (12-for-27), 3 2B, 1 HR, 6 RBIs, 2 BB, 2 K

Gino Cimoli .407 (11-for-27), 1 2B, 2 3B, 2 RBIs, 2 K

Ken Harrelson .391 (9-for-23), 1 2B, 1 3B, 1 HR, 2 RBIs, 5 BB, 3 K

Jerry Adair .385 (25-for-65), 5 2B, 3 3B, 1 HR, 9 RBIs, 1 BB, 5 K

Ted Williams .378 (17-for-45), 3 2B, 1 HR, 5 RBIs, 13 BB, 4 K

Eddie Bressoud .368 (14-for-38), 3 2B, 1 RBI, 1 BB, 1 K

Harvey Kuenn .365 (23-for-63), 4 2B, 1 HR, 5 RBIs, 4 BB, 1 K

Don Lock .356 (16-for-45), 5 2B, 2 HR, 5 RBIs, 4 BB, 11 K

Ken Aspromonte .341 (15-for-44), 2 2B, 2 HR, 7 RBIs, 5 BB, 4 K

John Romano .340 (17-for-50), 3 2B, 1 3B, 3 HR, 10 RBIs, 4 BB, 9 K

Al Kaline .339 (38-for-112), 3 2B, 0 3B, 3 HR, 16 RBIs, 16 BB, 5 K

Dick Brown .333 (18-for-54), 1 2B, 1 3B, 2 HR, 5 RBIs, 1 BB, 3 K

Jackie Jensen .321 (25-for-78), 3 2B, 5 HR, 10 RBI, 14 BB, 4 K

Floyd Robinson .321 (18-for-56), 2 2B, 1 HR, 1 RBI, 4 BB, 4 K

Ted Lepcio .314 (11-for-35), 1 3B, 4 RBIs, 5 BB, 6 K

Al Rosen .312 (19-for-61), 3 2B, 1 HR, 8 RBIs, 11 BB, 2 K

Walt Dropo .299 (26-for-87), 4 2B, 5 HR, 11 RBIs, 6 BB, 13K

Carl Yastrzemski .296 (16-for-54), 2 2B, 2 HR, 5 RBI, 5 BB, 10K

HOME RUN LEADERS OFF FORD

Jim Lemon 7 (3 in one game, 8/31/56)

Sherm Lollar 5

Roy Sievers 5

Rocky Colavito 5

Walt Dropo 5

Jackie Jensen 5

Al Smith 4

Larry Doby 4

Bob Allison 4

Zoilo Versalles 4

Vic Wertz 4

Chapter Four

Hank Aaron vs. Don Drysdale:
A Baseball Education

Sometimes the groan is audible. Sometimes, you can just read it on the face of that right-handed hitter when they go to the bullpen and bring in—yes, a sidearmer.

It is difficult enough to stand in a batter's box and try to hit. But when the ball appears to be coming from behind your head, a ball that seems to swoop in horizontally at your hands and move across the plate away from you at high speeds, no right-handed hitter wants to have to deal with that.

Typically, pitchers who don't have the velocity or the stuff to make it throwing overhand will sometimes resort to a most devious way of delivering the baseball—sidearm. And it can work. One of my son's former teammates, trying to make his high school team as a light-hitting infielder, ended up being cut. He transferred to my son's high school, found out he could throw underarm—sort of an extreme sidearmer—and ended up having a glorious career pitching at Florida State as an ace reliever, even managing a brief spin in the minors.

There have been a number of very successful sidearmers in the major leagues over the years; pitchers like Dan Quisenberry, Kent Tekulve, Mike Myers, Brad Ziegler, Ted Abernathy, Gene Garber, and Joe Smith all made a nice living as relievers. But a sidearming *starter*, now that's a different story.

When that sidearmer happens to be 6-foot-5, throws in the mid-90s, and possesses a mean streak as wide as the Mississippi River, you'd better hang loose once you step into the batter's box.

That was an accurate description of the late Los Angeles Dodgers Hall of Fame hurler Don Drysdale, an intimidating, sidearming slinger who led the National League in hit batters four consecutive years. Drysdale plunked 154 batters in his 14-year career, ranking him 20th on the all-time list. He's probably at the very top on a per-inning basis. Almost all the current pitchers ahead of him on the all-time HBP list— Tim Wakefield, Randy Johnson, Charlie Hough, Charlie Morton, Jim Bunning, Roger Clemens, and Bert Blyleven—threw more career innings than Drysdale's 3,432.

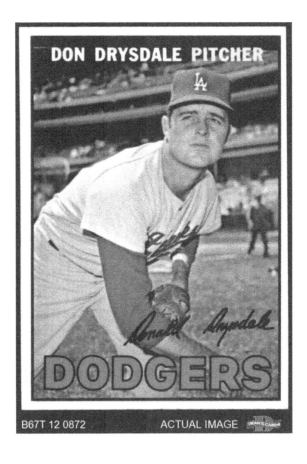

Enter Hank Aaron, a whippet-like right-handed hitter with a quick bat and an intense hatred of being thrown at. While it ended up that in 13 seasons and 249 at-bats facing Drysdale, Hank was never actually hit by a pitch, it wasn't that Don didn't try.

"I just feel that when you're pitching, part of the plate has to be yours," Drysdale told *New York Times* writer Dave Anderson some years after he retired. "The pitcher has to find out if the hitter is timid. And if the hitter is timid, he has to remind the hitter he's timid."

That was exactly the reminder Drysdale delivered to Aaron the first time he faced him in Drysdale's rookie season. He smiled as he recounted the story to Anderson, telling him manager Walter Alston had given Drysdale, then a 19-year-old rookie, orders to throw at Aaron. Dodger pitching coach Sal Maglie, known as "The Barber" in his day for the close shaves he'd give enemy hitters, reiterated Alston's point. One reason for Maglie's insistence might have been this: Hank Aaron batted .409 against him, clubbing four homers. That might have been one of the factors that nudged Maglie into the ranks of coaches.

Anderson continues his column.

"'Knock him down,' spoke up Sal Maglie, 'Knock him down.'

'No,' said Roy Campanella. 'If you knock him down, you'll get him mad.'

'Knock him down,' Sal Maglie said. After the meeting, Sal Maglie told Don Drysdale, 'Look over at me when Aaron comes up.' And when the rookie right-hander glanced into the dugout, Sal the barber nodded.

'That was his sign,' Don Drysdale recalled with smile. 'I knocked him down. And after a curveball strike looked over again and Sal nodded again. And down he went again.'"

Aaron wound up rapping into a double play. Drysdale's intimidating delivery made an impression and as the next season began, Drysdale continued knocking him down. A troubled Aaron went 1-for-18 for the season. Drysdale was, as the players say, "in his dome."

In Aaron's book *I Had A Hammer*, written with Lonnie Wheeler, former Braves publicity director Bob Allen remembered it well.

"'One game Don Drysdale threw at Hank a time or two, and Hank went down,' Allen explained. 'He complained about it after the game, which was rare, because Hank never complained about much. We had a staff meeting the next day, and I can remember John Quinn saying, 'Well, we've got a great young hitter in Hank. Now we'll find out if he can stay in the league. It will depend on how he gets back after being knocked down like that.'"

Make no mistake, Aaron knew how he handled this would be important for the rest of his career. If other pitchers saw there was a way to get Hank out, things could get ugly and dangerous. His stay in the big leagues would be over fast.

"Of all the guys who threw inside, Drysdale did it the most effectively," Aaron said. "God, Drysdale was rough. He would as soon knock you down as strike you out, and he was big and threw hard and came from the side—it seemed like he let the ball go about a foot from your ear. Drysdale was so rough on me that I thought he was going to put me out of the league—not by hitting me, just by making me look bad."

Indeed, while Drysdale never actually hit Aaron, he didn't have to. The intimidation factor was already there. He fanned Aaron 47 times, way more than Hank struck out against anyone else.

You could call it "Drysdale Dread." Dodgers catcher Johnny Roseboro recognized what a weapon it was and in calling pitches, he worked out a good plan.

"With an 0–2 count, Drysdale would come sidearm inside with a 96 mph," Roseboro said. "and when the hitter saw me move my glove inside, his intestinal fortitude will not let the batter look outside. So many a time Drysdale would just throw that ball on the outside corner—strike three."

Aaron knew he had to figure this pitcher out. And pronto.

"I batted so poorly against Drysdale at first that Fred Haney, our manager at the time, was going to bench me one day when he pitched," Aaron recalled. "Back then, sitting on the bench for a day wasn't like it is now. Now, with the guaranteed contracts and diluted rosters, guys are happy to get the day off. But back then, nobody wanted to come out of the lineup, because there was always somebody eager to take your place. I said, "Mr. Haney, you just let me play against him today. I can't sit on the bench. I've got to play. Drysdale got me the first couple of times that day—struck me out and made me look bad—and then I got a couple of hits. The last one was a bloop double that won the ball game. From that day on, I hit Drysdale."

Sure enough, Aaron would figure him out. After that 1-for-18 in 1957, Drysdale began the 1958 season by retiring Hank seven more times, so the great Aaron was actually just 1-for-23 against the guy!

But an Aaron mini-breakthrough on June 6, a pair of singles, was a sign that things were about to change. The key was to get the bat head out. Even if the ball came from the side, if the bat head was there to meet it, that would work.

Three weeks later, on a beautiful Sunday afternoon at Milwaukee's County Stadium, the Braves roughed up Dodger starter Stan Williams,

Henry Aaron vs. Don Drysdale

Regular Season: 249 PA , 267/.345/.579, 17 HR, 47 K
Playoffs: 0 PA

Henry Aaron vs. Don Drysdale: Batter vs. Pitcher

Henry Aaron vs. Don Drysdale: Year-by-Year Totals   Export Data ▾

Rk	Year	PA	AB	H	2B	3B	HR	RBI	BB	SO	BA	OBP	SLG	OPS	SH	SF	IBB	HBP	GIDP
1	1956	3	3	2	0	0	0	0	0	0	.667	.667	.667	1.333	0	0	0	0	1
2	1957	19	18	1	0	1	0	2	1	3	.056	.105	.167	.272	0	0	0	0	1
3	1958	26	25	8	3	0	1	4	1	2	.320	.346	.560	.906	0	0	0	0	0
4	1959	35	30	9	3	0	4	6	5	9	.300	.400	.800	1.200	0	0	1	0	0
5	1960	26	22	7	2	0	3	5	4	1	.318	.423	.818	1.241	0	0	0	0	0
6	1961	19	16	4	3	0	1	3	3	5	.250	.368	.625	.993	0	0	1	0	0
7	1962	17	14	0	0	0	0	1	3	5	.000	.176	.000	.176	0	0	0	0	0
8	1963	18	17	8	0	1	4	8	1	4	.471	.500	1.294	1.794	0	0	0	0	0
9	1964	19	17	3	1	0	0	2	2	3	.176	.263	.235	.498	0	0	0	0	0
10	1965	19	18	4	1	0	1	1	1	6	.222	.263	.444	.708	0	0	0	0	0
11	1966	21	19	7	1	0	2	7	1	3	.368	.381	.737	1.118	0	1	1	0	1
12	1967	15	13	3	0	0	1	2	2	4	.231	.333	.462	.795	0	0	0	0	0
13	1968	10	8	3	0	0	0	0	2	2	.375	.500	.375	.875	0	0	1	0	0
14	1969	2	1	0	0	0	0	0	1	0	.000	.500	.000	.500	0	0	0	0	0
	Totals	249	221	59	14	2	17	41	27	47	.267	.345	.579	.925	0	1	4	0	3

Regular Season

knocking him out early. On in relief was Don Drysdale. So when Aaron stepped into the batter's box against big #53 in the sixth inning, the bases were loaded with nobody out. Time for Hank to strike back.

Aaron lined Drysdale's first pitch over the right field fence for a grand slam, his first home run off the sidearmer and the first of Aaron's career-high 17 homers off Drysdale. Hank, by the way, wound up with 16 grand slams, eighth all-time, tied with Dave Kingman and some guy named Ruth.

By the time 1958 came to a close, Aaron had two more singles and three doubles off Drysdale. He wasn't sweating him anymore, hitting .320 against him for the year.

In 1959, Aaron—not particularly known at the time as a home-run threat—collected four homers off Drysdale, the most he hit off a pitcher in a single season, hitting .300. He hit three more off him in 1960, batting .318. Nobody would believe there was that 1-for-23 stretch now.

Hall of Famer Drysdale turned the tide back in his favor the next two seasons, holding Aaron to a .250 mark in 1961 (4–16 with three doubles, one home run) and an amazing 0-for-14 in 1962 which included three strikeouts in Aaron's last five at-bats against him. Drysdale must have thought he had finally turned the tide. He had Aaron figured out once again.

Nope. "Bad Henry" bounced back with a stunning 1963, clubbing Drysdale's offerings to the tune of .471 with eight doubles, four more homers, eight RBIs, his single best season against the sidearmer.

From there, it was back and forth between the two. Drysdale held Aaron down in 1964 (.176 in 1964 with no home runs allowed) and in 1965 (.222, one homer). Then it was Hank's turn—.368 in 1966 with a pair of dingers, and .375 in 1968.

In between, Drysdale held Hank to .231 in 1967, only allowing a pair of singles with four whiffs. But the last time Aaron faced him that year, September 3, he took him deep for the 17th and final time.

From there, Drysdale's career began winding down. He and Aaron faced one another just 11 more times over his final two seasons; Aaron had three singles, three walks, one intentional, no RBIs. The fireworks were over.

In 1969, Drysdale lost his last start against the Braves. He got Aaron to pop out his first at-bat, then walked him and was chased from the start one batter later, allowing an RBI single to Rico Carty.

Plagued by rotator cuff problems, Drysdale made just five more starts that season, retiring on August 11, quite a ways from the finish line.

Like a lot of National League hitters, Aaron wasn't disappointed to see him leave. When he looked back in *Hammer*, he remembered just what a challenge facing Drysdale was.

"In fact, when it was all over," Aaron recalled, "I'd hit more home runs against Drysdale—17—than I had against any other pitcher. We had a great rivalry going, and there was nothing bitter about it.

"Later, when Claude Osteen was pitching for the Dodgers—I hit 14 home runs against Osteen—Drysdale used to call him before the Dodgers played the Braves and give him a little pep talk, tell him to bear down and give me a few more home runs so the Big D could get his name off the books.

"There are some people who thought Drysdale didn't deserve to be elected into the Hall of Fame because he barely won 200 games (209), but I don't agree. Anybody who batted against him knows he was one of the dominant pitchers of his day."

When he sat down with Dave Anderson, Drysdale remembered Aaron, too.

"I wonder," Drysdale told Anderson with a chuckle, "how many more than 17 he would have hit if I hadn't pitched him inside. But the thing that Sal always told me about the knockdown pitch was, 'It's not the first one, it's the second one.' The second one makes the hitter know you meant the first one. And if you've got control, you can waste a pitch to put a little fear in the hitter."

HANK AT THE PLATE

In a strange way, Hank Aaron's career seemed to separate halfway through it. For the first half, he was seen as a soft-spoken, ruthlessly efficient offensive player. You never heard much about his defense, you never heard much about his baserunning. You just knew at the end of every season, you could look among the National League batting leaders and you'd see his name.

He won two batting titles (.328 in 1956, .355 in 1959), led the National League in home runs and RBIs four times each, but he never hit more than 47 in a season. He swatted 44 homers—his uniform number—four times.

It wasn't until later on, when Aaron's remarkable consistency got his home-run totals mounting, that we started to see him in a different light—Hank Aaron, the home-run threat.

He hit his 500th home run off the Giants' Mike McCormick in July 1968, got number 600 off another Giant, Gaylord Perry, in April 1971, and number 700 in July 1973 off Ken Brett of the Phillies. He was steaming along toward Babe Ruth's 714, hitting 40 home runs that season at age 39.

To add to the drama, Aaron hit his 40th home run of the season off Houston's Jerry Reuss in the fifth inning of the next-to-last game on the schedule, a homer which gave him 713 for his career, one shy of Ruth. Could he do it to end 1973 with a bang?

The answer turned out to be "No." He managed a single off Larry Dierker in the seventh and the next day, with 40,517 on hand in Atlanta to see if he could tie Ruth, Aaron managed three hits but no homers. He singled off Dave Roberts in the first, fourth, and sixth, but no home runs.

The closest he got to a homer was in his final at-bat of the season against Houston fireballer Don Wilson, who gave Hank a lot of trouble (.147). Facing Wilson in the eighth, Aaron popped the ball in the air all the way out to second base. The Braves ended up as 5–3 losers and all of baseball had to wait for the 1974 season to see if Aaron could tie and then pass The Babe.

It sure didn't take long. In his very first at-bat of the season against the Reds' Jack Billingham, he launched a three-run homer to tie the Babe. He passed Ruth days later with a fourth-inning home run off Al Downing. He went on to hit 40 more home runs in his career, retiring after the 1976 season when he had returned to Milwaukee, this time to play for the Brewers. He finished with 755 home runs, tops of all time until Barry Bonds came along.

WHO HE HIT, WHO HE DIDN'T

One sure sign that things were different in Aaron's day is looking at the list of pitchers he faced. There were 20 different pitchers that Hank faced over 100 times. So he knew what they threw and they knew him.

Of those starters, he had the most trouble—like a lot of National League hitters—with the Cardinals' Bob Gibson and the Mets' Tom Seaver. Gibson held Aaron to a .215 average, fanning him 32 times, surrendering eight homers. Seaver held him to .205 with four homers. But facing the best of the rest of NL starters in his era—here are 14 of 'em—you can see Hank did pretty darn well:

Dick Ellsworth (.451, 6 homers)

Johnny Antonelli (.409, 8 homers)

Larry Jackson (.363, 9 homers)

Sandy Koufax (.362, 7 homers)

Don Cardwell (.361, 10 homers)

Harvey Haddix (.358, 8 homers)

Bob Friend (.348, 12 homers)

Roger Craig (.347, 10 homers)

Bob Purkey (.308, 4 homers)

Chris Short (.304, 5 homers)

Gaylord Perry (.294, 3 homers)

Robin Roberts (.291, 9 homers)

Juan Marichal (.288, 8 homers)

Vern Law (.280, 8 homers)

Claude Osteen (.262, 14 homers)

The bottom line was this: Aaron was a machine. And if you've followed baseball for a while, you know how streaky the game can be. Aaron was a model of consistency.

For his career, Aaron hit .318 against lefties, .298 vs. righties, .304 at home, .306 on the road and monthly, he was a metronome—.297 in April, .298 in May, .305 in June, .310 in July, .310 in August, .307 in September/October.

When you sustain numbers like those over a 23-year career against the best in the game, hey, that's an amazing achievement.

Yes, there were a few pitchers that gave him a hard time. Jim Brosnan (.160) and Don Wilson (.147, mentioned above) were tough for him. Aaron also struggled with Dave Giusti (.213), Al McBean (.167), Jim Brewer (.179), Bob Bruce (.175), and Bill Stoneman (.194).

But for every one of those, there was a Tug McGraw (.444 with four homers in 27 at-bats) or Don Gullett (.462 with seven homers in 26 at-bats) or Don Elston (.472 with four homers in 36 at-bats) to boost that batting average right back up.

As people look back on Aaron's career, one of the lasting impressions of the player was his unflappable manner. Well, after he solved Drysdale. Nothing seemed to rattle him. And the way he handled things left people in awe.

Allen reflected on this in *Hammer*:

"Later on, of course, Hank made a career out of hitting Drysdale. I used to drive all around the state with Hank going to speaking engagements, and one time in the car I asked him why he never talked about hitting—about the way he hit Drysdale and everybody else. I'll never forget what he said. He said, 'If you can do it, you don't have to talk about it.' That's just the way he was."

Yet he knew what he was capable of and he knew where he stood. Some of his contemporaries such as Willie Mays, Bob Gibson, Pete Rose, and Johnny Bench might have gotten more publicity than he did, but Hank knew what he had done and how he measured up against the greats in the history of the game.

It might have taken him a few years but in *Hammer*, Hank finally spoke his piece about the player that seemed to draw most of those headlines in his day, the great Willie Mays.

"I considered Mays a rival, certainly, but a friendly rival," Aaron said, firmly. "At the same time, I would never accept the position as second best. I looked at Willie as my guideline. There were certain things that I couldn't do as well as he could, but I felt if I could do some things a little better, I should and maybe would be classified as the same type of ballplayer. I've never seen a better all-around ballplayer than Willie Mays, but I will say this: Willie was not as good a hitter as I was. No way."

Their final numbers:

Willie Mays: .301 AVG., 660 HR, 1,909 RBI

Hank Aaron:.305 AVG., 755 HR, 2,297 RBI

You tell 'em, Hank. You tell 'em.

CHAPTER FIVE

Iconic Matchups: Honus and Christy, Bye Cy, Babe and Dizzy, Yaz and Satchel, Mel's First

IF YOU'RE A DEVOUT BASEBALL FAN, YOU RECOGNIZE THE NAMES; YOU'VE heard the stories, maybe even seen the Cooperstown plaques. Names like Honus Wagner, the Flying Dutchman; Christy Mathewson, the Big Six; Dizzy Dean; the Bambino; Cy Young; Satchel Paige; and all the other colorful figures throughout baseball's rich history.

What we may forget is these guys *actually played the game*. That is, they were on the field, made errors, swung and missed, sweated, cursed, broke bats, dropped popups, gave up home runs, won and lost games.

If you can let your imagination take over for a bit as you run through some of these scenarios, you can almost see them on a sunny afternoon somewhere, the noise of the crowd, the sounds of bat hitting ball, ball sailing into glove, the shouts of the players.

Here are some moments from some of the game's icons that probably *weren't* iconic when they happened. They were just part of what they did, their job. It's only looking back across the years that we see these moments a little differently.

Honus Wagner vs. Christy Mathewson—
September 26, 1914

The season winding down, John McGraw's second-place New York Giants were playing out the string, facing the seventh-place Pittsburgh Pirates in a Saturday afternoon doubleheader at the Polo Grounds.

A late-inning rally by New York had broken a 2–2 tie and given the Giants the first game. Now McGraw turned to his ace, 24-game winner Christy Mathewson, to go for the sweep. Mathewson, 34, had turned in another fine campaign but now, especially at the end of the season, all those innings were starting to take their toll.

To a modern fan, Mathewson's inning totals seem impossible, almost inhuman. Four 30-win seasons, 390 innings in a single season, 10 300-inning seasons, including 303 heading into that afternoon's game, Mathewson had allowed the most earned runs of any NL pitcher that season. He had also allowed 15 home runs heading into that day's game, tops in the circuit. His strikeouts had dropped from a single-season high of 259 in 1908 to just 80 that year. That ol' fadeaway was truly fading away.

His opponent in the second game was Pittsburgh's Babe Adams, a 21-game winner the previous year, but struggling, like his Pirates, that season, 11–16 heading into the game.

Mathewson opened the game in Christy-like fashion, fanning Jim Viox and Dan Costello, getting Zip Collins to bounce out to short. When the Giants' leadoff batter Bob Bescher led off with a triple to deep left field, Pirates manager Fred Clarke thought this was going to be one of those days. Mathewson wins again. Then when Larry Doyle's sac fly made it 1–0 and after George Burns reached on an error by that old man over at third, Honus Wagner, that led to another run thanks to a Fred Snodgrass RBI single. Spotting Mathewson a 2–0 lead was not the way to go.

As the game continued, Adams himself got the Pirates' second hit, but when Viox lined into a double play back to Mathewson to shortstop Art Fletcher, it looked ominous.

But in the fourth, things took a turn. Costello led off with a single and one out later, the old man, Honus Wagner, hit a drive long and deep over the left field fence to tie the game, 2–2. That was Mathewson's 16th

Honus Wagner vs. Christy Mathewson

Regular Season: 67 PA , .308/.313/.462, 2 HR, 3 K
Playoffs: 0 PA

Honus Wagner vs. Christy Mathewson: Batter vs. Pitcher

Honus Wagner vs. Christy Mathewson: Year-by-Year Totals

Regular Season																	
Rk	Year	PA	AB	H	2B	3B	HR	RBI	BB	SO	BA	OBP	SLG	OPS	SH	SF	IBB	HBP	GIDP
1	1912	17	17	4	2	0	0	1	0	1	.235	.235	.353	.588	0	0	0	0	0
2	1913	20	19	9	2	0	1	4	1	1	.474	.500	.737	1.237	0	0	0	0	1
3	1914	17	17	4	0	0	1	3	0	1	.235	.235	.412	.647	0	0	0	0	0
4	1915	13	12	3	0	0	0	3	0	0	.250	.231	.250	.481	0	1	0	0	0
	Totals	67	65	20	4	0	2	11	1	3	.308	.313	.462	.775	0	1	0	0	1

homer allowed that season, tops in the National League. It also happened to be the 40-year-old Wagner's only home run of the season.

In the seventh, Mathewson began to tire. Pittsburgh's Ed Konetchy led off with a single to left, Mathewson wild-pitched him to second, and after Max Carey's deep flyout to right, Konetchy went to third and scored on Wally Gerber's single back through the box to give Pittsburgh and Adams a 3–2 lead.

The Pirates scratched for another run off Mathewson in the ninth, thanks to an error, Carey's bunt single, and Bobby Schang's sacrifice fly. Adams allowed a couple of singles in the ninth but held on and was a 4–2 winner. He had beaten Christy Mathewson.

And the great Mathewson started a slow fade. He went 8–14 the next season, only 16–22 over the next four seasons. As the innings took their toll, his stratospheric career returned to Earth. He retired in 1916.

Wagner managed just three singles in his next 15 at-bats against Mathewson over the next couple seasons. Christy did pitch one more time, returning to the slab in the second game of a Labor Day doubleheader when he was a player-manager for the Cincinnati Reds, besting old rival Mordecai "Three-Finger" Brown in a slugfest.

Improbably, Wagner played on for three more seasons until 1917, retiring at age 43. His final appearance came in a 15-inning loss to the Braves on September 17. Wagner came in for Red Smith in the 11th, played second for two innings, then was lifted for a pinch-hitter in the 13th. Pinch-hitter Bill Wagner promptly hit into a double play, so much for karma. Wagner's final at- bat was a seventh-inning strikeout against the Cardinals' Oscar Horstmann in a 5–2 Pirates loss six days earlier.

CY YOUNG'S FAREWELL—OCTOBER 6, 1911

Baseball is an unforgiving sport. There's no hint of sentimentality from the Baseball Gods and things often don't work out the way they should for anybody when they bid farewell, no matter their place in the history of the game.

That was certainly clear when I wrote *Last Time Out*, which documented these major-league finales. And to see Babe Ruth, Willie Mays, Lou Gehrig, Bob Gibson, and on and on, great players who basked in the spotlight for so long, then are summarily dismissed—if they can't do it anymore, it can be heartless.

That's the way it was for Denton "Cy" Young, winner of a never-to-be-challenged 511 major-league baseball games. He stood on a mound for the final time with a ball in his hand on an October day, at the end of the 1911 baseball season.

At 44, he was old, fat, and in five separate seasons had thrown over 400 innings and over 300 in nine of the next 10 seasons after that. And on the 16th of August, he suffered one of baseball's great indignities when the Cleveland Naps, his employer for the past two seasons, a team for whom he won 19 games in 1909, gave him his release. See ya, Cy.

The Boston Rustlers (not yet the Braves) snapped him up three days later, some said to sell tickets, the SABR folks tell us. He'd pitched well, throwing a pair of shutouts. But the schedule was cruelly against the Rustlers who had to close out the season with 24 consecutive games on the road. Throwing the second game of a doubleheader at Brooklyn's Washington Park, the old pro Young was back on the mound, for the last time.

Just 24 days earlier, Young started against Giants ace Christy Mathewson and couldn't get out of the third inning, allowing eight hits and nine runs. But here in the final game of the season and his career, Young was hoping things might turn around.

Young even drove in a run in the second inning to give himself a lead that wasn't going to last. Brooklyn came back with three runs in the bottom of the inning, Boston tied it in the fourth, and the two teams battled evenly until the bottom of the seventh when all proverbial hell, in baseball terms, broke loose for ol' Cy.

After he got the first out, he gave up a triple, four singles in a row, a stolen base, a double, another steal of third and a bad throw, another double and suddenly, it was 11–3, Brooklyn. Bob Coulson's double capped the rally, the 7,092nd and final hit Cy Young ever allowed. One of the game's greatest pitchers had allowed eight—count 'em—*eight consecutive hits*, chasing him out of the game that had been his life.

It was baseball's unflinchingly cruel way of sending one of the game's all-time greats a stinging goodbye note—"That's it. Enjoy your retirement, Cy. Sincerely yours, Baseball."

DIZZY DEAN VS. BABE RUTH—MAY 5, 1935

It almost didn't seem possible. Could a small stadium on the west side of Boston's downtown hold the egos and personalities of two of the game's greatest all-time performers?

Some 31,000 fans packed Braves Field at the corner of Commonwealth and Babcock on a Sunday afternoon in early May as the former hometown star, the one that got away, came back home, stuffed into a brown and baggy Boston Braves uniform. Here he was, standing behind home plate, smiling and shaking hands with the big, rawboned St. Louis Cardinals star, a 30-game winner the year before. One star descending, another on the rise.

Jerome Hanna "Dizzy" Dean had dreamed of this day, maybe ever since he first picked up a baseball and fired it from a pitcher's mound. Now, he was not only smiling and shaking Babe Ruth's hand for all the photographers, but in a few minutes, Dean would look in from 60 feet, six inches away, seeing that hulking figure in the left-hand batter's box in person for the first time in a regular-season game.

At 40, weighing 245 pounds, the great Ruth was at the end of one of the most remarkable trails in baseball history. The Braves had acquired him from the Yankees in February, and there were promises of Ruth possibly managing in the future.

Sure enough, in the season opener, The Babe rose to the occasion as he had so many times throughout his career, swatting a mighty home run off future Hall of Famer Carl Hubbell.

There wasn't much after that. Ruth had two hits in each of the first two games, then just two hits in the next nine games and was on an 0-for-13 streak when he stepped in against the hard-throwing Dean in the first inning on that Sunday afternoon.

The fans roared when Ruth was introduced, and Dean nodded as he stepped into the batter's box. Diz tipped his cap as he took the sign. "[Diz] had been looking forward to his first league showdown with Babe Ruth and telling everybody he'd have no choice in the matter," biographer Robert Gregory wrote. "He would have to strike him out."

But Dean knew Ruth recognized he was in for a challenge. "Babe was watching me pretty closely while I was warming up before the game," Dean told writer Vince State. "He had that old eagle eye of his on every move I made."

This time, the pitcher-hitter battle was a draw. Babe earned a walk.

Then it was Dizzy's turn. Batting in the second inning against Braves starter Ed Brandt, the Cardinals already up 3–0 on a Virgil Davis triple and Terry Moore home run, Dean one-upped The Babe. Dizzy clubbed a home run into the left-center field stands, laughing all the way around the bases.

When Ruth came up again with one out in the fourth, the hapless Braves trailed 6–0. It was Dizzy's day. And he knew it. Recalling that moment for biographers years later, Dean's memory was sharp.

"I figured that if I didn't steal the show he would," he said. As Ruth stepped into the box, taking his practice swings, Dean smiled and then turned around to face his outfielders. A la Satchel Paige, Dean had some instructions to share with them.

"He motioned them to play farther back," wrote Gregory. "They retreated a few steps, but Diz shook his head, no, no, that's not deep enough, and kept waving his glove until they were almost at the walls."

Then Dean took over. He worked the count to 1–2, then let loose with his best heater. Ruth unleashed his biggest swing—and missed. The Associated Press described it this way: "Babe almost broke his back going for that steaming third fastball."

An erudite sportswriter for the *Boston Globe* put it this way: "Dean whiffed the great man with marvelous eclat." It's good thing Dizzy didn't see that word. A wordsmith like him (wink) would have, no doubt, objected. (*Editor's note:* Eclat *is a French word meaning brilliant display or effect.*)

Ruth grounded out in his next at-bat but not before he gave Dean one more memorable moment. Going after a waist-high Dean fastball, Ruth took a wild swing and missed.

"I never saw a man take such a cut in my whole life," Dean told the *St. Louis Post-Dispatch*. "Lordy me, if he had hit that ball, it would have gone to New York or Pensacola. I had to laugh at him swinging like that and he was laughing because he hadn't expected to get a fast one like that, right through the heart of the plate." Ruth bounced one to short, came out of the game, and the Cardinals won handily, 7–0.

As it happened, the Babe got another chance to face Dean, two weeks later on another Sunday afternoon, this time in St. Louis. But he fared no better.

Ruth fanned in the first, lined into a double play in the third, bounced back to Dean in the sixth, and fouled out to third in the eighth. It turned out a Dizzy Dean three-run single (and an error) in the eighth lifted the Cardinals to a 7–3 win at Sportsman's Park.

Ruth played just 10 more games for the Braves, only five more games after the true end of his career, a three-homer game against the Pittsburgh Pirates at Forbes Field, his final home run, number 714, the first fair ball hit out of the stadium. The Babe knew it was the end, and he wanted to quit, but Braves management talked him into continuing for a few more games. Unfortunately.

Ruth finally did retire after injuring his knee chasing a drive by Lou Chiozza on May 30 at the Baker Bowl in Philadelphia, leaving the game after one inning. He grounded out to first in his final at-bat.

Dizzy Dean went on to win 28 games that 1935 season, 24 the next. Then after Cleveland's Earl Averill hit a line drive off Dean's toe in the 1937 All-Star Game, Dizzy tried to return before the injury was fully healed. In doing so, he altered his arm motion to compensate and was never the same pitcher again. By 1939, Dean was done as a starter, just four short seasons later.

He threw just one game in 1940, then hung them up. After a six-year hiatus in which Dizzy first became a Cardinals broadcaster, then got demoted to doing St. Louis Browns' games in 1947, he was challenged by the team owner to pitch the season finale. Apparently, Dizzy had been overly critical of the sorry Browns' staff all season long.

Tired of the criticism, the owner gave Dean a one-dollar contract, told him he was starting the next day against the Chicago White Sox. And he did. Once he found a uniform that fit him—Dizzy had added a few pounds over the years—Dean went out and threw four scoreless innings. Got himself a hit, too.

SATCHEL PAIGE vs. CARL YASTRZEMSKI—SEPTEMBER 25, 1965

It was one last show for Leroy "Satchel" Paige. On a lovely Saturday night in Kansas City, the greatest pitcher in the history of the Negro Leagues sat in a rocking chair out in the A's bullpen, a nurse at his side, watching the crowd file in.

The Kansas City A's were lousy and drew the way a lousy team would. Only 2,304 fans showed up to watch the A's Jim "Catfish" Hunter throw a two-hit shutout at the Boston Red Sox on Friday night so what was going to happen here? Satchel always liked to count the house.

Showman Charlie Finley had a grand idea to pack the stands for Saturday night's showdown with the Red Sox. He'd have 58-year-old Paige toss the first few innings for his A's.

True, nobody that age had ever pitched in a major-league game but then again, nobody else was ever like Satchel Paige. For Paige, pocket-ing a little coin ($3,500 or roughly eight times his old Negro League

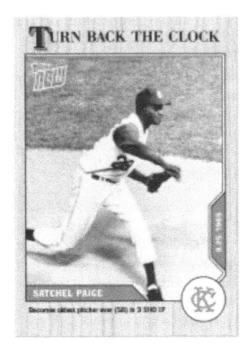

monthly salary), getting some publicity, a few headlines, sure, it was way too little and way too late. But it was better than nothing, better than a stick in the eye some people said.

The Boston Red Sox weren't much better in 1965. There were a couple of promising young players in left fielder Carl Yastrzemski and right fielder Tony Conigliaro, who, at 20, was going to lead the American League in homers that season. But the pitching was troublesome, there were a lot of holes in the lineup, and it was hard to see how they could get back into contention.

The A's would go on to lose 103 games and their attendance reflected that. A few days earlier, Finley's club drew just 690 fans to a game against the Senators. The stunt of signing Paige had to help things.

According to a story on MLB.com, there were other factors. "In 1965, Paige needed money," the article explained. "He had not pitched long enough to qualify for the MLB pension and his wife, LaHoma, was expecting their eighth child. They had written to 20 teams asking for a job in the game. Meanwhile, Paige signed with promoter Abe Saperstein, the Harlem Globetrotters owner who had been a Negro Leagues investor, to make personal appearances."

But basketball wasn't his game. When it came to throwing a baseball, Paige still had it. As the MLB story explained: "In June, Paige (at age 58!) threw batting practice before a benefit exhibition game between the Cardinals and Tigers at Busch Stadium. After one batter reached the wall, Paige stopped throwing batting practice fastballs and began using his assortment of off-speed pitches and off-beat deliveries, and none of the major-league hitters could get the ball out of the infield."

So that Saturday night in Kansas City, Finley advertised it as "Satchel Paige Appreciation Night" and 9,289 fans turned out, including a group of old Negro Leagues stars, including Cool Papa Bell and Buck O'Neil.

And here's Boston's Jim Gosger, a scrappy 22-year-old from Port Huron, Michigan, standing in the batter's box, staring out at a future Hall of Famer who was almost 60 years old. Talk about a mind-blowing experience.

"It was never brought up to us or our ballclub until we got to the ballpark that he was going to pitch," Gosger said recently. "And they had a hell of a crowd there."

Watching Paige's easy, almost three-quarters motion, it didn't take much for Gosger to imagine what the long-armed guy was like in his prime. "Everything was low and hard," he said. "He kept everything down. And at his age . . . ?"

Gosger swung and fouled out to first, opening the game. Dalton Jones followed, topping a slow roller to first, dove awkwardly into the bag, reaching on an error. He was caught trying to advance to third for the second out.

The next man up was Carl Yastrzemski, the American League batting champion in 1963, eventual runner-up to Tony Oliva for the batting crown in that 1965 season. In a couple of years, Yaz would lead the Boston Red Sox to the American League pennant, winning the Triple Crown with a .326 average, 44 home runs, and 121 runs batted in. Here's a 58-year-old man, facing one of the American League's best, in his prime. Yaz was 25.

As he stepped in, somebody in the stands mentioned that Yaz's father, a terrific sandlot player in his day, once faced Paige in a barnstorming game on Long Island 15 years earlier and tripled. Paige missed with his first three pitches and at 3–0, came in with his one mistake pitch, a high fastball that the younger Yastrzemski slammed off the left field wall for a double. You bet Dad had to laugh.

Next up was eventual American League home run king Conigliaro. Paige threw his famous hesitation pitch and Conigliaro missed it, popping it up to left field for the third out.

From there, Paige turned back the clock. Lee Thomas popped to third, Felix Mantilla grounded out, Eddie Bressoud flied to right. Then in the third, Mike Ryan popped to short, pitcher Bill Monbouquette struck out, ol' Satchel's final career whiff. Then Gosger stepped back in and rapped one at shortstop Bert Campaneris. Three outs.

Coming off the field after his three shutout innings, the 58-year-old Paige stepped like a younger man. He grabbed the arm of the young player he'd just induced to ground out. The final hitter of a remarkable career. "Hey young man," Paige told him, "good luck."

"It scared the hell out of me," Gosger said later. "I was just going to get my glove and he grabbed my arm. It was really something. I was the last man to face him. What an honor."

Of course, nobody in the majors got to bat against Paige in his prime, not in official league games anyway. Many of them had faced him in barnstorming games; Joe DiMaggio said he was the fastest pitcher he ever saw and the best. Paige was likely in his 40s when Bill Veeck signed him to pitch for Cleveland, but he could still pitch. He pitched for the Indians for two years, and even won 12 games in 1952 during his three-year stint with the St. Louis Browns.

Look at how he did against some of the game's best players, spotting them 10–15 years. Granted, it's a small sample size, but still . . .

Joe DiMaggio .000 (0-for-8)

Tommy Heinrich .000 (0-for-6)

Nellie Fox .211

Eddie Yost .125

Phil Rizzuto .191

Johnny Pesky .118

Ted Williams .222

A great story in John Holway's *The Last .400 Hitter* gives you a good sense about Paige's pitching smarts. Ted Williams remembered an at-bat against the old guy. "Well, I want to tell you, he still had a nice easy windup and a nice, easy hesitation pitch, and good control," Williams said. "He'd give you that nice easy motion, then he'd stop, and there it was! All that time I was hitting up there, I was thinking, 'Boy, this guy must have been some kind of pitcher, this guy must have been some kind of pitcher.'

"So Paige gives me that double windup, got his hands right in back of his head and turned his wrist. Everybody in the park saw it—he made damn sure I saw it. I said, 'Jesus, curve ball.' And, whoom, fastball, strike three."

Next day, Satchel popped into the Red Sox dugout. "Where's Ted? Where's Ted?" he demanded.

"Right here, Satch," Williams replied.

Paige grinned. "You bought to know better than to guess with ol' Satch."

The final hit Satchel Paige surrendered was one of 3,419 Carl Yastrzemski collected in a 23-year Hall of Fame career, the only hit he allowed in his final three innings in the major leagues. Yaz went on to a Hall of Fame career.

But facing the great Satchel Paige, Yaz had to remember this: His dad did better.

MEL OTT'S FIRST HOME RUN—JULY 18, 1927

He stood for a moment in the dugout at the Polo Grounds, staring at the lineup. At 18 years old, Mel Ott looked again at the New York Giants batting order. He didn't know this at the time, of course, but batting ahead of him was future Hall of Famer Freddie Lindstrom. He was hitting third. *Third!* Hitting fourth was future Hall of Famer Rogers Hornsby. Behind him was future Hall of Famer Bill Terry.

This was heady stuff. The Giants' gruff manager, John McGraw, the nail-spitting, profane wizard of baseball refused to let him, at age 17, play a single minor-league game. "I don't want anybody monkeying with that natural swing," he said, or something like that. Even though Ott, in what had to be as radical a batting stance as anybody ever saw, tended to lift his right foot *off the ground* before he swung.

Yeah, McGraw kept him apart from the old-timers, even 20-year-old Freddie Lindstrom who started and starred in a World Series at 18 years old. So don't be thinking old crusty McGraw wasn't radical. And he hit him third against these Chicago Cubs and veteran Hal Carlson, the 35-year-old righty the Cubs had just gotten from the Phillies in June.

As a 17-year-old, McGraw kept him with the Giants all season. Getting him 60 at-bats, giving him 10 starts in a row once August rolled around. And the kid hit, ending up at .383 for the season. At 17.

When 1927 started, McGraw kept him as a pinch-hitter until the final week of April, then gave him a couple of starts. He did the same in May and June and when mid-July got here, the Giants had a doubleheader set at the Polo Grounds, making up for a May 9 rainout and McGraw had him hitting third. At 18.

It was overcast and rainy, the Polo Grounds outfield grass was wet. And that mattered. Giants starter Fat Freddie Fitzsimmons surrendered a first-inning double to Eddie Pick, and Earl Webb sent Ott running deep into center field to track down his flyball. But Hack Wilson, who would drive in 191 runs in a single season three years from now, flew out to right to end the inning. Like Cubs catcher Gabby Hartnett, hitting seventh on this day, he was an eventual Hall of Famer, too.

Carlson worked quickly and struck out Eddie Reese to open the game, got Lindstrom to bounce out to second. Up stepped #4, the kid. Eighteen years old, just about exactly half as old as the major-league vet on the mound. Carlson fired and Ott swung and connected, a vicious line drive over the head of the stubby little center fielder Wilson, who may have been playing in. The sizzle of the line drive, the wet grass, and maybe

Wilson being caught out of position added up to trouble for the Cubs and the excited Ott tore around the bases as if he was being chased. He crossed home plate standing up and the Giants had a 1–0 lead. And Mel Ott had his first major-league home run.

His excitement wasn't over. Batting in the eighth, Ott slammed another deep drive to right- center, had Wilson chasing it again. He stopped at third base. Heinie Mueller pinch-ran for him and there was a celebration in the Giants dugout for the kid. Even though his club was losing, McGraw had to be laughing to himself about this prodigy he'd nurtured like a mother hen through a season and a half of cutthroat major-league baseball. He was on his way.

Ott would hit 510 more of those homers, retiring 20 years later. He'd hit 71 more triples, too. When Ott retired in 1947, he was third on the all-time home-run list between Babe Ruth (714) and Jimmie Foxx (534). So, John McGraw's prediction was right on the money. Mel Ott was a prodigy, all right, one of the greatest in the history of the game, lifting that right foot all the way to Cooperstown.

Chapter Six

Joe DiMaggio vs. Ted Williams: Taking a Long View

Like salt and pepper, Laurel and Hardy, Abbott and Costello, and other famous two-name combinations, it almost seems like it's against the law to mention Ted Williams without also mentioning his chief rival and simultaneous American League icon, Joe DiMaggio.

Their careers intersected for 12 seasons—DiMaggio broke in with the New York Yankees in 1936, Boston brought up Ted Williams three years later. The two of them each missed three years for World War II. Williams even missed parts of two seasons thanks to the Korean War. DiMaggio retired after a disappointing 1951 season with another World Series win and a double in his final Series at-bat. Williams retired nine years later, famously homering in his final at-bat on a chilly September afternoon at Fenway Park, immortalized in John Updike's classic *New Yorker* article, "Hub Fans Bid Kid Adieu."

As players, they were as different as Randy Johnson and Eddie Gaedel. Tall and imposing, almost movie-star handsome, Ted Williams was volatile, explosive, great copy, as driven and as scientific a hitter as there ever was. He was always willing to pose for the photographers with his marvelous swing, even did a series of shots bare-chested, in a skimpy pair of shorts. Day or night, Ted was always willing to talk hitting; it was his life.

Should you doubt that, leave it to legendary writer Roger Angell to get an amazing admission from Williams during a spring training visit long after Ted had retired. Williams was explaining that over the summer, he'd check in on the minor-league hitters he'd worked with in spring training to mark their progress—or the lack of it. Williams told Angell these modern players, many of whom had live-in girlfriends or wives, had their minds on something else. Angell was puzzled. Williams explained what he meant. "Roger, I didn't get laid for the first time until the All-Star Game break of my second year in the majors," Williams said. "I was thinking about hitting."

On the field in perfectly tailored pinstripes, Joe DiMaggio was graceful, effortless, always in control, emotionless. His manager said he'd never seen him make a great play because he was always in position. He was icily brilliant. Remember what a big friggin' deal it was when Joe kicked the dirt after Al Gionfriddo's famous snare of his long drive in

the 1947 World Series. It made all the World Series films—"Joe shows emotion, film at 11." Joe told *New York Times* columnist Arthur Daley that it took him a good week to get over Gionfriddo's snag.

Williams, on the other hand, had times when he would spit toward the stands or the press box or both. He seemed to be in constant combat with the intrusive Boston press, abusive fans, whoever. There was no repressing emotion with Ted, including his legendary jousts with the writers. Boston had seven daily newspapers at the time. And Ted was always good copy. As John Lardner wrote, "By the time the press of Boston has completed its daily treatment of Theodore S. Williams, there is no room in the papers for anything but two sticks of agate type about Truman and housing, and one column for the last Boston girl to be murdered on a beach."

Make no mistake, this explosive press treatment cost him. Take a look at the voting for the American League Most Valuable Player award over the course of his career and you'll see what a mighty price he paid.

DiMaggio was handled much more lovingly. He was lauded, glorified, and worshipped by the New York media or else he would cut them off. Period. There was no middle ground. As David Halberstam noted in his introduction to *The Best American Sportswriting of the Century*, DiMaggio "had always been treated with great delicacy by an adoring New York and thus national press corps. The essential portrait of DiMaggio which had emerged over the years was of someone as attractive and graceful off the field as he was on it. DiMaggio had rather skillfully contributed to this image—he was . . . as attentive and purposeful in controlling it as he was in excelling on the field, and he quickly and ruthlessly cut off any reporter who threatened to go beyond the accepted journalistic limits." Gay Talese's famous *Esquire* article "The Silent Season of a Hero" showed us a completely different side of DiMaggio, a much less appealing character, and made us wonder about the impact of media manipulation.

Now, in fairness, the Yankees were so good, DiMaggio so consistent, there wasn't any reason to be negative. Yet it's also fair to wonder how the impact of that sea of New York praise from their media circus all those years shaped our own opinions and those of baseball fans across the country about DiMaggio and other Yankees.

Ted Williams   Joe DiMaggio

Overall Stats		
121.8	WAR	79.1
2292	G	1736
9792	PA	7672
2654	H	2214
521	HR	361
1839	RBI	1537
24	SB	30
.344	BA	.325
.482	OBP	.398
.634	SLG	.579
1.116	OPS	.977
191	OPS+	155
Awards & Honors		
✓	Hall of Fame	✓
	Championships	9
19	All-Star	13
2	MVP	3
6	Batting Title	2
2	Triple Crown	

Joe DiMaggio
WIKIMEDIA COMMONS

As depicted in Talese's piece and several other unauthorized biographies, off the field, DiMaggio was aloof, wary, nervous, suspicious, an immaculately dressed chain-smoking wreck who dealt with insomnia, ulcers, and stress about money. Not necessarily in that order. His teammates would tell you he was obsessed with one question. He asked and asked and asked of them just one thing: "How do I look?"

When you think about how many years DiMaggio was the toast of the town, basking in the nightlife of New York City, up at all hours, banging showgirls and starlets, you wonder if it might have taken a physical toll. It turned out his career was essentially over in his mid-30s.

Generally speaking, Ty Cobb wasn't particularly complimentary of modern-era players. But he was especially harsh about DiMaggio.

"Joe is another modern who made a name for himself without scratching the surface of his talents," Cobb wrote for *Life* magazine in 1952. "Joe, like (Ted) Williams, never liked hitting to the opposite field. And even worse he was perhaps the outstanding example of how modern baseball players neglected to train and keep themselves in condition. He hated physical exertion, and as far as I know never took a lick of exercise from October till March. Naturally, he went to Spring Training with his muscles weakened and soft."

Cobb might have been overstating it, but DiMaggio's career did come to a pretty abrupt end. After a disappointing 1951 season (.263), DiMaggio retired at 37, a season that was capped by an embarrassing *Life* magazine article that came out just before the World Series. The article, which recounted an unflattering scouting report, explained how age had taken a toll on DiMaggio's once-immaculate game. DiMaggio was mightily embarrassed to read how he couldn't get around on the fastball anymore, how he had just one good throw in his arm and so on.

Later, DiMaggio even admitted as much to Daley. "What a dirty trick I'm playing on the runners. I'm giving this to you in confidence. I have only one throw a day in the old soupbone and even that kills me. Watch how I make one quick throw early in the game to keep the boys respecting me. Then I coast along on my reputation." He was, essentially, washed up at 36.

Williams, remember, turned 40 in the summer of 1957 when he batted .388, just a handful of hits away from a second .400 season. Then Ted went out and won another batting title the next year. In his final season, two years later, he hit .316, which would have put him just four points behind AL batting champ Pete Runnels, a teammate, if only Ted had enough at-bats to qualify.

In terms of longevity comparing the two careers, you certainly have to give the nod to Ted. Even with all his injuries, missing parts of several seasons due to military commitments and an assortment of other ailments—collarbone, elbow, etc.—Williams played 556 more games, had 440 more hits, hit 160 more home runs, drove in 302 more runs, and amazingly, drew 1,231 more walks.

Over the years since he retired, Williams's stature has seemed to grow among fans; the dramatic home run in his final at-bat, the .400 average, and the generous way Williams lived out the rest of his life: His remarkable out-of-sight charitable work with Boston's Jimmy Fund became quite a contrast to the reclusive DiMaggio, who, according to several biographers, didn't go much of anywhere unless someone was picking up the tab.

While Ted had mellowed, even apologetically doffing his cap at a Red Sox on-field ceremony in his later years—something he famously refused to do in his playing days—DiMaggio seemed to grow inward, fiercely protective of his legacy. Reportedly, he would not appear on a baseball field unless announced as "the greatest living ballplayer," a move which could easily have been interpreted as a slam to Willie Mays or Hank Aaron or Mickey Mantle or even Ted Williams himself. Some reports claim that when he heard Paul Simon's "Mrs. Robinson" which has the poignant line "Where have you gone, Joe DiMaggio?" DiMaggio's initial instinct was to sue.

As a ballplayer, DiMaggio was the consummate professional; a fine outfielder, an intelligent baserunner, a lifetime .325 hitter with at least medium power (361 home runs playing in a mighty big ballpark—over 400 feet to center field), somebody who people couldn't remember making a mistake on the field.

"Joe D. was so graceful, I mean, you didn't realize how fast he was because he looked graceful," former Dodger Ralph Branca told Fay Vincent in *We Would Have Played for Nothing*. "I watch video clips of him now and you realize he was really running hard, but when you saw him play, it looked like it was easy." And with the Yankees always winning, there wasn't a lot of room for easy criticism.

Williams was a decent, if not always interested outfielder, long and lanky, no speed merchant.

Like DiMaggio, Williams faced home field challenges, too. Boston management moved in the right field fences at Fenway Park, renaming it

"Williamsburg" early in his career. But it was still 388 feet away, a mighty wallop.

There was occasional talk of a swap between teams; DiMaggio, a right-handed hitter, eyeing that 315-foot Green Monster; Williams, a dead-pull hitter, training his sights on that 296-foot right field foul line at Yankee Stadium. It never happened—but almost did.

According to an Arthur Daley column in November of 1960, [then-retiring Yankees general manager] "George Weiss confirmed an ancient rumor in a now-it-can-be-told revelation as he was yielding active control of the Yankee empire last week. He admitted that agreement once had been reached on an even trade of Ted Williams for Joe DiMaggio. The architects of this fanciful swap were the presidents of the New York and Boston ball clubs, Tom Yawkey and Dan Topping." This was in 1950.

Daley continued. "They talked it over one night, said Weiss, and agreed to the deal. But Yawkey got cold feet the next morning and called it off."

"Smart man, Yawkey," Daley writes. "DiMadge quit after an indifferent season in 1951 while Williams continued at so productive a pace that he won unanimous selection as the Player Of The Decade."

The New York rumors continued. In December 1951, a *New York Times* headline read "Yanks 'Interested' in Getting Williams from Red Sox If DiMaggio Retires," which probably was news to Ted.

As you might expect, since he played longer, Williams's lifetime cumulative stats are considerably better—521 home runs to Joe's 361, a career batting average 19 points higher (.344 to .325) and an on-base percentage almost 100 points higher (.482 to .398).

Yet as impactful a player as Williams was, he could have done so much more. Though Williams played until 1960, nine years after DiMaggio's departure, he only amassed 886 more at-bats, roughly a season and a half. Why? Walks! Williams's 2,021 lifetime walks were almost three times DiMaggio's 790. That includes one season where Ted was intentionally walked 33 times. He was 40 at the time.

There are those who criticize Williams for taking those walks. Hall of Fame pitcher Ted Lyons, for example, said Ted "was too choosy." Williams hit .333 against Lyons with just four walks in 40 plate appearances.

If you're a believer in WAR or Wins Above Replacement, it's a Williams landslide. Baseball Reference gives Williams a 123.1 WAR, 14th all time. DiMaggio's is 78.1, 68th all time. Do you know anyone who thinks there were 67 major-league ballplayers better than Joe DiMaggio? Were there 13 players more important than Williams? The argument rages on.

Reading about their careers, you also had to wonder how they did against each other head-to-head. We know, for example, Williams hit .345 against the Yankees over his career, a point higher than his career mark. How did he do in the games when he saw DiMaggio out there playing center field? We know DiMaggio hit .334 against Boston, nine

Ted Williams vs. New York Yankees
Regular Season: 327 GP, 62 HR, 229 RBI, 72 2B, 2 SB
Playoffs: 0 GP

Ted Williams vs. New York Yankees: Batting

Ted Williams vs. New York Yankees: Totals   Export Data ▾   Glossary

Regular Season

Rk	Season	Team	GP	PA	AB	R	H	1B	2B	3B	HR	RBI	SB	CS	BB	SO	BA	OBP	SLG	OPS	TB	GIDP	HBP	SH	SF	IBB
1	1939	BOS	18	77	60	19	21	8	6	1	6	17	0	1	17	14	.350	.494	.783	1.277	47	0	0	0		0
2	1940	BOS	19	84	68	17	24	14	4	0	6	14	0	1	15	6	.353	.476	.676	1.153	46	2	1	0		1
3	1941	BOS	22	92	68	23	32	25	5	0	2	14	0	2	24	5	.471	.609	.632	1.241	43	2	0	0		1
4	1942	BOS	22	96	77	14	23	13	4	0	6	16	0	1	18	6	.299	.438	.584	1.022	45	2	1	0		5
5	1946	BOS	22	93	69	18	13	7	2	1	3	10	0	0	24	7	.188	.398	.377	.775	26	6	0	0		2
6	1947	BOS	22	94	74	11	17	7	8	0	2	7	0	0	20	6	.230	.394	.419	.813	31	2	0	0		4
7	1948	BOS	22	101	83	16	29	15	7	2	5	30	1	0	17	7	.349	.465	.663	1.128	55	1	1	0		6
8	1949	BOS	22	99	78	17	30	21	4	0	5	18	0	0	21	7	.385	.515	.628	1.143	49	5	0	0		2
9	1950	BOS	18	81	59	18	20	11	5	0	4	16	1	0	22	2	.339	.519	.627	1.146	37	4	0	0		0
10	1951	BOS	18	79	67	12	24	16	3	2	3	13	0	0	12	8	.358	.456	.597	1.053	40	1	0	0		0
11	1953	BOS	7	20	17	2	8	4	3	0	1	6	0	0	3	0	.471	.550	.824	1.374	14	0	0	0		0
12	1954	BOS	19	89	57	18	23	16	3	1	3	15	0	0	30	5	.404	.596	.649	1.245	37	2	0	0	2	4
13	1955	BOS	14	50	36	4	13	9	2	0	2	4	0	0	14	4	.361	.540	.583	1.123	21	1	0	0	0	3
14	1956	BOS	20	72	56	3	11	9	1	0	1	6	0	0	16	3	.196	.375	.268	.643	15	5	0	0	0	0
15	1957	BOS	20	73	53	10	24	14	4	0	6	13	0	1	20	7	.453	.603	.868	1.471	46	2	0	0	0	3
16	1958	BOS	14	56	42	10	19	11	5	0	3	13	0	0	12	3	.452	.554	.786	1.339	33	1	0	0	2	1
17	1959	BOS	14	39	31	6	12	7	4	0	1	8	0	0	8	4	.387	.513	.613	1.126	19	2	0	0	0	2
18	1960	BOS	14	56	40	7	14	9	2	0	3	9	0	1	16	5	.350	.536	.625	1.161	25	1	0	0	0	3
	Totals		327	1351	1035	225	357	216	72	7	62	229	2	7	309	99	.345	.495	.608	1.103	629	39	3	0	4	37

points higher than his career mark of .325. What about when he saw Ted out there in left field or after Williams had done something dramatic at the plate? Did they push one another? What were those dozen years of baseball combat really like?

THE RIVALRY BEGINS—1939

The first time the two met was on April 20, 1939, Opening Day at Yankee Stadium. Rookie Ted Williams found himself hitting sixth against veteran Yankees right-hander Red Ruffing, who opened Williams's Hall of Fame career with a strikeout. Batting in the fourth, Williams ripped his first major-league hit, a double in the right-center field gap. Then, batting in the sixth, Ruffing struck him out again.

Facing Boston's ace Lefty Grove, DiMaggio was walked twice, once intentionally, singled, and was called out on strikes. A Bill Dickey home run and a Jake Powell triple and score on an error gave Ruffing a 2–0 win in that season opener.

The very next time Williams faced Ruffing, he homered in the first inning. So did Joe Cronin and Jimmie Foxx as the Red Sox beat him 8–4 in the first game of a Memorial Day doubleheader. In the second game, Williams hit number 8 against Monte Pearson, but the Yankees clobbered Red Sox pitching for a 17–9 win. DiMaggio skipped the opener and drew a seventh-inning walk as a pinch-hitter in the nightcap.

When the Yankees came to Fenway at the start of July for a three-game set, the rookie Williams and the four-year veteran DiMaggio each put on a show—on defense! Boston won Saturday's game 5–3 as Williams slammed a triple off Marius Russo. DiMaggio collected a single but also threw two Boston runners out on the bases (Jim Tabor at the plate, Jimmie Foxx trying to stretch a single at second).

In Sunday's game, Boston's Lefty Grove picked up his eighth win, outdueling Lefty Gomez, 7–3. It was Ted Williams's turn to pick up a couple of outfield assists, throwing out both Tommy Heinrich and Joe Vosmik at the plate. Williams also had the game-winner, too, slamming a three-run homer off Gomez in the seventh. DiMaggio, who came into the game hitting .419, had three hits, including a double off Grove. The rivalry was on.

As the season rolled into September, the 1939 Red Sox weren't half-bad (74–49), but the Yankees (88–37) were just humming. After the second game of a Sunday doubleheader in Boston, DiMaggio had three hits, including a two-run homer (his 25th) off Charlie Wagner to raise his average to .410! With just a few weeks left in the season, DiMaggio was that close to .400 two years before Ted did hit the .400 mark. Williams had a pair of home runs off Bump Hadley, giving him 24 on the season. But Ted also made his 17th error, playing right field, which perhaps explains his subsequent move to left. He made 19 errors that season. DiMaggio himself made 17 errors in his second year. Official scorers must have been tough, the gloves just not as big.

DiMaggio's run at .400 faded in the closing weeks. An eye infection helped cause DiMaggio's average to dip to .381, still good enough to give him his second batting title. That season, DiMaggio was named AL MVP with his 30 home runs and 126 RBIs, the first of his three MVP

Joe DiMaggio vs. Boston Red Sox

Regular Season: 253 GP, 46 HR, 223 RBI, 58 2B, 4 SB
Playoffs: 0 GP

Joe DiMaggio vs. Boston Red Sox: Batting

Joe DiMaggio vs. Boston Red Sox: Totals   Export Data ▾   Glossary

Regular Season

Rk	Season	Team	GP	PA	AB	R	H	1B	2B	3B	HR	RBI	SB	CS	BB	SO	BA	OBP	SLG	OPS	TB	GIDP	HBP	SH	SF	IBB
1	1936	NYY	19	92	90	17	25	11	7	4	3	22	1	0	2	6	.278	.293	.544	.838	49		0	0		0
2	1937	NYY	20	95	82	22	34	23	5	2	4	22	0	0	12	7	.415	.489	.671	1.160	55		0	1		3
3	1938	NYY	17	72	63	15	23	11	8	1	3	13	2	1	9	2	.365	.444	.667	1.111	42		0	0		2
4	1939	NYY	18	67	61	10	29	21	3	0	5	16	1	0	5	2	.475	.515	.770	1.286	47	1	0	0		1
5	1940	NYY	21	98	80	16	28	19	3	0	6	25	0	0	18	5	.350	.469	.613	1.082	49	2	0	0		6
6	1941	NYY	19	83	71	9	19	13	4	0	2	19	0	0	12	2	.268	.373	.408	.782	29	0	0	0		4
7	1942	NYY	22	96	87	17	20	15	2	1	2	12	0	0	9	6	.230	.302	.345	.647	30	2	0	0		1
8	1946	NYY	22	94	84	14	22	13	5	0	4	13	0	0	9	5	.262	.333	.464	.798	39	4	0	1		1
9	1947	NYY	19	81	69	15	27	20	4	1	2	15	0	0	11	4	.391	.481	.565	1.047	39	3	1	0		3
10	1948	NYY	22	95	88	16	35	22	8	2	3	24	0	0	7	4	.398	.442	.636	1.078	56	1	0	0		3
11	1949	NYY	13	55	42	14	16	6	3	1	6	14	0	1	12	4	.381	.527	.929	1.456	39	2	1	0		0
12	1950	NYY	21	94	81	18	24	15	4	2	3	14	0	0	13	8	.296	.394	.506	.900	41	2	0	0		2
13	1951	NYY	20	81	69	10	21	15	2	1	3	14	0	0	12	8	.304	.407	.493	.900	34	1	0	0		1
	Totals		253	1103	967	193	323	204	58	15	46	223	4	2	131	63	**.334**	**.415**	**.568**	**.982**	549	18	2	2		27

awards. It may have been the only one of his three there wasn't much of an argument about.

Ted Williams sure didn't swing like a rookie, hitting .327 with 31 home runs and a league-leading 145 RBIs. One thing was clear; these were two players worth watching.

HEADING TOWARD HISTORY—1940

Wandering through the box scores from the Red Sox-Yankees games that 1940 season, you see a few things that are surprising. They played four doubleheaders, with the Yanks taking six of the eight games. What was amazing was on August 7, the Yankees were at .500, a 50–50 record. DiMaggio had been out, their pitching was erratic, and they were unusually inconsistent.

The Red Sox, meanwhile, were 56–47 and in good shape. All of a sudden, someone flipped a switch and the Yanks decided to play like the Yankees and ran off a 25–7 streak while Boston struggled, playing just .500 ball down the stretch. It meant another disappointing finish to a Red Sox season at the hands of the damn Yankees.

DiMaggio continued to lead the Yanks, Williams settled in as one of the league's most feared hitters, but what was surprising was that neither player's excellence ensured wins. In examining the box scores, it wasn't as if there were a lot of games where you could say Williams or DiMaggio's heroics won it for their team. True, there weren't a lot of 0-for-4s by either guy, but more often than not, it was somebody else who ended up being the decisive performer.

DiMaggio won his second batting title in 1940 (.352) along with 31 home runs and 133 RBIs. Williams's sophomore season was dandy—Ted matched his career average (.344) with 23 home runs and 113 RBIs. In an August 13 doubleheader, for example, DiMaggio swatted two homers and drove in eight runs in a three-hit game as the Yankees completed a sweep with a 19–8 victory. Williams had a pair of hits and his 15th homer, then hit another off Red Ruffing the next day, and a grand slam off Tiny Bonham the day after that. But Williams alone couldn't stop the Red Sox skid.

Raising the Stakes—1941 and 1942

To many people, the 1941 season was one of the most amazing in baseball history. DiMaggio had his historic 56-game hitting streak, finishing the season at .357 with 30 home runs and 125 RBIs to win his second MVP.

Williams won his first batting title with his remarkable .406 (it actually should have been .419 or .412, since in those days, sacrifice flies counted as outs) with 37 home runs and 120 RBIs. But Williams lost out on the MVP award. Ted, incidentally, hit .412 during Joe's historic streak, closing out his season with the dramatic 6-for-8 in that last-day double-header against Philadelphia, raising his final average to .406. There were some who complained that Williams's brilliant season-long achievement deserved the MVP. But Joe got the nod.

In 1942, Ted won his second batting title (.356) with 36 home runs and 137 RBIs while DiMaggio, just 27, fell off the pace. Though he played in every game—a career-high 154—Joe hit just .305 with 21 home runs and 114 RBIs. It looked like the American League MVP was going to belong to Williams. And it should have.

Somehow, the MVP award slipped from Ted's grasp again, going to Yankee Joe Gordon, who hit .322 with 18 home runs and 103 RBIs, impressive production for a second baseman, but come on.

One baseball fan from New Jersey stood up for Williams in a letter to the *New York Times* printed in the sports section titled "Betrayal of Williams." "The award for the most valuable player in the American League fires one's indignation to the boiling point. Ignoring the batting feats of Ted Williams of the Red Sox and disregarding precedence, the baseball writers voted the prize to Joe Gordon of the Yankees for his defensive ability.

"The attitude of the baseball writers towards Williams makes it evident that the cards were stacked against him since that day early in July when he was accused of loafing. These so-called, fair-minded members of the press have allowed their personal prejudices to blind them to the merits of the greatest left-handed batter of our day.

"They have made a farce of what once was considered one of the highest honors a baseball player could receive. Their sense of justice makes them suitable for the Reichstag . . . Robert E. Krouse, Elizabeth, N.J."

Then came the war. Both Williams and DiMaggio missed the entire 1943, 1944, and 1945 seasons due to World War II. When they returned, Williams at 27, DiMaggio at 31, things had changed.

BACK FROM THE WAR—1946–1951

Back in pinstripes, Joe DiMaggio fell under .300 for the first time in his career at .290, with 25 home runs and 95 RBIs while Williams batted .342 with 38 home runs and 123 RBIs and a staggering, league-leading 156 walks, earning his first MVP award in 1946. He was second to Mickey Vernon in the batting race (.353 to Ted's .342), second in homers to Hank Greenberg (44 to Ted's 38) and second to Hank in RBIs (127 to Ted's 123).

Not only that, Boston won 104 games to take the American League pennant—the only one of Ted's career—and met the St. Louis Cardinals in the World Series, falling in seven games. And Williams, possibly still feeling the effects of a bum elbow injured in a postseason exhibition game, didn't hit a lick in the Series. Neither did his Cardinals counterpart Stan Musial, but Williams's only shot at postseason was anything but memorable. He often later talked about it as the biggest disappointment in his career. And for the boobirds, who were always looking for reasons to criticize Williams, it was enough ammunition to last them the rest of his career.

In 1947, something weird happened to Ted's MVP vote again. Somehow, DiMaggio edged Ted out—the numbers didn't explain it. Joe hit .315 with 20 home runs and 97 RBIs in leading the Yankees back to the World Series. But frankly, his numbers paled in comparison to Williams's .343, 32 homers, and 114 RBI with 162 walks and a 1.133 OPS, all tops in the league, a damned Triple Crown! Was this an example of media bias? You tell me. New York pitcher Joe Page got seven first-place votes to Ted's three. Go figure. Can anyone *not* in pinstripes explain or justify that one?

The 1948 seasons were terrific for both Joe and Ted; DiMaggio hit .320 with 39 home runs and 155 RBIs, leading the league in those last two categories. Williams hit a stunning .369 with 25 home runs and

127 RBIs as both Boston and New York fell behind the Cleveland Indians, who beat the Boston Braves in the World Series that year.

Once again, Williams struggled in a key moment. Though Williams had himself a sensational September, helping the Red Sox catch Cleveland down the stretch and force a one-game playoff, his great work ended there.

In the playoff game at Fenway Park, the Tribe started left-hander Gene Bearden, a war hero and a 20-game winner that season, the only 20-win season of his career. Bearden simply dazzled the Red Sox on that chilly October afternoon, throwing only sliders and knuckleballs. He threw one fastball that Bobby Doerr hit onto the left field screen, but it was too late.

Indians player-manager Lou Boudreau almost singlehandedly beat the Sox with a pair of home runs in the 8–3 win. And yes, Boudreau was also the guy who came up with the cursed "Boudreau Shift" against Williams. Ted had but one seventh-inning single and the Tribe's win advanced them to a World Series date with the Boston Braves. Think of it! There could have been a Subway Series in Boston, too! Cleveland ended up winning the Series in six games.

In 1949, Ted nearly had another Triple Crown season, losing the batting title to Detroit's George Kell on the last day of the season. He hit 43 home runs and added 159 RBIs with a league-leading 162 walks, winning his second MVP. Injuries, meanwhile, were taking a toll on Joe, who only played 76 games that year, batting .346 with 14 home runs and 67 RBIs. Though he was just 34, the end was near.

In 1950, a late surge from DiMaggio managed to get his average up over .300 with five hits in a doubleheader against the Washington Senators on September 25. He managed four walks off Boston's Mel Parnell in the season finale at Fenway to stay there.

Williams was off to a sensational season when he injured his elbow in the All-Star Game, limiting him to 89 games. He still managed 28 home runs, 97 RBIs, and a .317 average. The Red Sox won 94 games, good enough for second place behind the Yankees' 98. New York swept the Phillies in the World Series, rookie Whitey Ford almost throwing a complete-game shutout in Game 4.

THE FINAL SEASON FOR JOE

In 1951, there were lots of issues for #5 in his last season for the Yankees—neck spasms, heel problems, a slowed-down bat. Though the Bombers won another pennant and beat the New York Giants in the World Series, DiMaggio was a shell of himself.

He closed out his season with hits in 14 of his last 16 games, the final seven in a row to wind up at .263 with 12 home runs and 73 RBIs. He hit his final homer, number 361, in the second game of a doubleheader against the Red Sox, a sixth-inning shot off Chuck Stobbs in an 11–3 win. He got his final hit two days later, a first-inning single off Boston's Harley Hisner in a 3–0 Yankee end-of-the-season win.

He closed out his World Series and career with an eighth-inning double off the Giants' Larry Jansen. When he announced his retirement in December, there had already been speculation in the *New York Times* that the Yankees were going to go after Ted Williams. It didn't happen.

As for Williams, Ted's 1951 season was solid—.318 average, 30 home runs, 126 RBIs with 144 walks after a rough start in April and May. The Red Sox were also a solid team at 87–67, but the Yankees won 98 and won themselves yet another World Series.

Though at 33 with DiMaggio gone, Williams might have been ready to take over the American League, Uncle Sam called. Again. Williams lost most of the '52 and '53 seasons to the Korean War. When he came back in 1954, he might have won the batting title with a .345 average, except playing in 117 games, he didn't have enough at-bats to qualify for the title. Cleveland's Bobby Avila won the crown at .341.

TED'S FINAL SEASONS

Injuries held Ted to just 98 games in 1955 and cut into his impressive numbers—.356, 28 home runs, and 83 RBIs. As happened several times throughout his career, Williams didn't have enough at-bats to qualify for the batting title.

The qualifications changed several times throughout his career. In 1955, Ted actually hit 16 points higher than the recognized batting champion, Detroit's Al Kaline, but Al got the crown.

In 1956, Williams batted .345 with 24 home runs and 82 RBIs, runner-up to MVP Mickey Mantle, who hit .353. Not bad for a 37-year-old.

In 1957, Williams left them all behind. On May 8, a guy who couldn't outrun a statue was hitting .474. After briefly dipping to .369, he was back at .411 heading into June. In mid-July, his average slid to his career average—.344—before climbing back to .377 by the end of August. He turned 39 in Baltimore that summer before a mystery virus laid him low for a couple of weeks.

When he returned to the lineup, there was a pinch-hit homer off Whitey Ford in the ninth inning, his only home run off the little lefty, and the hits kept on coming. He had 12 hits in his final 18 at-bats including his final two hits of the season, a double and RBI single off Yankees starter Art Ditmar on a Sunday afternoon at Fenway Park, raising his average to .470 against the Yankees that year. His two hits on that final day raised Ted's final average that season to an amazing .388.

Ted won another batting title the next year, edging out teammate Pete Runnels with a closing rush, hitting .328 for his sixth batting crown. A variety of injuries, including a serious neck problem, ruined Williams's 1959 season. He wound up at .254, was hitting below .200 at the end of May, and there were those who called for him to hang it up. Williams, of course, had his own ideas. He asked for—and received—a $30,000 cut in pay (let's face it, something DiMaggio never would have done) and went out and hit .316, passed the 500-home-run mark, and of course, left the game with that final dramatic home run on his final swing.

THE BEST VS. THE BEST

In wandering through all these nearly ancient box scores, you had to wonder how each guy did against the premier pitchers of their time. Like great heavyweight fighters who never seem to match up when both boxers are at their peak—an aging Joe Louis murdered by up-and-comer Rocky Marciano, an aging Larry Holmes flattened by a terrifying young Mike Tyson, a rusty Muhammad Ali, returning to the ring after a three-year layoff facing a hungry tiger in Joe Frazier after just six months of training—we got to see DiMaggio and Williams pretty much in their primes for a good long while.

Having read a lot about both men, examining their track record in close detail, you can't help but wonder how different each man's career might have been had they swapped cities from the start. Though Williams's rapport with the Boston press was tumultuous at best, in reading many of Arthur Daley's columns on Williams over Ted's lengthy career, there was a warmth, a respect between the two men that transcended the printed page.

For example, here's an exchange between Daley and Ted from February 1957. It was about one of Williams's passions, fishing, and the catching of a particularly impressive marlin.

"Who caught the big one," Daley asks. "That's the most intelligent question I've heard in years," roared the laughing, delighted Ted. He shook hands fervently and screamed his answer, "ME."

You had to think the Boston writers, when they read that, wondered if it was the same guy.

Or look at this example from September 1949 called "Ted Williams Does the Talking":

> "Ted Williams was sitting in front of his locker at the Yankee Stadium yesterday. It never is difficult to get him talking. The difficulty usually is the restless Red Sox slugger rarely remains stationary long enough to get any conversation out of him."

Daley greets the Red Sox star harshly. He writes: "The greeting from the dressing-room visitor hardly could be classed as being a model in diplomacy. 'A fine bunch of bums you are,' was the opening salute. 'You should be a dozen games in front by now and where are you?'"

Imagine a Boston writer saying that. Now measure Williams's response. Daley continues: "'Isn't that the truth?' said Mr. Williams sadly, too much of a realist ever to take umbrage at the remark—which probably was why there was no risk in uttering it. He shrugged his shoulders hopelessly as to how the Red Sox, the best team in the league, should be in a trailing position.

"'Is there anything more unpredictable than baseball?' he asked, his bubbling good nature speeding a grin to his face." *(Editor's note: Let me quote Daley again. "HIS BUBBLING GOOD NATURE SPEEDING A GRIN TO HIS FACE.")*

Daley continues: "It was strictly a rhetorical question. But a reply was tossed in anyway.

'Golf,' was the answer offered.

"'Or women,' he added mischievously and started to laugh.

"Then Williams, always the most sensitive of players, offered a stunningly candid self-critique. 'I guess I didn't help too much in the early part of the year,' said Ted slowly. 'I don't remember whether it was after our first Western trip or the second one but I was down to .290. But I always have hit best in July and August. However, September usually is a tough month. That's especially true of day games. The shadows lengthen earlier—you don't get those shadows under arc lights—and the days are cooler.'"

Daley sought a second opinion—from Joe DiMaggio, who revealed a somewhat less scientific approach than Williams.

"I agree with Ted about the shadows," said the Yankee Clipper, "but I'll be darned if I know what months are my best hitting months. I never bothered to look. When I'm hot, I'm hot."

And you can be sure the Boston sportswriters gagged when they read Daley's close.

"This Williams guy is such a likeable cuss that it's a shame the fans who boo him so much don't know him better even though his stubborn streak impels them to treat them with rock-headed disdain on occasions. The crowds think he's arrogant when he isn't. They think he's a bad fielder when he actually is a good one. They think he's a selfish individualist when he's the fiercest team fighter of them all. He was rarin' to go yesterday when the rain washed out the game to his vast disappointment. When it's replayed, it may be much too late."

Some years later, Daley looked back. Writing in February 1969, Daley spun an entirely different look at the cantankerous Ted Williams, the scourge of the Boston press. He wrote: "The portrait of Ted Williams as painted by his detractors among the baseball writers pictured him as something of an ogre. They have said he was rude, crude and uncivil. He brushed them off and bawled them out. Since Boston fans never tired reading about Williams, the uncooperative hero often placed the task of chronicling him in depth somewhere between the difficult and the impossible.

"But no one ever could get me to put the rap on him. At all times I found him wonderful, a guy who went out of his way to help me."

Ted Williams? *Helping* a writer? Daley goes on to explain how Williams, injured in a spring training game, was supposedly unreachable. He called the hotel housing the Red Sox, was warned that Williams never returns calls and five minutes later, the phone rang. "Hello, Arthur. This is Ted. How are you?"

Some years later, Williams was in his sacred place—the batting cage—when he noticed Daley looking on. Daley tells the story in another column.

"I thought you're a friend of mine," he said, coiling for another swing.

"I thought so, too," I said. He sent a ball screaming over the fence.

"What's the idea then of that column you wrote about me last winter?" he said. "I see your stuff. You can't get away with anything with me." He cracked a line drive to center, still frowning.

"You big fathead," I said. "You can't even read. I didn't knock you. For the most part that was a highly complimentary column."

"It was?" he said in a small boy's voice, taking a final swing. He walked out of the cage and started to laugh.

"Hello," he said, sticking out his hand. Only Williams would be so unembarrassed as to drop his hello into the middle of a conversation."

Of course, it's difficult to just grab a handful of columns over the years and try to project an entire career. But might our perception of Ted Williams and maybe Williams's behavior itself been altered had the coverage of his career, understanding his natural volatility, his eagerness to get things straight been handled the way Daley did? Did it take an out-of-town writer to see the real Ted Williams?

The stories of Williams's stormy relations with the Boston press are legendary as are some of the snide, sometimes horribly unprofessional ways in which he was covered by the ferociously competitive Hub papers.

Some of the criticism of Williams was warranted, certainly. But notice these Daley columns came over a span of 30 years. Note also that at times, Williams would give a lengthy, insightful interview to an out-of-town writer, knowing it would piss off the Boston press. Which it did.

"I know in my heart I got a lot of rotten remarks written about me," Williams told a Boston TV interviewer years later, "Things that weren't true. And I was rebellious enough at times to throw a little static at them and they didn't like that. I know I brought a lot of it on myself by not being as mature as I should have been."

Had Williams's extraordinary achievements been cast in the remarkably glowing light that shone down on DiMaggio's from the beginning of Joe's career, you wonder how we all might have viewed Williams, what additional awards might have been his, how DiMaggio's superb 13-year run—somewhat abbreviated compared with Williams's unusual longevity—might have made us reconsider both men, both careers.

Maybe not. Williams has said more than once that the constant criticism in Boston fueled him. "That nobody made them eat more crow than Ted Williams," he often said. Maybe having something to fire him up every single day rose his talent to a level he might not have approached with the complimentary, daily, regular pats on the back that Joe read.

Even the great Red Smith, one of the most accomplished of all sportswriters, one who continually spoke of his early editors warning him about "godding up the ballplayers" sort of did just that in his farewell column. "I told myself not to worry," Smith wrote, closing what turned out to be his final sentence. "Someday there would be another Joe DiMaggio."

Since those were the last words Smith wrote, maybe we can cut him some slack. He died a few days later, after all.

No, Ted Williams wasn't going to win a game for you with his glove, though DiMaggio, clearly a vastly superior defender, still had four seasons of double-digit errors in center field, just like Ted did in left or right.

Williams wasn't going to win you games with his legs, though, as he once noted, Ted led the league in runs scored six times, DiMaggio did it only once, batting in the middle of a lineup that was generally more productive.

Williams posted a much higher career batting average, had more seasons over .300, drew almost three times as many walks, hit 160 more home runs in a park not particularly favorable to a left-handed hitter, all the while playing for a team that was, except perhaps for one or two seasons, clearly inferior to those surrounding and supporting DiMaggio.

But after examining these box scores, looking at the DiMaggio-Williams matchup in depth and in context, having read a lot about both men, examined the coverage of each man, you have to wonder if we're shortchanging the Boston slugger and perhaps his overall place in the history of the game. Joe DiMaggio was a great player, certainly. So was Ted Williams. And he did it longer. With parts of five seasons twice interrupting his career.

Maybe the good folks at Cooperstown unintentionally have things in proper perspective. For as you enter the Baseball Hall of Fame, there are two statues there to greet you. One is of the Bambino, the great Babe Ruth. The other is Ted Williams.

"The [statue] one that I had in Cooperstown," Williams recalled, "I shed a tear that day. There I was, my statue there and it was a hitting shot. As I looked at that statue of me, I could look over about 60 feet and there was a statue of Babe Ruth. And that brought a tear to my eye because there was only one, always and forever, Babe Ruth. As a kid, I thought that. And there's my statue right there, with the mighty Ruth."

How Did Ted and Joe Match Up with the Best of Their Peers?

For comparison's sake, let's look at how Ted and Joe handled the stuff from these Hall of Fame hurlers:

Bob Feller

	Hits-At-Bats	Avg	2B	3B	HR	RBI	BB	K
DiMaggio:	66–193	.342	11	7	11	46	23	12
Williams:	53–154	.344	13	4	10	34	38	13

Bob Lemon

	Hits-At-Bats	Avg	2B	3B	HR	RBI	BB	K
DiMaggio:	18–58	.310	4	0	0	12	9	2
Williams:	31–116	.267	4	1	4	21	31	7

Whitey Ford

	Hits-At-Bats	Avg	2B	3B	HR	RBI	BB	K
Williams:	17–47	.378	3	0	1	5	13	4

Hal Newhouser

	Hits-At-Bats	Avg	2B	3B	HR	RBI	BB	K
DiMaggio:	45–115	.391	8	5	9	37	15	4
Williams:	20–79	.253	0	2	2	12	16	3

Early Wynn

	Hits-At-Bats	Avg	2B	3B	HR	RBI	BB	K
DiMaggio:	27–98	.276	3	1	3	17	10	9
Williams:	42–133	.316	9	0	8	30	31	9

Ted Lyons

	Hits-At-Bats	Avg	2B	3B	HR	RBI	BB	K
DiMaggio:	26–73	.356	0	2	4	17	1	2
Williams:	12–36	.333	2	2	1	3	5	4

Jim Bunning

	Hits-At-Bats	Avg	2B	3B	HR	RBI	BB	K
Williams:	23–61	.377	5	0	8	17	15	7

Lefty Grove

	Hits-At-Bats	Avg	2B	3B	HR	RBI	BB	K
DiMaggio:	26–72	.361	7	1	2	10	6	5

And these top-of-the-line starters:

Tex Hughson

	Hits-At-Bats	Avg	2B	3B	HR	RBI	BB	K
DiMaggio:	14–59	.237	3	0	2	9	4	8

Dizzy Trout

	Hits-At-Bats	Avg	2B	3B	HR	RBI	BB	K
DiMaggio:	21–97	.217	1	2	5	18	6	5
Williams:	27–64	.422	5	1	5	16	15	8

Billy Pierce

	Hits-At-Bats	Avg	2B	3B	HR	RBI	BB	K
DiMaggio:	4–30	.133	0	0	1	1	4	4
Williams:	22–89	.247	4	2	2	11	33	14

Virgil Trucks

	Hits-At-Bats	Avg	2B	3B	HR	RBI	BB	K
DiMaggio:	17–55	.309	3	1	2	12	4	5
Williams:	39–113	.345	8	1	10	28	25	10

Mel Harder

	Hits-At-Bats	Avg	2B	3B	HR	RBI	BB	K
DiMaggio:	19–83	.229	5	2	0	9	7	7
Williams:	22–71	.310	4	0	4	14	12	7

CHAPTER SEVEN

Duke Rounds the Bases

The progress of an education, whether that of a candidate for the Presidency or that of a candidate for the heavyweight championship always interests me. So when I read in a newspaper that Marciano had been matched to fight Jersey Joe Walcott for the title in the Philadelphia Municipal Stadium on the night of September 23, 1952, I went."
—"NEW CHAMP" BY A. J. LIEBLING IN *THE SWEET SCIENCE*

IT MAY BE A LEAP OF FAITH TO SEE THE BATTLE BETWEEN A PITCHER and a hitter as a challenge of one man's intellect vs. another man's physical skills, what A. J. Liebling was hinting at in that passage about the Rocky Marciano–Jersey Joe Walcott fight.

When an encounter is repeated over a number of years with varying degrees of success, the drama mounting, the experiences shaping each and every on-field decision on every single pitch, it's a matchup that grows more fascinating with every successive at-bat. Baseball games, of course, are a series of these matchups, and when you're able to add a little context and a healthy dash of history to these ball-and-strike showdowns, watching things unfold can be exciting.

Such was the case between the former Brooklyn and Los Angeles Dodgers great Duke Snider and the Philadelphia Phillies' Hall of Fame hurler Robin Roberts, who faced off against one another on the diamond 260 times from 1948 to 1961. Of all the major-league batters who have ever stepped into a batter's box, it's Duke Snider who is the all-time leader for home runs against a single pitcher, swatting a record 19 home runs off the whistling deliveries of the durable Roberts. He batted .295 off Roberts, exactly his career average. Oddly, Ted Williams and Bob Feller had precisely the same thing—Ted batted .344 against Feller and he hit the same for his career!

Duke Snider
WIKIMEDIA COMMONS

Snider's first career at-bat against Roberts came in a Wednesday night game at Philadelphia's Shibe Park in 1948. With two on and one out in the first inning, Roberts got Snider on a swinging strikeout. But Roberts's wild pitch to the next batter—Pee Wee Reese—ended up letting in the game's only run in a 1–0 loss.

His last at-bat against the righty came all the way across America, a seventh-inning leadoff single at the Los Angeles Memorial Coliseum 13 years later. But earlier in the game, Roberts had gotten Snider to rap into a double play and hit a grounder to first. It was that kind of back-and-forth battle between pitcher and hitter.

In all, there were 19 times that a Snider swing resulted in a Roberts pitch landing in the seats. But the moment that Snider will always remember happened in Brooklyn. "I got the last home run off Robin Roberts, got my 40th home run [of] 1957, at Ebbets Field, the last home run that was hit there," Snider recalled years later. "And we had two more games that I could have played. Manager [Walt] Alston came to me and asked me if I wanted to play. I didn't. I'm sort of sentimental about that last at-bat at Ebbets Field being a home run."

Interestingly, Roberts doesn't go into that in his 2003 book, *My Life in Baseball*. He does mention Snider a few times—there are seven references to him in all but no mention of the 19 home runs—tops in the history of the game—specifically. Near the end of the book, Roberts did allude to surrendering home runs.

"I did give up a lot of home runs," Roberts wrote, "but they only bothered me if they cost me a ballgame. If I won 6–3 and gave up three solo home runs, I had won the game and didn't give a thought to the home runs. Of course, I didn't know anybody was counting. Maybe if I had known, I would have changed something, but I doubt it. I was mainly a one-pitch pitcher, although I sometimes mixed in a curveball when I was ahead in the count. I could put my fastball where I wanted it.

"I was sometimes criticized for not pitching inside more and not knocking hitters down. Dizzy Dean broadcast the *Game of the Week* on network television during the fifties and every time he saw me, he would tell me, 'Robin, you've got to knock somebody on their ass.'

"Well, lots of people talked about knocking batters down, but few did it. And it just wasn't me. I just went after people with my best stuff and let the batters hit it if they could. That was my act, and it got me through 18 years in the big leagues."

Tracing their matchup over those 13 years and 260 at-bats, Roberts was going to live or die with his fastball. "If I had a game where I threw 115 pitches," Roberts said, "90 of them were fastballs."

Hall of Famer Ralph Kiner agreed. "Probably the best fastball I ever saw was Robin Roberts," he said. "It would rise six to eight inches and it had plenty on it. And he had great control."

But challenging hitters the way he did, Roberts also allowed 505 career home runs, second all-time to Jamie Moyer's 522. Roberts held the all-time gopher ball title until Moyer passed him on July 7, 2010, allowing number 506, a two-run shot by the Braves' Matt Diaz in the sixth inning. (On a personal note, I covered Diaz's sensational career at

Florida State. That kid could hit!) Moyer, as many baseball fans remember, had a 25-year career, even pitching in his 49th year for the Colorado Rockies, throwing 53.2 innings and allowing 11 more home runs.

Funny enough, there didn't seem to be anything unusual about the Roberts-Snider duel that began in 1948. In his first 45 at-bats against the hard-throwing Roberts, the sweet-swinging lefty hit just three home runs and collected only eight hits (.178). But Snider began to figure him out.

He hit .367 with a home run in 1951, no homers in '52, but reached Roberts for three homers in '53 (.286). Then he really turned it up. In the 1954 season, Snider ripped Roberts for a .546 average, a pair of homers, then, over the next three years, Snider slammed eight homers off Roberts, including a dramatic pair of them in Robin's final pitching effort in Ebbets Field, including that home run in his last Ebbets Field at-bat.

When the Dodgers moved out to Los Angeles, Roberts had the edge again on Snider, shutting him out in 1958, 0-for-8 with a pair of strikeouts. In 1959, Snider slammed his final two homers off Roberts, a homer to left in June, and a homer to right in August which was his last hit off the righty until the very last time they faced one another. Roberts turned the table back in his direction, fanning Snider five times in his final 14 at-bats. But in his final at-bat, Snider drove a groundball single through the middle in the seventh inning on April 11, 1961. Don Drysdale and the Dodgers won that game, 6–2, spoiling Roberts's first start of that season.

The two of them kept on playing but never faced one another again. Snider played for three more seasons, including one in New York with the Mets and one in San Francisco with the Giants. Roberts left Philadelphia for Baltimore, Houston, and the Chicago Cubs before retiring in 1966. Nobody wrote about the Snider-Roberts duels coming to a halt.

DUKE'S HOME RUN CHALLENGERS

Oddly, the home-runs-off-one-pitcher all-time record wasn't something that many people knew or ever talked about. Maybe it isn't that much of a surprise to find out that after Snider's totals, the duel for the runner-up spot ended up being quite a battle between three of the game's greatest players: Willie Mays, Hank Aaron, and the mighty Babe.

Duke Snider vs. Robin Roberts
Regular Season: 260 PA , .295/.341/.614, 19 HR, 33 K
Playoffs: 0 PA

Duke Snider vs. Robin Roberts: Batter vs. Pitcher

Duke Snider vs. Robin Roberts: Year-by-Year Totals   Export Data

Regular Season

Rk	Year	PA	AB	H	2B	3B	HR	RBI	BB	SO	BA	OBP	SLG	OPS	SH	SF	IBB	HBP	GIDP
1	1948	5	5	1	1	0	0	2	0	1	.200	.200	.400	.600	0	0	0	0	0
2	1949	8	8	1	0	0	1	3	0	3	.125	.125	.500	.625	0	0	0	0	0
3	1950	33	32	6	0	1	2	2	1	4	.188	.212	.438	.650	0	0	0	0	0
4	1951	31	30	11	1	1	1	5	1	4	.367	.387	.567	.954	0	0	0	0	1
5	1952	20	19	5	0	0	0	0	0	2	.263	.263	.263	.526	1	0	0	0	0
6	1953	29	28	8	2	0	3	6	1	5	.286	.310	.679	.989	0	0	1	0	2
7	1954	26	22	12	2	1	2	7	4	0	.545	.615	1.000	1.615	0	0	1	0	0
8	1955	26	26	9	1	0	2	6	0	1	.346	.346	.615	.962	0	0	0	0	2
9	1956	26	22	6	3	0	3	5	3	4	.273	.360	.818	1.178	1	0	0	0	1
10	1957	21	19	5	1	0	3	6	2	2	.263	.333	.789	1.123	0	0	1	0	1
11	1958	10	8	1	0	0	0	0	2	2	.125	.300	.125	.425	0	0	0	0	0
12	1959	12	10	5	1	1	2	8	2	1	.500	.583	1.400	1.983	0	0	1	0	0
13	1960	10	9	0	0	0	0	0	1	4	.000	.100	.000	.100	0	0	0	0	0
14	1961	3	3	1	0	0	0	0	0	0	.333	.333	.333	.667	0	0	0	0	1
	Totals	**260**	**241**	**71**	**12**	**4**	**19**	**50**	**17**	**33**	**.295**	**.341**	**.614**	**.955**	**2**	**0**	**4**	**0**	**8**

Beginning with his first major-league hit, Willie Mays ended up whacking 18 home runs off Warren Spahn, just one behind Snider's lifetime total off Roberts. Hank Aaron was next, swatting 17 longballs off Dodgers great Don Drysdale, which happened to be the same total as the inimitable Babe Ruth, who set the standard with 17 homers off lefty Rube Walberg from 1923 to 1932. Babe reached him for four homers in Ruth's record-setting season of 1927, the most we were able to find for one hitter off one pitcher in a single season.

When you look at the list of double-figure home-run hitters off a single pitcher, it's not hard to notice there are few players of recent vintage. Some of the game's most celebrated home-run hitters won't reach double figures off one pitcher again. The game has changed so much, pitchers don't face hitters three, four times a game anymore. So it sure looks like The Duke will be the all-time champ for career homers off one pitcher. And to think he had just three home runs in his first 45 at-bats against the guy before he started hitting them out of the park.

THE HIT PARADE—HOME RUNS OFF ONE PITCHER

Duke Snider—Robin Roberts 19, Murry Dickson 10, Bob Purkey 10, Warren Hacker 10

Willie Mays—Warren Spahn 18, Vern Law 15, Don Drysdale 13, Lew Burdette 12, Bob Buhl 11, Harvey Haddix 10, Johnny Podres 10

Babe Ruth—Rube Walberg 17, Hooks Dauss 14, Howard Ehmke 13, Milt Gaston 13, Lefty Stewart 13, George Uhle 12, Tommy Thomas 11, Earl Whitehill 11, Walter Johnson 10, Eddie Rommel 10, George Earnshaw 10, Horace Lisenbee 10, Ted Lyons 10. Babe also hit nine off Tom Zachary, who surrendered the historic number 60 of 1927.

Hank Aaron—Don Drysdale 17, Claude Osteen 14, Bob Friend 12, Don Cardwell 10, Roger Craig 10, Larry Jackson 10

Jimmie Foxx—Tommy Bridges 16, Red Ruffing 16, General Crowder 16, Willis Hudlin 14, Lefty Gomez 14, Ted Lyons 14, Bump Hadley 13, Mel Harder 11, Jack Knott 11, Johnny Rigney 10, Wes Ferrell 10, Earl Whitehill 10

Stan Musial—Warren Spahn 15, Preacher Roe 12, Johnny Antonelli 11, Murry Dickson 11, Don Newcombe 11, Robin Roberts 10, Bob Rush, 10

Ernie Banks—Robin Roberts 15, Lew Burdette 12, Bob Friend 10

Mickey Mantle—Early Wynn 13, Pedro Ramos 12, Camilo Pascual 11

Frank Howard—Dave McNally 13

Roy Campanella—Robin Roberts 13

Johnny Bench—Don Sutton 12, Steve Carlton 12, Phil Niekro 11

Eddie Mathews—Bob Friend 14, Robin Roberts 13, Jack Sanford 11, Roger Craig 11, Vern Law 11, Bob Purkey 10

Mel Ott—Lon Warneke 13, Larry French 12, Paul Derringer 12, Max Butcher 11, Charlie Root 10

Willie McCovey—Don Drysdale 12

Yogi Berra—Early Wynn 11, Ted Gray 10

Dick Allen—Ken Holtzman 11

Ted Williams—Virgil Trucks 12, Bob Feller 10, Virgil Trucks 10

Frank Robinson—Larry Jackson 10

Al Kaline—Jim Kaat 10

Roger Maris—Jim Perry 9

Jim Thome—Rick Reed 9

Barry Bonds—Greg Maddux 8, Curt Schilling 8, John Smoltz 8, Terry Mulholland 8, Chan Ho Park 8

Albert Pujols—Ryan Dempster 8

Alex Rodriguez—Tim Wakefield 8, David Wells 8, Ramon Ortiz 8, Bartolo Colon 8

Ken Griffey Jr.—David Wells 8

Sammy Sosa—Curt Schilling 7, Jose Lima 7

Mark McGwire—Frank Tanana 7

It Don't Mean A Thing if You Ain't Got That Swing— and Miss

In baseball, a "golden sombrero" signifies striking out four times in a single game. Through the 2024 season, baseball's all-time golden sombrero king is Giancarlo Stanton of the New York Yankees with 28 separate major-league games where he fanned four times. That gives Stanton a one-sombrero edge on former Philadelphia Phillie Ryan Howard, who had 27 of 'em. Former Baltimore Oriole Chris Davis is next with 26 four-whiff games, but all these marks, even Stanton's, might not be safe. The number-four-ranked whiff king is absolutely capable of many more and is renowned as one of baseball's breeziest batters, the Washington Nationals' Joey Gallo. Two Hall of Famers are sandwiched around Arizona Diamondbacks whiffer Eugenio Suarez's 21. Reggie Jackson had 23 four-strikeout games, three more than Hall of Famer Jim Thome. Believe it or not, there is such a thing as a silver platinum sombrero which, at least to this point, is fairly rare. That means five strikeouts in a single game, one of those days that the hitter couldn't hit a beach ball. The all-time king there, kind of breezy here, is Sammy Sosa who fanned five times in a single game four separate times. From what we could find, only one other player, Ray Lankford, had a five-whiff game three times.

There are other whiff episodes of note. Baltimore Orioles occasional slugger Sam Horn once struck out six times in an extra-inning game. Sammy Sosa, Ray Lankford, and Javier Báez are—so far—the only players to have more than one platinum sombrero. Interestingly, Báez and Seattle Mariners' Nelson Cruz had five-strikeout days on the same day—July 25, 2017. There are many other instances and with the way the game is trending, likely more to come. But just because you have a silver platinum night, doesn't mean you can't be productive. In a seventeen-inning Orioles game on May 6, 2012, Chris Davis went 0-for-8 with five whiffs. He also threw two innings of relief and earned the win, the first American League positional player to earn a win in 44 years.

CHAPTER EIGHT

Home Runs of Every Variety

BASEBALL'S BANTY ROOSTER, FORMER BALTIMORE ORIOLES MANAGER Earl Weaver, was famous for many things, among them (A) fighting with umpires, all of whom seemed to tower over him, (B) smoking in the dugout—he tagged reliever Don Stanhouse "Full Pack" because his walking-a-tightrope method of relieving games drove Weaver to ransack his Raleighs, (C) arguing with Jim Palmer about pitching (Palmer: "The only thing Earl knows about a curveball is he couldn't hit it") and (D) being a quote machine. He left us with these two quotes, which, taken together, seemed to forecast where his game was headed long after he left it.

First, Earl offered this: "When you play for one run, that's usually all you get. I have nothing against the bunt in its place, but most of the time, that place is in the bottom of a long-forgotten closet."

Then this: "The key to winning baseball games is pitching, fundamentals and three-run homers." Amen.

Let's face it, folks, you would be hard-pressed to find any current major-league manager who would disagree with the stated philosophy of The Earl of Baltimore. That certainly seems to be the way the game is trending. Everybody—except pitchers and outfielders who might strain their neck—loves those three-run home runs. Yet, when it comes to keeping track of an important event like those across the history of the game, we have no idea. Nobody ever talks about who is accumulating them.

When it comes to four-run homers, grand slams, we like to call them, we know all about that. Alex Rodriguez is the all-time grand slam home run leader with 25. A-Rod is two ahead of Lou Gehrig's 23, four ahead of Manny Ramírez's 21, six more than Eddie Murray, seven more than Willie McCovey and Robin Ventura, eight more than Jimmie Foxx, Carlos Lee, and Theodore Samuel Williams, nine more than Hank Aaron, Babe Ruth, and Dave Kingman.

But three-run homers? Two-run homers? Walkoff homers? Solo homers? Game-tying home runs? They all seem to be lost in the shuffle. Until now.

The answers to all of those questions were provided by the great Stathead site and the Home Run Log and my crackerjack correspondent who, incidentally, is well named—Katie Sharp. Though Katie was quick to note that these statistics only go back to 1914, back in the day when Philadelphia's "Home Run" Baker would lead the AL with nine, chances are we didn't miss anyone from those days in compiling these all-time lists.

Three-Run Homers

For a player to connect on a three-run homer, that means that the pitcher in question thinks he can get him out instead of walking him to load the bases and set up a force at any base. Some 60 times, that pitcher happened to be the venerable Jamie Moyer, who surrendered the most homers in baseball history, 522 in a 25-year career!

In the near future, it may well be that the strategy of the game will almost always insist on the intentional walk. Before that, many pitchers were willing to take their chances and got burned. You'll see for yourself.

As you might expect, the names are familiar on the all-time three-run home run list. If you're someone who already ranks among the game's overall all-time leaders in homers, chances are you'd be up there in the three-run shot territory, too.

The three-run homer king competition came down to four of the greatest home-run hitters of all time—Sammy Sosa, Babe Ruth, Hank Aaron, and Jimmie Foxx. The champ was former Chicago Cubs great Sammy Sosa, who slammed 97 three-run homers in his career, 43 of them with men on first and second, 31 of them with men on first and third, and a whopping 23 with men on second and third, far and away the most homers in that spot. Shoulda walked him!

The legendary Babe Ruth was just two behind with 95 three-run homers, slamming 59 with men on first and second, 28 with men on first and third, and nine with men on second and third, and first base open. Intentional walks were rare in Ruth's day—here's a statistical anomaly: Ruth received 28 intentional passes in 1924 and 13 in 1926 but only three in his 1927 60-home-run campaign (maybe because Lou Gehrig was hitting behind him). Stats on intentional walks don't show up until 1924, so that may explain Ruth's low career intentional walk total: 79. Barry Bonds would get that before the All-Star break.

Aaron was next with 94 three-run homers, just seven with men on second and third. The intentional walk *was* in vogue in Aaron's era, Hank collecting 293 of them, a high of 23 in his 1968 season, an off-year for him: .287, 29 homers, 86 RBIs. Who says baseball makes sense?

The great Jimmie Foxx was close with 92 three-run shots with only eight coming with first base open. He had 134 career intentional walks with a single-season high of 17 coming in 1934 when Foxx hit .334 with 44 homers and 130 RBIs with a league-leading 111 walks. He was just 10th in the MVP voting that year, behind Hal Trosky, Wes Ferrell, and Marv Owen, names that don't exactly roll off the tongue.

Among the rest of the crew collected from Baseball-Reference.com's Home Run Log, there are just a handful of players who made pitchers regret *not* walking them with first base open. Manny Ramírez hit 15 of those, Ernie Banks 13, while Fred McGriff, Harmon Killebrew, Albert Pujols, and Mike Schmidt each had 11.

Albert Pujols just missed the 90-three-run-homer club with 89. Three other sluggers hit 80 or more three-run shots: Mel Ott his 83 of his 511 career homers with two men on, a whopping 52 of them with men on first and second! Jim Thome and Mike Schmidt each hit 81 three-run shots.

Next up is the all-time home run king Barry Bonds, who is tied with Ken Griffey Jr. with 78 but likely could have had a lot more. As his career wound down and his home run totals (and reportedly his helmet size) grew, Bonds did get 688 intentional walks, 377 of them *after* he turned 37. In 2004 alone, Bonds drew *120* intentional walks.

Across his career, Bonds was intentionally walked 111 times when he was facing a lefty pitcher (Bonds, of course, batted left-handed), 41 times overall when the bases were empty, 75 times when a runner was on first, 108 of them when his team was losing, and 95 of them in the very first inning! The big intentional walk inning for Bonds was the third inning with 103.

So, whether artificially aided or not, how might Bonds have added to his home run and RBI totals if teams had been a little more willing to really pitch to him in those statistically-out-of-whack closing seasons?

There were four other sluggers who managed to club 70-plus three-run shots: Ted Williams (76), Ernie Banks (75), and Gary Sheffield, Jeff Bagwell, Alex Rodriguez, and Lou Gehrig each with 70.

The 60-plus three-run homer club included some of the game's greatest sluggers—Frank Robinson (69), Reggie Jackson (68), Manny Ramírez (68), José Canseco (68), Mickey Mantle (67), Willie McCovey (67), Willie Mays (67), Mark McGwire (66), David Ortiz (66), Willie Stargell (66), Eddie Murray (65), Frank Thomas (65), Harmon Killebrew (62), Mark Teixeira (60), Johnny Bench (60), and Juan González (60). Now, who would have thought Mark Teixeira hit as many three-run bombs as Johnny Bench or Juan Gone? Baseball doesn't make sense.

When we get down to those players who swatted 50-plus three-run homers, there were some surprises there, too. Yankees great Joe DiMaggio led the 50-club with 58 three-run shots. Interestingly, DiMaggio only had 111 career intentional walks with a high of 21 in his magical 1941 season. Williams had 25 intentional passes that season, 258 for his career.

Next in the 50 club is a surprise entry, Boston's superb right fielder Dwight Evans, who wound up his career with Baltimore, hit 57 three-run homers, tied with Rafael Palmeiro and Adrián Beltré (57). Cal Ripken had 55, while Miguel Cabrera, Jeff Kent, Gil Hodges, Carl Yastrzemski, and Gary Gaetti all hit 54. Fred McGriff (53), Stan Musial (52), and Eddie Mathews (51) rounded out those with 50-plus three-run shots over their careers.

The 40-plus club included Rogers Hornsby (47), a trio of third base-men—Scott Rolen, Ron Santo, and Darrell Evans—all with 44, along with Cecil Fielder and Raúl Ibañez. Robinson Canó, Darryl Strawberry, Billy Williams, Dante Bichette, and Andre Dawson had 42 three-run homers with Brian McCann hitting 40 over his long career.

Would you care to guess which pitcher allowed the most three-run homers? Naturally, the pitcher who allowed the most home runs of all time, Jamie Moyer, allowed 60 three-run bombs of the 522 he surrendered, tops on the list. Don Sutton is next with 52 allowed, then there's a three-way tie of CC Sabathia, Tim Wakefield, and Early Wynn, each of whom gave up 46 three-run homers throughout their careers.

TWO-RUN HOMERS

The circumstances surrounding a two-run homer are a bit different. With one runner on, especially if he happens to be on first base, you have the opportunity for the hitter to roll one over for a double play. And you can see that some pitchers were willing to take a shot at that. Consequently, there are some names that pop up here that didn't on the three-run homer list.

The great Babe Ruth leads the career two-run homer list with 248 career blasts, two more than runner-up Hank Aaron's 246. Aaron hit 181 homers with a man on first, Ruth 175. They both clubbed 48 with a man on second base, but with a man on third, Ruth slammed 25 two-run homers, eight more than Aaron, giving him the slight edge.

Sure enough, Aaron ranks among the all-time list of grounded into twin-killings with 328, fifth behind leader Albert Pujols (426), Miguel Cabrera (364), Cal Ripken Jr. (350), and Iván Rodríguez (337). Since Ruth's stats for hitting into double plays weren't tabulated, we have no idea how many times The Babe hit into a DP. He might have been up there, too.

Back to the two-run homer hitters. Alex Rodriguez is next with 226 two-run shots, three ahead of Barry Bonds and Harmon Killebrew with 223, then Willie Mays with 220, Albert Pujols 216, and Ken Griffey Jr. with 200 lifetime two-run shots.

From there, the names are who you might expect on the two-run homer list—Mark McGwire (197), Ted Williams (193), Manny Ramírez (191), and Sammy Sosa (190).

Then came Jim Thome (185), Frank Robinson (185), Stan Musial (182), and Mel Ott (180). What was interesting was seeing some of the game's most famous sluggers in a row from 176 to 162—Reggie Jackson (176), Miguel Cabrera (175), Rafael Palmeiro (171), Mike Schmidt (169), Lou Gehrig (166), Jimmie Foxx (163), and Mickey Mantle (162)

As for those hurlers who rolled the dice by pitching to dangerous hitters with a runner on but gave up those two-run homers, there are few new names on that list as well. Moyer led the way, surrendering 148 two-run shots, a dozen more than runner-up David Wells (136) and 14 more than Ferguson Jenkins and 16 more than Phil Niekro.

Solo Shots

As for the individual hitters, are you wondering who hit the most solo bombs? It's about who you would think. The first number listed is their rank on the all-time HR list, then the total number of solo HRs out of their total home runs, then the percentage of the home runs they hit with nobody on base.

(1) Barry Bonds 450 of 762 (59%)

(2) Hank Aaron 394 of 755 (52%)

(4) Albert Pujols 382 of 703 (54%)

(5) Alex Rodriguez 375 of 696 (54%)

(6) Willie Mays 362 of 660 (55%)

(7) Ken Griffey Jr. 337 of 630 (53%)

(8) Jim Thome 337 of 612 (55%)

(3) Babe Ruth 331 of 714 (46%)

(13) Rafael Palmeiro 329 of 569 (58%)

(9) Sammy Sosa 326 of 609 (54%)

(10) Frank Robinson 324 of 586 (55%)

(14) Reggie Jackson 308 of 563 (55%)

(11) Mark McGwire 306 of 583 (55%)

(17) David Ortiz 305 of 541 (56%)

(18) Mickey Mantle 297 of 536 (55%)

(16) Mike Schmidt 291 of 548 (53%)

(20) Frank Thomas 287 of 521 (55%)

(20) Willie McCovey 282 of 521 (54%)

(37) Nelson Cruz 277 of 464 (60%)

(12) Harmon Killebrew 277 of 573 (48%)

(15) Manny Ramírez 275 of 555 (50%)

One of the raps on Ted Williams was he was always too willing to take a walk instead of going outside the strike zone, especially with men on base. Williams hit 521 home runs and 240 of them were solo shots, just 46 percent. So, like Babe Ruth, whose numbers he precisely matched, more than half of Ted Williams's home runs came with men on base. Former Twins great Harmon Killebrew was third on that list. "The Fat Kid," as he was referred to in *Ball Four*, hit just 48 percent of his homers with nobody on.

On the other hand, for Barry Bonds, Nelson Cruz, and Rafael Palmeiro, about six out of every 10 career home runs came with the bases empty.

ROBERTS GAVE UP SOME BOMBS

If you had occasion to wander through earlier pages, you may have noticed comments from former Philadelphia Phillies workhorse Robin Roberts, who said as long as he won the game, that was all that mattered.

As Roberts explained in his own book, "I did give up a lot of home runs," he said, "but they only bothered me if they cost me a ballgame. If I won 6–3 and gave up three solo home runs, I had won the game and didn't give a thought to the home runs. Of course, I didn't know anybody was counting. Maybe if I had known, I would have changed something, but I doubt it."

So, it's probably not all that surprising that when we look at the list of big-league hurlers who have allowed the most solo shots, at the top of the list, go to the head of the class, it's Robin Roberts with a considerable edge on runner-up Fergie Jenkins. Roberts allowed 324 solo home runs in his career, 14 more than Jenkins and 18 more than Jamie "throw and duck" Moyer's 306 and 24 more than knuckleballer Phil Niekro.

NL hitters who connected for longballs vs. Roberts were Duke Snider with an all-time best 19, Ernie Banks 15, Hank Sauer 15, Roy Campanella 13, Eddie Mathews 11, Gil Hodges 10, with Hank Aaron, Jackie Robinson, Wally Moon, and Stan Musial each with nine apiece.

After Roberts, we spot some different names on the gopher ball list: Jenkins, Moyer, and Niekro. At the top of each pitcher's individual home runs allowed list, we see three different sluggers; Tony Pérez reached Jenkins for eight, Moyer surrendered 10 to Manny Ramírez, and Niekro gave up 11 bombs to Johnny Bench.

Other longtime hurlers who rank among the leaders in solo homers allowed are the ageless Bartolo Colón (287), Don Sutton (285), Frank Tanana (282), Bert Blyleven (275), Warren Spahn (268), Tom Seaver (256), and Catfish Hunter and Randy Johnson (both 250). You pitch enough innings, you're going to give up some home runs.

GAME-TYING HOME RUNS

Baseball strategy being what it is these days, this is the category that makes managers and pitching coaches cringe—giving up a game-tying home run. As technology has played a larger role in game management, skippers scouring data charts to find favorable matchups, there may be fewer circumstances where this kind of thing happens. Managers these days are more likely to just walk the potentially dangerous hitter and take their chances with the next guy. But it wasn't always that way. When you take a look at this list, imagine the groans in the dugout, the cheers in the stands, that magical moment when there's a swing, a long drive headed for the stands . . .

Perhaps it's not surprising that this time, it's the all-time home run king who tops the list. Barry Bonds launched game-tying home runs 87 different times, eight more than runner-up Hank Aaron's 79.

Third on the list—and this is a bit of a surprise—is Rafael Palmeiro with 70. Willie McCovey is next with 65, one more than Ken Griffey Jr.'s 64. A-Rod and Willie Mays are next with 62 game-tying shots. The next names are the usuals—Thome and Killebrew (60), Frank Robinson (59), Mark McGwire and Albert Pujols (58), Sammy Sosa (57), Stan Musial (56), and Adrián Beltré tied with another third sacker, Mike Schmidt, along with Ernie Banks, with 55. Then comes Reggie Jackson (54) and Mickey Mantle (53), Frank Thomas (52), Mel Ott, Lou Gehrig and Manny Ramírez (51), and Babe Ruth (50).

WALKOFFS

Hall of Fame hurler Dennis Eckersley had himself a remarkable major-league career. He was a 20-game winner as a starter, a phenomenal closer, and after he retired, a much-beloved color commentator on the game, with the emphasis on "color."

"Eck" had his own vocabulary where hair was "moss" and money was "iron." And, according to William Safire of the *New York Times*, Dennis Eckersley was credited with the origination of the phrase "walkoff" referring to a home run that concludes a ballgame.

It is, of course, the most dramatic of all baseball blows. Nothing stops fans in their tracks like the walkoff. Listen to Russ Hodges's excited radio call of Bobby Thomson's home run off Ralph Branca to give the Giants the pennant. That was a walkoff.

As we examine the list of regular-season walkoff home runs, you have to consider that in many cases, the player who *could* decide the game won't get that opportunity. Sometimes, the player that gets the walkoff is a hitter that the manager thought the pitcher on the hill could get out. And they couldn't.

We respectfully hope that the estimable Bill James, he who suggests that you can't really truly judge whether someone is a "clutch" hitter or not, take a look at this list and see some names that even their parents would be surprised to see ranking among the greatest players in history.

For example, nobody would be surprised to see Babe Ruth, with 12 walkoff homers, had more than just about everybody who ever played the game. Actually, he had one less than the all-time king, Jim Thome, with 13.

And Ruth was tied with five other terrific "clutch" players—Frank Robinson, Stan Musial, Jimmie Foxx, Albert Pujols, and Mickey Mantle, each of whom had a dozen walkoff home runs.

Right behind them were four other "clutch hitters"; at least one of whom will surprise you. Tony Pérez and David Ortiz had 11 walkoff shots. But the surprise is former Washington Nationals star Ryan Zimmerman had 11 walkoff homers. Zimmerman hit just 284 career home runs, so to have 11 of them win games, that's a pretty impressive number.

WALKOFF GAME-WINNERS

Taking a look at the remaining list of all-time walkoff home run winners, it's an interesting list of players, some Hall of Famers, some a long way from Cooperstown.

Barry Bonds 10

Adam Dunn 10

Harold Baines 10

Mike Schmidt 10

Dick Allen 10

Sammy Sosa 10

Jason Giambi 10

Reggie Jackson 10

Baines, Schmidt, and Jackson are the only three in the Hall of Fame. Dunn, as one-dimensional a player as the game ever saw, has no chance. Allen, who in the eyes of most, was a far more feared hitter than Baines ever was, hasn't gotten the nod. Thanks to their involvement with steroids, admitted or not, Bonds, Sosa, and Giambi are on the outside looking in. Maybe forever. As you run down the all-time list of walkoff game-winners, it's a bit surprising that some of the all-timers aren't on this list. Evidently, getting a walk-off homer just isn't as easy as you might think.

As great a player as Hank Aaron was, he had just nine in 3,298 games, same as Chipper Jones achieved in 2,499 games. Yogi Berra managed seven; Al Kaline, George Brett, Fred Lynn, Willie Mays, and Willie McCovey six; Rogers Hornsby, Jim Rice, Jackie Robinson, Mark McGwire, and Johnny Bench five; Joe DiMaggio, Mel Ott, and Carl Yastrzemski four; Pete Rose, Lou Gehrig, Roberto Clemente, and Ted Williams three.

When you think that Pete Rose played in 3,562 games and only found three walkoff homers in there, that goes to show you how difficult getting those walkoff opportunities can be. It seems hard to believe that two big RBI guys, Ted Williams and Lou Gehrig, only had three walkoff homers each. Surely, they had way more chances than that to win games. Very likely, opposing pitchers wisely just didn't give them the chance.

As for the relievers who ended up taking the loss, allowing these walkoff home runs, the all-time leader in walkoff homer runs allowed is former Pirate Roy Face, who took it on the chin 16 times. Rollie Fingers was next with 13 walkoff home run defeats. Next was Randy Myers with 12, then six players tied with 11 walkoff losses on home runs each—Eddie Guardado, Ron Davis, Troy Percival, Lindy McDaniel, Rich Gossage, and Jim Brewer.

The man who coined the phrase—Dennis Eckersley—was victimized seven times by walkoff home runs during the regular season. His most famous walkoff loss, of course, was surrendering that dramatic pinch-hit home run to Kirk Gibson in the 1988 World Series. You also can't forget the Twins' Kirby Puckett hitting a walkoff homer in the

11th inning off the Braves' Charlie Leibrandt, forcing a Game 7 in the 1991 World Series.

But as iconic as those moments were, two other World Series walkoff homers were more important. Pittsburgh's Bill Mazeroski and Toronto's Joe Carter each did Kirk Gibson one better.

Mazeroski's Game 7 ninth-inning home run off Yankee Ralph Terry gave the Pirates the 1960 World Series title. And Carter's walkoff homer off Phillies reliever Mitch Williams in the bottom of the ninth of Game 6 gave the Blue Jays the Series title in 1993. When you're walking off into a championship and the offseason, now *that's* a walkoff.

Chapter Nine

Homers in the First, Homers in the Ninth!

WHETHER THEY WORK OR NOT, PREGAME STRATEGY SESSIONS WITH THE pitcher of the day have long been an important part of baseball tradition. Ever since the early days of the game, managers and pitching coaches have always gone to great lengths to map out a particular way *they think* the game should be pitched.

There never is a shortage of advice on exactly how a pitcher should proceed. Jim Bouton's uproarious baseball tell-all *Ball Four* wryly recounts the inane quality of one of these pregame pitching strategy sessions to great comic effect.

"They were going over the Twins lineup—it's a tough one," Bouton recalled, "and the conversation went about like this:

'Pitch him high and tight.'

'Hell, he'll hit that one over the left-field wall. You got to pitch him low and away.'

'Pitch him away and he'll go to right field on you.'

'I don't know about all of that. I do know you got to curve him.'

'Oh, no, he's a hell of a breaking-ball hitter.'

"Finally [pitching coach] Sal Maglie said: 'Well, pitch around him.'

"When the meeting was over, Gary [Bell] added up the pitch-around-hims and there were five, right in the beginning of the batting order. So according to Sal Maglie, you start off with two runs in and the bases loaded.'"

Talk is cheap. So is baseball strategy. And in the case of facing some of the game's greatest hitters, strategy doesn't help a whole bunch. That's why they're great hitters. They're up there to do damage.

And let's face it, about the worst thing that can happen to a starting pitcher is allowing a first-inning home run. There goes your lead, there goes momentum for the other team, there goes your starting pitcher's confidence. There's damage.

So, of all the hitters who've stepped into a batter's box over the years, which one has done the most first-inning damage?

Former Cardinals folk hero Albert Pujols is at the top of the list. He clubbed 703 career home runs with 154 of them in the game's opening inning, driving in 459 runs, by far the most RBIs he ever accumulated in a single inning. Pujols was somebody who ruined a lot of pitcher's starts. And 160 times out of his 703 homers, he hit the first pitch.

The Stathead site offers a lot of intriguing information, breaking down Pujols's home runs by count. His lowest home-run total of nine came when he was ahead 3–0. The most productive count for him was 1–1. Pujols hit 100 home runs on that count and 30 on an 0–2.

Pujols's nearest challenger for first-inning home run damage was Barry Bonds, the all-time home-run king. Bonds swatted 133 first-inning homers, driving in 403 first-inning runs. He also drew 456 first-inning walks, almost twice as many as he drew in any other inning except the third (334). Bonds was a little more deadly on the first pitch, hitting 219 homers on that first swing.

In third place is the mighty Babe. Babe Ruth hit 129 first-inning homers out of his career total of 714. He drove in 374 runs in that first inning.

Eight other players managed to hit over 100 first-inning home runs: Hank Aaron, 124 of his 755; Willie Mays, 123 of his 660; Alex Rodriguez is next with 122 of his 696.

From there, it's Gary Sheffield (118 of 509), Ken Griffey Jr. (111 of 630), Frank Thomas (109 of 521), Sammy Sosa (106 of 609) and Mickey Mantle (103 of 536). Two players just missed the 100 club—Mark McGwire with 98 and Reggie Jackson with 97.

The player that some say was the greatest leadoff hitter of all time, Rickey Henderson, hit 82 first-inning home runs.

BARRY AND THE BABE

When it comes to hitting home runs in baseball's most dramatic stage of all, the ninth inning, it's somehow fitting that baseball's all-time home-run king is the champ. There are those, of course, who insist Bonds's home-run total was artificially aided. Maybe so. But the numbers are the numbers and the record is the record.

So yes, when it comes to ninth-inning home runs, Bonds barely edged out the Sultan of Swat, Babe Ruth, 53 to 51.

Ruth seemed to be hovering over Bonds's shoulder throughout that record-breaking 2006 season. How he tied the Babe's all-time mark of 51 ninth-inning home runs was fittingly dramatic.

It happened on a Wednesday afternoon game at San Francisco's AT&T Park in late April 2006 as the Mets were trying to close out a 7–4 win. New York brought in closer Billy Wagner but the Giants weren't done.

Omar Vizquel led off with a single. Wagner, one of the hardest-throwing relievers in the game, fanned José Vizcaíno and Randy Winn, moving the Mets just one out away.

Then, the Giants got a break. Moisés Alou rapped one on the ground to third baseman David Wright and Wright's throw sailed. Vizquel came around to score from second to make it 7–5.

Then things got even more interesting. For coming out of the San Francisco dugout was Barry Bonds, the game down to the final out.

Sure enough, Bonds blasted one to deep center field at AT&T, tying the game. It was Bonds's 51st ninth-inning HR, tying the great Ruth.

Though the Giants went on to lose that game in extra innings, Bonds had tied Ruth's ninth-inning mark with his 711th career home run.

On May 20, Bonds tied Ruth's all-time home-run total with number 714 off Oakland's Brad Halsey, then bettered it eight days later off Byung-Hyun Kim with a fourth-inning shot at AT&T Park.

When it came to ninth-inning homers, he passed Ruth with two more ninth-inning home runs later that year, hitting a three-run shot off Arizona's José Valverde in mid-June, then a solo shot off Colorado's Brian Fuentes in mid-September.

Bonds finished 2006 with 734 homers.

And in 2007, he went after Aaron. Bonds hit number 755 to tie Aaron off Clay Hensley in San Diego on August 4, then, before a roaring crowd in San Francisco three days later, he slammed number 756 off Washington's Mike Bacsik. He hit six more home runs before the end of his career, his 762nd and final homer coming off of Ubaldo Jiménez on September 5 in Colorado. Bonds seems to be the only big leaguer we could find who hit more than 100 home runs in three separate innings; the first (133), the third (103), and fourth (102).

Other Ninth-Inning Heroes

A look through the Home Run Log showed a dozen players who managed to hit more than 40 ninth-inning homers. Hank Aaron, Willie Mays, and Reggie Jackson were all locked with 48 homers in the ninth, trailing Bonds and Ruth.

Mike Schmidt and Mickey Mantle were next with 47, then Ted Williams and Harmon Killebrew with 46, Mel Ott and Albert Pujols with 45, Alex Rodriguez and Ken Griffey Jr. with 43, Willie McCovey with 42, and Frank Robinson with 40.

There were some surprises. Despite his impressive record as a clutch hitter and an RBI guy, Gehrig hit just 22 ninth-inning home runs. He did receive 29 intentional walks in the eighth and ninth innings.

His predecessor in the batting order, Babe Ruth, received 36 intentional walks in those two innings. Interestingly, Ruth received 32 intentional first-inning walks, Gehrig 12.

Here are the ninth-inning totals for some other big-time home-run hitters:

Sammy Sosa—39	Miguel Cabrera—34
Jim Thome—38	David Ortiz—32
Jimmie Foxx—38	Duke Snider—31
Eddie Murray—36	Carl Yastrzemski—31
Stan Musial—35	Mark McGwire—30
Gary Sheffield—34	Rafael Palmeiro—30

IN OT, WILLIE MAYS IS NUMBER ONE!

If Willie Mays wasn't the greatest all-around player in the history of baseball, he was certainly the most dangerous hitter when it came to extra-inning games. The great Mays was the all-time leader in extra-inning home runs with 21, five more than Frank Robinson, the runner-up.

One of the greatest of all his extra-inning blasts came on July 2, 1963, when his home run decided one of the most remarkable pitching duels of all time. That was the day when Milwaukee ace Warren Spahn and Giants ace Juan Marichal put on the once-in-a-lifetime performance—matching zeroes for 15 consecutive innings at windy Candlestick Park. Finally, in the bottom of the 16th with one out, Mays connected with a home run over the left field fence to win it, 1–0. It was Mays's 15th home run off Spahn. He upped the mark to 18 before Spahnie retired.

Mays's very first major-league hit was also a home run off Spahn, on May 28, 1951. Mays had started his career 0-for-12. Spahn later joked that if he'd have gotten Willie out in that at-bat, they might not ever have had to deal with him!

Here are the extra-inning home run leaders:

Willie Mays—21	David Ortiz—12
Frank Robinson—16	Stan Musial—11
Albert Pujols—15	Barry Bonds—11
Hank Aaron—14	Harmon Killebrew—11
Jimmie Foxx—14	Willie McCovey—10
Mickey Mantle—14	Eddie Murray—10
Babe Ruth—13	Reggie Jackson—10
Ted Williams—12	Sammy Sosa—10
Jim Thome—12	Willie Stargell—10
Rafael Palmeiro—12	Yogi Berra—9
Mark McGwire—12	Mike Schmidt—9

Alex Rodriguez—9

Billy Williams—9

Ken Griffey Jr.—9

Dick Allen—9

Ernie Banks—8

Frank Thomas—7

Lou Gehrig—4

Chapter Ten

Pedro Martínez: Nine in 1999

He stood on that mound, that raised pile of dirt not quite in the middle of that ancient ballpark on the evening of July 13, 1999. It was the same spot where Babe Ruth and Walter Johnson took turns throwing scoreless innings at each other 13 times, Ruth winning 1–0, 83 years earlier. The same location where Smoky Joe Wood stood, whirled, and beat Christy Mathewson in 10 innings 87 years earlier to give the Boston Red Sox the 1912 World Series.

So many of the game's great hurlers had dug in their cleats on that hill. Bob Feller, Lefty Grove, Whitey Ford (when Casey Stengel would let him), Jim Palmer, Bob Gibson, Sandy Koufax, and now, Pedro Martínez.

History was already in the air that night. Baseball's All-Century Team had been announced before the 1999 All-Star Game and folk heroes from all over the country, showing up in suits and ties, were on the emerald diamond once again, waving to the fortunate Fenway Faithful.

And when Boston's larger-than-life Hall of Famer Ted Williams came rumbling in on a golf cart from center field amid a sea of noise, all the current All-Stars crowded around Ted like a visit to the Pope, it was the kind of past-meets-present baseball moguls could only imagine. It was thrilling, all the current millionaires gathering around a genuine baseball legend who looked as happy to see them as they were to see him.

Then, after an almost scold from the public address announcer to get everyone off the field, the actual 1999 All-Star Game began. And with Boston's All-Star starter Pedro Martínez's sizzling first pitch to Cincinnati's Barry Larkin, it was an evening to envision where the game would be headed. For not only was Martínez in the middle of perhaps the greatest single season any pitcher ever delivered from any mound, witnessing how he was able to dominate the game's finest hitters—many of them buoyed by steroids—was, in retrospect, immensely satisfying. At the time, it was merely shocking.

Remember that just a few months earlier, the nation was enthralled in the Great Home Run Chase between the ebullient Sammy Sosa of the Chicago Cubs and the steely giant Mark McGwire of the St, Louis Cardinals. Here, on this national stage and home field, Martínez's natural baseball talents and ferocious competitiveness made them look like Little Leaguers. They may have seemed larger than life a year earlier when they stomped on Roger Maris's record of 61 homers—McGwire swatted 70, Sosa 66—but here, Pedro dismissed the cheaters (along with a few others) in brutal, "not in my league" fashion.

Cincinnati's star shortstop Larkin started the festivities. Martínez was clearly amped for the assignment. With ancient Fenway Park packed to the rafters, fans seeing so many of the game's giants of the past, topped by Ted Williams in the flesh, how could any baseball fan not be lifted up?

And Pedro Martínez delivered. He showed future Hall of Famer Larkin all three of his unhittable pitches; a sizzling, darting fastball, a sharp, late-breaking curve, and an undetectable out-of-the-hand changeup that arrived at the plate just slow enough—after the eye-blurring heat that preceded it—to get the hitter to swing well before it arrived, since it was delivered with the precisely same arm motion. It was unfair.

Larkin managed a couple of desperate fouls on overwhelming 98-mile-per-hour heat on the black for strikes one and two, then chased a tantalizing 85-mile-per-hour down-breaking changeup for strike three. There was only one word for it—dazzling.

Colorado's Larry Walker, also a future Hall of Famer, was next, a bruising left-handed hitter and an exceptional two-way player often overlooked. Walker came in hitting a tidy .382 with 25 homers, a most formidable opponent.

Martínez caught him off-guard, flippantly flipping in an 84-mile-per-hour changeup. Strike one. Next came a high-and-away heater at 98 that Walker barely clipped foul. 0–2. Martínez next barely missed with a 98-mile-per-hour heater, the ball streaking to the outside corner. Liking that idea, he then threw the same pitch, just an inch closer, catching the outside corner for strike three. Walker, a stunned expression on his face, quietly walked to the dugout. You could tell what he was thinking. *What have I just seen?*

Shortly before the third strike, the Fox cameras caught American League manager Joe Torre watching solemnly from the dugout. A fine hitter in his day, a guy who once hit .363 and collected 230 hits in a season, his expression read "Thank God, I'm retired."

Up third was Sosa, who'd already whacked 32 home runs midway through this '99 season. His knees buckled as Martínez broke off his first curveball that darted low and away and missed. With a delightful sense of humor—no doubt he enjoyed the knee buckle—Martínez repeated the same pitch, moving it in closer. Again, Sosa, a major-league hitter with thousands of at-bats, saw his knees buckle once more as Iván Rodríguez snagged it for strike one.

After a 96-mile-per-hour heater up missed, its sizzle cutting through the night air, Martínez came back with an 86-mile-per-hour changeup that had Sosa so far out ahead of it, he almost had time to swing twice. To finish off this most poetic at-bat, Pedro reached back for a high, sailing 98-mile-per-hour fastball, one soaring up toward Sosa's hands. With a swing that said, "I know I'm not hitting this but I might as well try," Sosa swung and missed for strike three, ending the first inning to raucous cheers from the Fenway Faithful and maybe from the Baseball Gods, too.

The other major steroid boy, McGwire, with 28 homers already, would lead off the top of the second and he was treated just as rudely. An imposing 6-foot-5 giant with sloping shoulders and a haunted stare, he stepped into the batter's box as you might dip your toe into a chilly pool. Martínez started him as he had Sosa, with a breaking ball low and away that missed. He followed that up with an even slower breaking ball, one that dipped in for strike one at 80 miles per hour. It's one thing to change speeds on different pitches; it's another to do that on the pitch you just threw. McGwire looked back at the ump. Written across his wrinkled forehead was this—"I'm supposed to be able to hit THAT?"

Pedro followed that with a mean-spirited, 85-mile-per-hour changeup so deceptive, McGwire's feeble swing was so far ahead of the ball, he was bringing the bat back as Rodríguez was snaring the pitch. Strike two! Now, keep in mind that as all this is happening, McGwire is thinking, any hitter *has* to be thinking, this guy has 98 in his arm and I haven't seen it yet . . .

Once more we see the diminutive Martínez, all arms and legs, bring his hands up in front of the Red Sox across his chest, turn, lift a leg and sure enough, wham, here it is, a 97-mile-per-hour high-riding fastball, sailing up under McGwire's meaty arms. He had to swing and miss and most certainly did, offering as desultory a strikeout as you've ever seen, perhaps short of a few pitchers looking lost at the plate.

Nobody had treated the great home-run king so disrespectfully. It was almost blasphemy, a mismatch of the highest order against the game's great home-run hero. It was also four consecutive strikeouts, which gave Fox archivists a chance to bring out dusty old black and white film of Carl Hubbell's strikeout streak in the 1934 All-Star Game, Hubbell fanning Babe Ruth, Lou Gehrig, Jimmie Foxx, Al Simmons, and Joe Cronin in order.

Hubbell, of course, featured a trick pitch, a screwball, something perhaps most American League hitters hadn't seen all that often. There was no interleague play then. Judging from the flailing film clips they showed of Ruth, Gehrig, and Foxx, they'd never seen anything like that before. At least, that's how it looked.

Another screwballing lefty, the Dodgers' Fernando Valenzuela, did the same five-strikeout gig in the 1986 summer classic. But that, of course, was before steroids, the home run surges, and the shattering of Roger Maris's record. It was nowhere near as dramatic as what Fenway fans were witnessing.

Stunned by what he had seen happen to McGwire, the Giants' Matt Williams was next and he happily swung at the first pitch, an 80-mile-per-hour changeup, just catching it off the end of the bat, and topped a slow roller to second that Roberto Alomar, perhaps caught by surprise that someone actually hit the ball, mishandled. Williams was safe.

Next up was Houston's Jeff Bagwell, a stumpy, crouching hitter who, like McGwire, had somehow clubbed 28 homers out of that puzzling, sitting-on-a-kitchen-stool stance. He stepped into the batter's box and if it wouldn't have been bad form before a national audience, he might have laughed.

He was feeling it now and here came Pedro's steaming 96 on the black for strike one. A show-me curveball missed, Bagwell said a silent prayer, then Pedro flipped in a darting changeup at 86 which found the range for strike two.

Like McGwire and Sosa before him, you could see that Bagwell was setting himself for gas—you can't adjust to 96–98 if you're not looking for it to begin with. Even if you *are* anticipating it, you have barely a split-second to connect. Pedro could see what he was looking for and didn't want to disappoint.

After a blurring 97-mile-per-hour heater missed away and another 97 missed up—Martínez's ball was not only blazingly fast, it was tailing and moving out and up—it filled the count, three balls, two strikes. Surely, he'll not want to walk me, Bagwell thought. I've seen two fastballs in a row. Ready . . .

What does Martínez go to on 3–2? How about a perfectly delivered 83-mile-per-hour changeup, unhittably low and inside off the plate—a day/night difference from what he expected, and the hapless Bagwell waved at it for strike three as Rodríguez fired a bullet to second base to get the sliding Williams to end the inning. Fenway fans considered booing the out so they could see Pedro Martínez keep pitching.

With five extraordinary whiffs of the six outs he needed, Martínez was easily selected the All-Star Game MVP. Not only was Pedro utterly unhittable—he looked that way quite often—you had to remember he made the finest hitters in the National League look as if they had been yanked out of Williamsport's Little League World Series and tossed in against an impossible big-league ace pitcher.

Looking back at that wonderful moment in Boston, the delicious irony now is at least a couple of those hitters—Sammy Sosa and Mark McGwire—players who were dead central in the middle of the steroid scandal that nearly upended the game a few years later—were dismissed, routed, abused in such an off-hand manner, watching their hapless at-bats now, a quarter-century later, feels like justice.

It was such a night that Pedro may also unwittingly have planted the insidious idea that one unhittable pitch—he featured three—might be enough for future bullpen men. Learn how to throw one unhittable pitch, throw until further notice, and we'll bring in somebody else for the next inning. That was where Major League Baseball would be in 2025.

You could almost think the Baseball Gods in the sky who have stewarded the game through troubles before knew this All-Star Game was back at the baseball's oldest park for the first time in 38 years, and they set all it up so that little Pedro Martínez, the one guy certainly beyond suspicion in the steroid matter, ended up being centerstage in a nationally televised showcase that happened to be smack in the middle of arguably the greatest single season by a pitcher in the history of the game.

With 15 wins in hand that night, Martínez went on to a stirring 25–4 record with a miniscule 2.07 ERA, fanning 313 hitters in just 213 1/3 innings, allowing just 160 hits and only 37 walks. And it should not

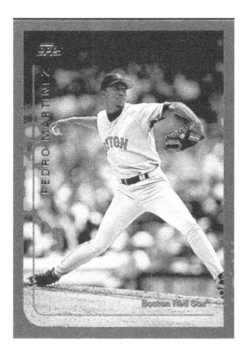

be lost on us that he achieved these numbers in the middle of Steroid Mania.

To take this a bit further, while roided-up sluggers were clouting home runs out of major-league ballparks at a record clip, the amazing Martínez only allowed nine home runs all season long. That, folks, is domination.

Who were these Mighty Nine? Some will surprise, some will shock, some will remind you that the one game you cannot predict is baseball. Even with a dominating hurler like Pedro Martínez on the hill.

In chronological order, here are the Mighty Nine:

No. 1—April 5, Joe Randa of the Kansas City Royals at Royals Stadium: The second batter Pedro Martínez faced in this remarkable 1999 season was Joe Randa of the Kansas City Royals. After Martínez opened the bottom of the first by fanning Carlos Beltrán looking, Randa took a 3–2 fastball to right-center field over the wall. Martínez allowed five more hits over the six innings he worked. Boston was a 5–3 winner, giving him his first victory of the season.

No. 2—May 12, David Bell of the Seattle Mariners at Fenway Park: After compiling 10 strikeouts through five innings en route to his seventh win, David Bell connected on a 2–2 pitch, a line drive to deep left-center field for a home run. Martínez followed that up by striking out Ken Griffey Jr. for the third time. He worked eight innings, allowed four hits and one other run, while fanning 15 to raise his record to 7–1.

No. 3—June 4, Ryan Klesko of the Atlanta Braves at Fenway Park: Pedro showed no mercy on the visiting Braves, fanning 16 and allowing just three hits in besting Tom Glavine for his 11th win. He fanned Brian Jordan four times, Gerald Williams three, and Chipper Jones twice. Before Klesko's seventh-inning solo homer, Javy López singled leading off the second and Andruw Jones managed a fifth-inning double. Pedro threw 114 pitches in the complete game, one of five that season, throwing 78 strikes (28 swinging, 24 looking, 26 fouls).

No. 4—June 26, Chris Singleton of the Chicago White Sox at Fenway Park: After catching Frank Thomas looking at strike three (The Big Hurt vs. Pedro: 2-for-24, .083) to end the first, the Red Sox put up 11 runs for Pedro in the bottom of the first. With two outs in the top of the second, Chris Singleton turned around an 0–1 pitch, sending it into the Red Sox bullpen. Pedro worked just five innings with the big lead, raising his record to a stunning 14–2.

No. 5—July 2, Magglio Ordóñez of the Chicago White Sox at Comiskey Park: Raising his record to a stunning 15–2 with eight innings of otherwise shutout work, Ordóñez connected with a 2–1 pitch in the fourth inning and launched it deep to left field.

PEDRO'S NUMBERS AT THE ALL-STAR BREAK
Wins: 15, Losses 3, ERA: 2.10, Innings 132 2/3, Hits 104, Walks 24, Strikeouts, 184

No. 6—August 3, Jim Thome of the Cleveland Indians at Fenway Park: Oddly, just as in a couple other instances, Pedro fanned Manny Ramírez to open the second inning, then Jim Thome slammed a 3–0 pitch out of the ballpark. He threw five innings, allowing just that one run, fanning seven. He got a no decision as Tim Wakefield blew the save and took the loss.

No. 7—August 14, Alex Rodriguez of the Seattle Mariners at Fenway Park: Arriving at Fenway too late to make his scheduled start, Pedro entered the game in the sixth with the Red Sox up 7–1. Starter Bryce Florie left with two outs in the fifth so when Pedro took over in the sixth and finished the game, he earned win number 17. After getting Ken Griffey Jr. to fly out, Martínez left one up for Alex Rodriguez who slammed it over the left field fence for his 30th home run. He later added a double off Pedro. A-Rod batted .291 over his career against Pedro with 19 strikeouts in 60 plate appearances.

No. 8—August 19, Miguel Tejada of the Oakland Athletics at Fenway Park: After reaching Pedro for a single earlier, Tejada broke a 2–2 tie with a sixth-inning blast over the left field wall. When a faltering Red Sox bullpen let the game get out of hand, Martínez suffered his fourth loss of the season.

No. 9—September 10, Chili Davis of the New York Yankees at Yankee Stadium: With the Red Sox in desperate pursuit—again—of the Yankees, Pedro Martínez came a single pitch away from absolute perfection, fanning 17 Yankees in a 3–1 win, allowing just a single hit—a second-inning homer on an 0–2 count to Chili Davis. After dropping a curveball in for a strike and a fastball on the inside corner for strike two, Martínez tried to go away with another heater and it caught too much of the plate. Davis smacked it in the middle of the right field bleachers for the game's first run. After that, not a single Yankee reached base.

The next day, Buster Olney of the *New York Times* wrote, "Boston's Pedro Martinez humbled the Yankees in their home park in a manner never seen before . . . Martinez faced 28 batters, one over the minimum, and those making the loudest noises among the 55,239 at Yankee Stadium were Red Sox fans. Boston pulled to within five and a half games of the Yankees in the American League East, hoisted almost single-handedly by a pitcher with a sagging face, the body of an oversized jockey, and an arm and confidence of a comic book superhero.

"Derek Jeter was Martinez's first strikeout victim, on a 97 mile-an-hour fastball in the first inning, and Chuck Knoblauch was his 17th, the last out of the game, on a 97 mph fastball. Every Yankee hitter struck out at least once, including Darryl Strawberry, who pinch-hit in the ninth inning.

"It was as if the Yankees were swinging within a darkened closet, for Martinez was throwing all three of his pitches for strikes. His fastball was moving, Tino Martinez said, and he was spinning his curveball for strikes, and when you looked for the fastball, he would then throw his changeup, the ball dropping away as if Pedro Martinez were manipulating it like a marionette."

You don't generally get that sort of passion and awe in the pages of The Old Grey Lady.

And Olney added one quote from Yankee manager Joe Torre, who was no doubt remembering the All-Star Game performance.

"That is about as close to unhittable as you can find," Torre said. "You can't fault the hitters."

There are some who insist Martínez's 2000 campaign was even more impressive, but those who saw that All-Star Game as well as that September performance against the Yankees might differ. That Yankees team, remember, would go on to win their second straight World Series, both four-game sweeps.

In 2000, Martínez was 18–6, had a 1.74 ERA, fanned 284 in 217 innings, walking just 32. For those who are into the ERA+ statistic, Pedro's 291 that season was the finest in the history of modern baseball.

Some may rank Pedro's brilliance in 1999, especially in Boston's All-Star Game, with the great Carl Hubbell. History is like that, always looking for comparisons. But if you saw Pedro Martínez in action in 1999, you know this. There *was* no comparison.

Who Hit Pedro?

Gregg Jefferies .469 (15-for-32), 2 2B, 1 3B, 1 HR, 3 RBIs, 2 BB, 1 K

Luis Gonzalez .388 (19-for-49), 5 2B, 0 3B, 2 HR, 7 RBIs, 5 BB, 7 K

Mike Piazza .385 (10-for-26),. 1 2B, 0 3B, 6 HR, 8 RBIs, 0 BB, 4 K

Barry Bonds .333 (11-for-33), 3 2B, 1 3B, 1 HR, 3 RBIs, 10 BB, 8 K

Kenny Lofton .327 (16-for-49), 3 2B, 0 3B, 0 HR, 3 RBIs, 5 BB, 5 K

Tony Gwynn .314 (11-for-35), 1 2B, 0 3B, 0 HR, 4 RBIs, 1 BB, 0 K

Craig Biggio .302 (13-for-43), 6 2B, 1 3B, 0 HR, 2 RBIs, 6 BB, 7 K

Alex Rodriguez .291 (16-for-55), 2 2B, 0 3B, 1 HR, 4 RBIs, 5 BB, 19 K

WHO DIDN'T

Frank Thomas .083 (2-for-24), 1 HR, 2 RBIs, 1 BB, 11 K

Edgar Martínez .120 (3-for-25), 7 BB, 11 K

Roberto Alomar .148 (4-for-27), 2 RBIs, 8 K

Sammy Sosa .160 (4-for-25), 2 RBIs, 1 BB, 15 K

Jason Giambi .160 (8-for-50), 1 2B, 1 HR, 5 RBIs, 5 BB, 19 K

David Justice .164 (9-for-55), 2 2B, 4 RBIs, 8 BB, 20 K

Manny Ramírez .167 (5-for-30), 2 2B, 1 BB, 13 K

Jim Thome .171 (6-for-35), 1 2B, 3 HR, 3 RBIs, 9 BB, 14 K

Jorge Posada .183 (11-for-60), 2 2B, 1 3B, 4 HR, 10 RBIs, 8 BB, 33 K

Bernie Williams .184 (14-for-76), 3 2B, 3 HR, 7 RBIs, 11 BB, 20 K

Jeff Bagwell .192 (5-for-26), 1 HR, 5 RBIs, 4 BB, 9 K

Chipper Jones .204 (10-for-49),. 1 2B, 3 HR, 10 RBIs, 10 BB, 10 K

Rafael Palmeiro .206 (7-for-34), 2 -RBIs, 5 BB, 8 K

CHAPTER ELEVEN

Christy Mathewson vs. the Truth

FOR LIFETIME FOLLOWERS OF BASEBALL, THE NAME CHRISTY MATHEWson has a glow around it. Mathewson was movie-star handsome, a giant (for his time) at 6-foot-1; also, he was a college graduate, a rarity in those days when baseball was a roughhouse sport.

Mathewson was able to rise above a hard-scrabble game with immense dignity, class, and pride. He was a sort of Ivanhoe or Sir Galahad, a player whose presence on the mound, fans just seeing the guy in uniform, somehow helped establish the game of baseball with all of America just after the turn of the century.

As the legendary sportswriter Grantland Rice put it, "He was the only man I ever met who in spirit and inspiration was greater than his game."

Christy Mathewson was seen as a role model for America's youth, a dream husband and partner for every woman, someone you'd want to count on as your pal to every man—Mathewson always operated above the fray. And there was a lot of fray in those early days of baseball, much of it generated by the man who managed him, John McGraw. There was a yin and yang clarity between the two, McGraw and Mathewson, yet they may have been as close as any manager and player ever.

When you take a long look at Mathewson's extraordinary career and his immaculate reputation, it can be a bit jolting to watch a video representation of Lawrence Ritter's classic book about the early days of the game, *The Glory of Their Times.*

When you actually listen to Richard "Rube" Marquard, then an old-timer, offer a most revealing reminiscence of his former roommate, Christy Mathewson, it will stop you in your tracks. "He was a wonderful fella, wonderful, wonderful," you hear Marquard say. "And he loved to gamble. If you had a dollar in your pocket, he never would be satisfied until he got that dollar from you. He always carried a thousand dollars with him because he played craps, poker, anything at all. You could win that thousand dollars if you were lucky with that one dollar. He would stand downstairs in the lobby of the hotel, wait for the ballplayers after they got through breakfast before they had to go out to the ballpark and he'd have a pair of dice in one hand and a deck of cards in his pocket. He'd say 'Let's go for a little while.' I'd seen him lose seven, eight thousand in one night."

What? Are we talking about Christy Mathewson or Pete Rose? From what they say on the internet, losing $7,500 in 1907 or so would be equivalent today of losing around $242,000. In a single night. With no stopping. This was *Christy Mathewson?* Do we have a problem here, America?

When Marquard was interviewed decades after Mathewson's tragic death at the hands of tuberculosis, the old roommate had no reason to spill the beans on him. It wasn't as if there were any lingering doubts about Christy's integrity; Marquard was just trying to describe a man he knew exceedingly well, a man who, in person and in his behavior, was quite different, evidently, from the way he had been written about.

Understanding that aspect of Mathewson's personality should perhaps make us look at other elements of his life—like when he ended up covering the 1919 World Series for the *New York Times*.

If this discrepancy makes you reflect on an earlier chapter—about the way Joe DiMaggio was covered as opposed to Ted Williams—good. It should. Mathewson himself was somewhat uncomfortable with the way people wrote about him. At the time, certainly nobody wrote a thing about Mathewson's penchant for gambling.

Considering the way fate or karma seems to work out in one's life, it was indeed ironic that Christy Mathewson was hired by the *Times* to cover the infamous 1919 World Series.

Yes, folks, it was *that* World Series, the one that eight members of the Chicago White Sox thought it would be more fiscally sound for them to try to lose. Sure enough, there was Mathewson, sitting in the press box in Chicago and Cincinnati through the entire Series, seated directly next to journalist Hugh Fullerton, who was one of the first to smell a rat down on the field.

As a correspondent, it was Mathewson's duty to write about what he saw. And he did. But surprisingly and publicly, *he did not write* what he had been sharing with Fullerton in these press boxes; namely that something fishy was going on.

On October 16, a week after the Cincinnati Reds had wrapped up the questionable Series, there it was, in the pages of the *New York Times*, the great Christy Mathewson defusing the rampant rumors of a World Series fix. The question is, why?

"The rumors and mutterings about the honesty of the series are ridiculous to me," he wrote. "It seems that there are some irrefutable arguments against the possibility of any arrangement being made which would conflict with the natural outcome."

A graduate of Bucknell, Mathewson had his own literary style and wrote quite clearly and distinctly. And at times, he could be pretty brutal.

As Joe Posnanski notes in *The Baseball 100*—he rates Mathewson number 36—"In 1914, Matty wrote a story for something called Everybody's magazine. The story was titled 'Why We Lost Three World's Championships' and it was about the Giants' failure in three World Series. In it, he tore apart his teammates ('With very few exceptions the men are not of championship caliber'), ripped everybody for caring only about what the press said about them ("The Giants are the greatest 'newspaper ball club' I know. Most of the men read everything that is printed about them") and, yes, he ripped his dear friend McGraw for building a team of 'puppets' that would do anything and everything he said and, as such, fold in the biggest moments.

"Now the Giants that have won the last three National League championships do not stand on their own feet," Mathewson wrote. "They are McGraw. His dominant personality is everything. . . . Unlike McGraw [Philadelphia manager] Connie Mack had not been forced to build a team of puppets worked from the bench by a strike. The Athletics could stand on their own feet. Mack has long encouraged them to do that."

Whew! We didn't see that kind of candor a few years later. And you wonder why. Writing as someone who evidently loved the whole idea of wagering—it was part of his daily routine—this had to be an emotional topic for him. Especially since the integrity of his sport was on the line. And he evidently was reluctant to put the rap on his fellow ballplayers. He had his image to think of, and he was right to consider that. What would it have meant if Christy Mathewson himself called out the players for the fix? This was before the arrival of Babe Ruth. Why, it might have meant the end of the sport!

To the modern reader, it's clear that Christy could have used some editing. Starting three separate paragraphs in his account with the phrase "In the first place" was a gamble he didn't win.

But having one of the greatest and most respected players in the history of the game there to record its darkest hour, well, that *is* interesting.

"In the first place," Mathewson wrote in the *Times*, "I believe—and I have been associated with baseball for many years—ballplayers are inherently honest. Only once or twice during long experience with the game have I seen more than one or two players who have made any peculiar moves, and they were very quickly detected and the banana peel placed under them. They skidded out of baseball. [He's likely alluding to the dark cloud that seemed to follow Hal Chase.]

"In the first place," Mathewson continued, again, "there is the future of a player in a series of this sort to figure on, and there would be too many men to fix to do it successfully. There is no one man on a team, no matter who he is, who can throw a game . . .

"No pitcher could guarantee to toss a game. As soon as he started to go bad, he would be ousted to the shower. Even the fans know enough about baseball to holler 'Take him out!' as soon as a twirler begins to display signs of weakness . . .

"In the first place," he added a third time, "it would cost too much. The difference between winning and losing in the last series meant a difference of approximately $2,000 per man. In addition to this any one of them would be risking his whole future in baseball. Once found out, no player could work in the big league again."

Mathewson was on target on that one. While the news of the fix would not come out until the end of the 1920 season, his prediction of a lifetime banishment for those involved would come true.

But Mathewson's closing paragraph on this whole matter seems in direct contrast with what was going on *during* the Series if Eliot Asinof's *Eight Men Out* account of that Series is accurate.

For public consumption—and maybe this was his way of telling baseball fans everything was going to be all right—Mathewson closed with this paragraph, which he had to know in his heart was not true.

"There was too much betting on this series for the good of baseball, and disgruntled gamblers can start disagreeable rumors . . . The odds in this past series would have reflected it if there had been any truth in the reports . . . Baseball is honest and will stay honest in spite of the abuse it has taken from time to time. (Copyright, 1919 Christy Mathewson)."

In fact, it *wasn't* honest, and he knew it. And according to Asinof's account, "Matty" had a pretty good suspicion about the whole Series all along, doubts which he shared with sportswriter Hugh Fullerton, who eventually broke the story in 1920.

Asinof recounts a meeting between Bill Burns, a former ballplayer and attempted fixer and Fullerton at the Gibson House, a saloon across from the Hotel Sinton where the Reds were staying.

"[Fullerton] invited Burns to have a drink at the Gibson House, across the street from the Sinton [Hotel in Cincinnati], and casually asked how he was betting. Burns replied that he was sinking it all on the Reds, and added confidentially: 'Get wise, Hughie, and do the same!'

"Fullerton returned to the Sinton . . . where he ran into his roommate, the former Reds manager, Christy Mathewson, was lying on the bed, reading the late paper . . . Matty had been assigned to cover the Series . . . Fullerton told him what he'd heard, adding his own revised opinion: it was possible that something was up! . . . Fullerton decided to send out a warning. He wired all papers that used his accounts of the ball games: ADVISE ALL NOT TO BET ON THIS SERIES. UGLY RUMORS AFLOAT . . . He probed into Matty's great baseball experience, digging for every possible way in which ballplayers might throw a ball game. Matty explained the simplicity of it, describing the ultra-thin line that separated an effective pitch from a disastrous one, a beautiful fielding play from a spectacular near-miss. As for a hitter, there was simply no way of knowing how hard he was trying. They arranged to sit together in the press box and go over every doubtful play. And just for the record, Fullerton decided he would pencil a circle on his scorecard around every play that was really suspect."

So here's how it went. Mathewson and Fullerton watched the Series side by side, and shared their ideas as illustrated in John Sayles's film *Eight Men Out*, based on Asinof's book. When, in the deciding game, which was intentionally lost early by fixer Lefty Williams, Mathewson makes it a point to tell Fullerton that Williams is just throwing fastballs, slow ones. Clearly, he knew what was up. The question is, why didn't Mathewson share that with his readership in the *Times* a week later? Why didn't he come clean?

He did offer hints. On October 7, in mid-Series, Mathewson shared these observations in the *Times*: "Pitchers have held their opponents to three hits or less, but never before in the big series have six successive sluggers, not the weaklings of the team but the best, strode to the plate and then, one by one, slouched away again dimly conscious of the fact that the umpire was singing that sickening song 'Three strikes you're out.' That happened today in the second and third innings when Gandil, Risberg, Schalk, Williams, Liebold and Eddie Collins took the count in succession. The six of them in eighteen strikes fouled only four balls."

Later, in the same article, Mathewson wrote: "The showing of the White Sox outfield was a disappointment to me after hearing so much about their great work. The fielding of Felsch and Jackson was not up to the advertisement. Jackson allowed one to go over him without even seeming to get started after the ball until it was past him and Felsch misjudged one hit by Roush that put an end to all doubt."

Hints? Sure. But Mathewson did not take the step he might have— saying the Series was as crooked as a three-dollar bill. Would the great Christy Mathewson, a man whose judgment was so respected that umpires would turn to him on a controversial close play, let something like that go? He did.

All these years later, we can only speculate why he didn't want to blow the whistle. He certainly had his reasons. As a pitcher, Mathewson was beyond question. He was a legend in his time and that mattered to him. Especially considering the way his career started.

Christy A Dual Threat?

Though he actually spent some time playing first base and the outfield when he first arrived with the New York Giants, once John McGraw took over as manager of the Giants in mid-July of 1902, he saw Mathewson as a pitcher, his ace, even though Mathewson had just one pre-McGraw win on his record. His first base days were over.

Christy went on to win 13 games, including eight shutouts, and wound up with a 2.12 ERA. A star was born.

Looking at Christy's record with the long view of history, you wonder how in the world he did it? How any human arm could do it! The inning totals alone are staggering, never mind the amazing won-loss record.

Year—Innings—W–L

1901—336—20-17

1902—276—14-17

1903—367—30-13

1904—368—33-12

1905—339—31-9

1906—267—22-12

1907—315—24-12

1908—391—37-11

1909—274—25-6

1910—319—27-9

1911—307—26-13

1912—310—23-12

1913—306—25-11

1914—312—24-13

How did he do it? How did he last? He *pitched*. In other words, he figured he had seven other players behind him, all eager to try to help him win. Instead of trying to strike every single batter out—remember Crash Davis's great line in *Bull Durham*, "Strikeouts are boring. Besides that, they're fascist. Throw some ground balls, they're more democratic"—that was Mathewson's method. Or as William Kashatus put it in *Pennsylvania Heritage*: "Mathewson partly owed his pitching success to his knowledge of each hitter's idiosyncrasies and weaknesses, as well as his pinpoint control. Seldom did he rely on his blazing fastball to strike out a batter. Instead, he mixed in his vicious curve or tricky 'fadeaway' (screwball) to force ground balls and pop-ups. Only when there were runners in scoring position did he go for the strikeout."

His old catcher, John "Chief" Meyers, who ought to have known, wholeheartedly agreed.

"I caught almost every game he pitched for seven years," Meyers told Lawrence Ritter in *The Glory of Their Times*. "What a pitcher he was! The greatest that ever lived. He had almost perfect control. Really, almost perfect. In 1913 he pitched 68 consecutive innings without walking a man. That record is still standing, I think. That season he pitched over 300 innings and I doubt if he walked 25 men the whole year. Same thing in 1914. I don't think he ever walked a man in his life because of wildness. The only time he might walk a man was because he was pitching too fine to him, not letting him get a good ball to hit. But there was never a time he couldn't throw that ball over the plate if he wanted to."

As corny as it might sound, it almost seems as if Mathewson felt *his* wins would feel more like a *team* win if everybody was involved. That this philosophy—counting on his teammates for big outs—would end up costing him some key games, including the Merkle "boner" in 1908 not to mention the three successive World Series losses of 1911, 1912, and 1913 where Mathewson went 2–5 despite a stunning 1.13 ERA.

Of course, Christy's longstanding World Series record is the three shutouts he threw in a six-day span in 1906 to lead the Giants to the title. That record may be even more unapproachable than Cy Young's 511 wins.

One of his contemporaries, Max Carey, offered his own explanation for Mathewson's enduring success. "Mathewson has the ability and all that," said Carey, "but I believe the main factor that has held him up so long has been his love of the game. Thirteen years is a long time to be under fire. I'm no veteran myself—only a youngster at the game; but there are times when I'm tired out and would give a farm to break away for a long rest.

"But I've watched Mathewson closely and I've never seen him pitch a ball-game in which he didn't look as if he were having a lot of fun. He

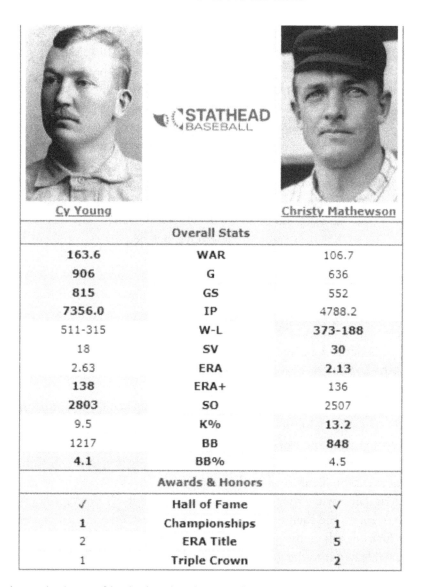

Cy Young		Christy Mathewson
Overall Stats		
163.6	WAR	106.7
906	G	636
815	GS	552
7356.0	IP	4788.2
511-315	W-L	373-188
18	SV	30
2.63	ERA	2.13
138	ERA+	136
2803	SO	2507
9.5	K%	13.2
1217	BB	848
4.1	BB%	4.5
Awards & Honors		
✓	Hall of Fame	✓
1	Championships	1
2	ERA Title	5
1	Triple Crown	2

always looks as if he had rather be out there pitching than doing any-thing else. It doesn't look to be work with him, but only pure sport—an afternoon's romp as a businessman might go out to play golf or tennis.

"But after thirteen years baseball is still Mathewson's favorite sport. He either likes it immensely or he is the greatest actor I ever saw. He never has to drag himself out to the lot and force himself to play. The game appeals to him and he finds a lot of new things to study and work over all the time."

The great American writer Ring Lardner, who got to watch Mathewson in his prime, offered his own wonderfully colloquial description of how Christy worked and how, unlike most pitchers of today, Mathewson had his priorities and was skilled at finding a way to coast through a ballgame.

"Take him in a common ordinary ball game, agin a average club, and every day pitchin', and what he's tryin' to do is stick the first one over so's he won't have to waste no more'n one ball on one batter," Lardner wrote. "He don't stick it over right in the groove, but he puts it just about so's you'll get a piece of it and give the Giants a little easy fieldin' practice. If the Giants gets a flock o' runs and goes way out in front, he'll keep right on stickin' that first one over, and maybe he'll allow a little scorin'. But if the guy workin' agin him is airtight, and the game's close, and you get a couple o' men on and a base hit'll do some damage, he unlocks his safe and pulls out some o' the real stuff he's got and lets go of it. Maybe the curve he'll show you ain't as good as some you've saw, but it'll come where you can't get a good hold of it.

"Or if it's a fast one you don't like, that's what you'll get, and even if it ain't as fast as Johnson's, you'll find that it comes past you a couple of inches higher or lower or this side or that side of where you could wallop it good. Or maybe you'll see this fadeaway that he got up himself, and it's about as easy to hit as this here Freddie Welsh. That's the way he works in a reg'lar game, when they ain't much dependin' on it. He don't really pitch till he's got to, and then he sure does pitch. The rest o' the time, he's puttin' that first one where they either got to hit at it or have a strike called on 'em, and leavin' it to the guys back of him to take care o' what's hit. That's why he's been good so long and that's why he's goin' to be good a whole lot longer. And McGraw's smart enough to help him save himself."

That about covers it, doesn't it?

Mathewson's legacy endures. He was the topic of a recent story in the *New Yorker* magazine that discussed his youth novels. His instructional book *Pitching in a Pinch: Baseball from the Inside*, published in 1912, was well known. His young adult novels, not so much.

As Luke Epplin wrote in the *New Yorker*: "An even more entertaining distillation of Mathewson's philosophy can be found in the series of young-adult novels that he wrote with the *New York Herald* writer John Wheeler, from 1910 to '17. Mathewson's unparalleled fame—Wheeler remarked that schoolboys across the country were 'acquainted with the exact figures which have made up Matty's pitching record before they had ever heard of George Washington'—helped them find a large audience. Long since out of print, these novels sought to convince young readers and parents alike that baseball was an edifying pursuit that fostered character and intellect.

"In Mathewson's 1914 novel, 'Pitcher Pollock,' Tom Pollock, a farm boy, moves to the city of Amesville, Ohio, to attend high school. Mr. Cummings, the owner of the department store where Tom works after school, notices his baseball skills and teaches Tom how to mix up his pitches to fool batters. During one of their practice sessions, Tom declares that he needs a break. When Mr. Cummings asks if Tom's arm feels sore, Tom replies, 'No, sir, it's my head. I never knew before that a pitcher did so much pitching with his head!' Tom develops into the town's star pitcher, so much so that a former athlete, Mr. George, asks Tom's coach, Bat Talbot, about the possibility of Tom trying out for a professional club. When Bat declares that Tom is too smart to play baseball for a living, Mr. George says: I don't know, Bat. Baseball isn't what it used to be, and ball players aren't like what they were once. . . . There's a pretty fine, self-respecting lot of men playing professional ball these days. Why, say, it's just as respectable a profession as—as medicine or law, isn't it?"

While Mathewson's contention in *Pitching in a Pinch* that players would soon need to be educated to keep up with their competitors proved to be wrong—one winces at the idea of an Albert Belle–penned young adult novel—it revealed a baseball player who got by on more than just sheer physical talent.

"His writings advanced the idea that baseball players aren't empty vessels in the field, operating primarily through instinct and raw talent,"

Epplin wrote. "They are analytical thinkers who must be able to execute and amend strategies on the fly in order to outsmart their competitors."

Mathewson, no doubt, would be saddened to see today's game's emphasis on sheer stuff. What teams perhaps learned from the likes of Pedro Martínez and others is that if you have one virtually unhittable pitch, the hell with strategy. Keep throwing that pitch until further notice. And when you're tired, we'll bring in somebody from the bullpen who can do about the same thing until the game's over.

From Ring Lardner to Grantland Rice to those that played against him, almost everybody who saw Christy Mathewson had something positive or uplifting to say about him. His style, charisma, and reputation were essential in establishing baseball as America's game.

Yet the gambling thing bugs me. These days, you can't watch a Boston Red Sox game on NESN without seeing a little daily gambling spot and hearing the odds on Rafael Devers getting a hit and so on.

We certainly know Pete Rose's passion for gambling, evidently much like Mathewson's, was essentially responsible for his lifetime ban from the sport that made him famous. We know the toll it can take.

We've also read so much about Mathewson's personal dignity, and his brief turn as a manager for the Cincinnati Reds, that we can't imagine him, like Rose, also a manager of the Reds, calling up bookies to play $50 on the Dodgers tonight or even wagering one way or another on a game his team was involved in, a game that, as manager, he *might* have impacted.

Christy Mathewson was always above the fray. And you want to believe that he always would be. But that would also mean a gambler, an apparently inveterate one like Mathewson, would be able to set limits, to be able to understand the difference between a high stakes game of craps or poker that cost him thousands in those idle afternoons or evenings, and placing some sort of wager on the contest about to unfold, one that he knew one hell of a lot about before the first ball was even thrown; in other words, a sure bet.

CHAPTER TWELVE

Pete Rose vs. the Truth

PETE VS. HALL OF FAMERS

Warren Spahn .531 (17-for-32), 2 2B, 1 3B, 2 HR, 5 RBIs, 1 BB, 0 K

Jim Kaat .361 (13-for-36), 2 2B, 2 3B, 0 HR, 6 RBIs, 2 BB, 1 K

Juan Marichal .342 (42-for-123), 7 2B, 1 3B, 4 HR, 11 RBIs, 11 BB, 20 K

Don Sutton .339 (60-for-177), 15 2B, 2 3B, 4 HR, 10 RBIs, 14 BB, 15 K

Don Drysdale .328 (19-for-58), 4 2B, 1 3B, 1 HR, 6 RBIs, 0 BB, 8 K

Jim Bunning .318 (28-for-88), 4 2B, 4 3B, 1 HR, 6 RBIs, 7 BB, 4 K

Ferguson Jenkins .316 (36-for-114), 9 2B, 1 3B, 4 HR, 11 RBIs, 9 BB, 15 K

Bob Gibson .307 (35-for-114), 6 2B, 1 3B, 1 HR, 10 RBIs, 12 BB, 11 K

Gaylord Perry .304 (42-for-138), 6 2B, 0 3B, 1 HR, 9 RBIs, 10 BB, 18 K

TOTALS: .332 (292-for-880), 55 2B, 13 3B, 18 HR, 74 RBIs, 66 BB, 103 K

When it comes to numbers, a topic that always interested Pete Rose on and off the diamond, the former Cincinnati star's totals are hard to beat. Not only lifetime—where he had more hits than anybody who ever played the game—but especially when he faced off against the best of the best. In this case, all Hall of Famers. Take a look at his career numbers above.

Stepping into either batter's box—he was a switch-hitter—against nine of the finest pitchers from his era, roughly 1963 to the mid-1980s (arguably the strongest and most dominant era of starting pitchers in the history of the game), Rose *averaged* an impressive .332.

While Rose wasn't a home-run hitter, he did pile up doubles (746 of them, second all-time to Tris Speaker's 792). He also surely slid headfirst into third at the end of his 135 triples (75th all time) and raced around the bases the 160 times he actually hit one out.

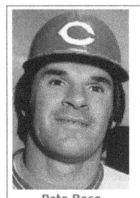

Pete Rose		Ty Cobb
	Overall Stats	
79.5	WAR	**151.5**
3562	G	3034
15890	PA	13103
4256	H	4189
160	HR	117
1314	RBI	**1944**
198	SB	**897**
.303	BA	**.366**
.375	OBP	**.433**
.409	SLG	**.512**
.784	OPS	**.944**
118	OPS+	**168**
	Awards & Honors	
	Hall of Fame	✓
3	Championships	
17	All-Star	
1	MVP	1
3	Batting Title	12
2	Gold Glove	
1	Silver Slugger	
1	WS MVP	
	Triple Crown	1

Rose also played more games than anyone else, 3,562 (254 more than Boston's Carl Yastrzemski), hit more singles, 3,215 (162 more than Ty Cobb), and played about the hardest, no-holds-barred brand of baseball anybody ever saw. All-Star Games, exhibition games, spring training, they were all the same to Pete Rose.

After a career like that—again, just looking at Pete's numbers—you'd think the guy would be remembered and honored as one of baseball's immortals. To some people, perhaps, he still is.

To many others though, Pete Rose remains a pariah. It was the problem Pete had with those *other* numbers, wagers, debts, taxes, the ages of his occasional afternoon dalliances, all of which got him into the hardest brand of trouble *off the field* of any player you can name. Truthfully, it seems as if the trouble has really never let up on the guy ever since he was unceremoniously drummed from the game in 1989 after being accused of gambling on baseball, in particular, the team he was managing at the time, the Cincinnati Reds.

While the lifetime ban agreed upon with then-commissioner Bart Giamatti was purposely vague on the matter of Rose's actual wagers, it was pretty clear that there wasn't a soul in Christendom who doubted Pete hadn't done *something* wrong. If one of baseball's most visible players is getting booted from the game in midseason, it had to be pretty bad. It was.

The evidence that Rose bet on baseball was simply overwhelming. So much so that Giamatti insisted lead prosecutor John Dowd share all the evidence he had with Rose and his attorneys before they even went to a hearing. In order to avoid the press, the two parties actually met in the cafeteria of a small Catholic elementary school in Dayton, Ohio. Dowd showed Rose what evidence he had and years later, Dowd explained perhaps one reason why Rose resorted to betting on baseball.

"He was paying, by the way, six for five on half-a-million dollars to a loan shark on Long Island," Dowd told the Emory School in 2015. "That's six dollars for every five he owes. He could never pay it off."

Giamatti asked Dowd to show his hand to Rose for this reason. "I didn't want him to ever say that he didn't know what the evidence was.

That we played hide the ball," Giamatti told Dowd. Pete knew what he was up against and accepted the lifetime ban.

However, he continued to deny he bet on baseball for many years. In 2004, Rose finally did admit that Dowd's report was right; he did bet on baseball—a mea culpa to coincide with the release of a new book. Instead of the intended cleanse, all the confession seemed to do was further muddy the already murky waters around the guy's ankles or maybe even his knees by this time.

From there until now, it seemed whatever move Rose made, whether it was a goofy TV reality show, or endless autograph sessions in casinos all over the place, shameless money grabs, the occasionally profane interview, once Pete Rose was *out* of uniform, it was as if he didn't know how he was supposed to behave. Hey, what *was* a retired baseball icon supposed to do when he wasn't sliding headfirst somewhere? Never the shy, retiring, humble ex–baseball player, a soft-spoken fella just thankful to have a chance to play the game, somebody grateful to be acknowledged by even a single fan, this was not something he understood. He was *Pete Rose*, dammit!

Though there were certainly many bets that Pete made that didn't pay off over the years, his biggest—and most fateful miss—was his bet on Giamatti. It seemed pretty clear at the time of the ban that Major League Baseball had him dead to rights; the best he could negotiate with Giamatti was a lifetime ban—with the implicit understanding that if he "reconfigured his life" (whatever that means) he might someday reapply for reinstatement in the game. And with that, a chance at the Baseball Hall of Fame.

But Giamatti up and died, just eight days after announcing Rose's ban. Maybe Pete was naïve, but he sincerely believed that Giamatti was going to give him another chance. So far, from what we know, no other commissioner, not Fay Vincent, not Bud Selig, not Rob Manfred has seriously given Pete's potential reinstatement genuine consideration. At age 84 in 2025, that betting window is closed.

First Time Back

With that lifetime ban in place for a decade, the first time Pete Rose was allowed back on a major-league field was for Game 2 of the 1999 World Series in Atlanta in late October because of the announcement of the All-Century Team. Rose had been voted onto the team and it took a special dispensation from then-commissioner Bud Selig to allow Rose to participate.

Before the game, as the greatest living players in the history of the game were trotted out at Turner Field—Willie Mays, Ken Griffey Jr., Mike Schmidt, an 81-year-old Ted Williams—they were there and happy and proud, waving to the fans, smiling at one another, their baseball duels done.

When it came time for the introductions, Pete Rose received the longest and loudest ovation for any All-Century Team member—even louder than for hometown hero Hank Aaron! It was the kind of noise he hadn't been allowed to hear for a decade. Pete looked a bit embarrassed. He looked around at his peers, the game's all-time heroes, spread out across the diamond around him. And he was there, among the best to ever play the game. He was back, even if it was only for one night.

Moments later, Rose found himself behind some microphones in a small room overflowing with writers who came to hear some sort of confession, a plea for forgiveness. Perhaps they were hoping to see the cocky Pete Rose, the guy who once had the world by the balls—probably exactly how *he* would have described it—throwing himself on the mercy of the court.

What we didn't know was before he even uttered a word, Pete faced a formidable task. On that evening, he was still denying that he bet on baseball, a stance he would shift to the truth five years later to coincide with the release of a brand-new tell-some book.

Here he was in Atlanta, back inside a major-league ballpark, trying to win the support and perhaps the affection of a roomful of writers, folks who had been eyewitnesses to his glory days, guys whose words just might tip public opinion back in his favor. You know, like they did back when he was inarguably great.

You could almost read what Rose was thinking as he looked out at all those empty notebooks and whirring tape recorders. "Guys, you remember those days, right? Back when I was the man?" Judging from the on-field announcement, it sure sounded like he had the crowd on his side. Could he get the writers, too? One more time?

"I would do anything in my power to change what has happened to me in the last ten years, I would," Rose said, addressing the room. "But I can't change what has happened. You know how I feel. You know I'm sorry.

"I mean, I guess maybe when I got the hit to break Ty Cobb's record, I shouldn't have cried at first base because no one thinks I'm sorry unless I cry. I got feelings like everybody else has feelings, obviously. If anybody in this group doesn't think I'm sorry for what happened."

But of course, the ultimate question is this: Is Pete Rose really sorry for what he did? Or is he just sorry he got caught?

Scanning that Turner Field room full of baseball writers, or as he might have imagined them—eyewitnesses—Pete reached out to them as only he could.

"I must tell you this," he said then, gesturing with a wave of his hand, "that I'm sitting here looking at a lot of friends out there, and I can't think of anybody I'm looking at that I hurt."

As Rose spoke, esteemed author Roger Angell of the *New Yorker*, a peerless chronicler of the game and a future Hall of Fame honoree himself, responded under his breath.

"Baseball," Angell said.

In many ways, it was a pivotal moment; one that peeled back the layers of Rose's dilemma. Here he was, sitting for a captive audience hanging on his every word—just like the old days—while at the same time, trying to hide an ugly truth. Somehow, he thought it was okay to be asking for penance from these writers, men (mostly) who had written so glowingly of him not that many years ago.

Yeah, those were Pete Rose's glory days all right; him stuffing their notebooks with wonderfully sassy, inimitable quotes, always available, always quotable, chatty and funny. He was at the top of his sport, you know, hey, everybody wins!

Now that was all gone. He must have sensed it was never coming back.

The Jim Gray Moment

And there was this. A few moments *before* he was herded into the writers' room, NBC's Jim Gray had grabbed the exiled one for an interview that was as uncomfortable to watch as it must have felt, standing in Rose's sneakers.

The world had just seen the guy stand among the greats of the game on the Turner Field infield. He was inside a ballpark for the first time in a decade. Pete Rose was back, back from Baseball Purgatory. Some of us thought he might do a headfirst dive into a base just for old times' sake.

Gray was unmoved. With the air of an assassin, he thrust a microphone in Pete's face, asking searing, probing, aggressive questions that truly, in the large scheme of things perhaps weren't unfair—Pete wasn't telling the truth, after all—but at that particular celebratory moment in Atlanta seemed terribly out of place.

Those of us downstairs, patiently waiting for Pete, had no idea this was happening above us. With Rose in his sights, Gray was simply relentless.

> Gray: "Pete, let me ask you now. It seems that there is an opening, the American public is very forgiving. Are you willing to show contrition, admit that you bet on baseball and make some sort of apology to that effect?"
>
> Rose: "Not at all, Jim. Not at all. I'm not going to admit to something that didn't happen. I know you're getting tired of hearing me say that. But I appreciate the ovation. I appreciate the American fans voting me on the All-Century Team. I'm just a small part of a big deal tonight."
>
> Gray: "With the overwhelming evidence that is in that report, why not take that step?"
>
> Rose: "No. This is too much of a festive night to worry about that because I don't know what evidence you're talking about. I mean, show it to me."

After all that, Pete Rose had to come down and meet us writers like nothing happened.

In Gray's book, *Talking to GOATs*, he tells us after the interview, he got supportive phone calls from the likes of Jack Nicholson, Don King, and Marlon Brando. Later, Gray was asked by NBC to apologize "to the fans" for disrupting a festive evening, not to Pete.

Naturally, the players detested what Gray did and let him know it over the next few weeks, shunning interviews, asking him to leave the dugout. Later in the Series when Gray arrived at Yankee Stadium, George Steinbrenner made it a point of supporting him. Make of that what you will. Welcome to modern journalism. Pick a side.

WHAT ABOUT THE HALL?

If you've ever had a chance to sit and chat with Rose, it's like you're riding shotgun on a delightful, occasionally off-color, rambunctious, careening ride through an action-packed, foot-stomping career. Story after story throughout his long and tumultuous career painted Rose as an entertaining, dynamic, captivating performer at the top of his game and when you interview him, you see why.

Of course, what should be the crowning achievement of this extraordinary career, a spot in Baseball's Hall of Fame in Cooperstown, has been—and apparently will always be—denied him. A recent, desperate appeal to Commissioner Rob Manfred was rejected, almost out of hand. Why? Why is the answer always "No" to Pete Rose? Because of those *other* numbers we talked about before.

Now it's not as if all the current 342 Hall of Fame members were Boy Scouts. Of the 270 elected players as of 2024, there are several with scurrilous moments in their past, some in the present. There are some with questionable actions post-baseball—drug busts, DUIs, maybe even sexual assaults and who knows what else. Some we know about, some we never will.

But so far as we know anyway, there weren't *any* of them who decided it was a good idea to put a wager down on the team he was managing. Like Pete.

Or if they did—and there are some very odd moments in baseball's past that would raise our eyebrows now—nobody ever found out about it.

The profound question that lies at the bottom of the Pete Rose controversy is this one: Are you recognizing the *person* in Cooperstown? Or are you recognizing the *player*? Should there be a difference?

Yeah, there is some sort of vague morals clause that says candidates "shall be chosen on the basis of playing ability, sportsmanship, character, their contribution to the teams on which they played and to baseball in general."

In other words, would it be wrong and unjust to strictly celebrate whatever achievements that player had vs. his peers during the length of his career, regardless of what he did off the field? Should Rose's personal foibles, his off-the-field actions, impact whether Cooperstown's doors would welcome him or not? Are we evaluating him as a player or as a person? And is it the person we think we know from the media coverage or the real guy? We might know more about these guys now than in the days when writers basically glorified the players. But do we really?

We certainly all want our baseball heroes to be just that—heroic. But they are, like us, human. And often find themselves in predicaments caused by their fame, sometimes caused by poor decisions, selfishness, stupidity, immaturity, greed, sexism, the things we all struggle with.

PETE KNEW BETTER

And on principle, what Pete Rose did—placing bets on a game where he possessed a whole lot of inside information (which didn't help him much, reportedly since he lost money on his baseball bets) in order to try to beat the system—is, in the eyes of many, unforgivable. And maybe it is.

It wasn't as if he didn't know better, he did. And as a student of baseball history, he certainly knew all about the scandal of the 1919 World Series! It was his hometown Cincinnati Reds who ended up winning the Series, courtesy of the White Sox, at least eight of whom were *trying* to lose. Sure, he knew all about it. And he knew the rule about betting on the game, too.

The integrity of the sport is up for grabs, some insist. You can't ever let Pete in, they say. Or those other alleged (and some admitted) cheaters

(Barry Bonds, Roger Clemens, Sammy Sosa, Mark McGwire, etc.) It is a compelling argument.

But if we look at what Pete Rose did a little differently than most, if we see *what* he did as one more thing he thought he could get away with because of *who* he was, and where he was, why, the guy was practically a living monument in Cincinnati.

At that point in his life, Rose hadn't heard the word *no* in years or if somebody said it, he wasn't listening. The always deadly combination of hubris, fame, poor judgment, and flat-out ignorance—sorry, Pete, but it's true—led him down a desperate path where he needed the action or needed the money to cover other dumbass things he did or was trying to keep some of his low-life friends off his back or a million other reasons—or maybe we should say several million reasons—we don't know about. If we think of these bets that way, maybe we can see his wagering a little differently. Maybe.

He was trying to beat the system, thanks to what he figured he had—inside knowledge—and his ability to anticipate results. From all reports, he did a rotten job of it.

To me, that's different than what Clemens, McGwire, Sosa, Bonds, etc. did, using a banned substance to give them a considerable advantage in every game they participated in, helping them excel and set records that will never be broken. These records can't be expunged from the baseball record book because we can't say with absolute certainty who used steroids and who didn't. That's a lifetime scar on the game.

For years, baseball fans wondered if anybody would beat Roger Maris's record, just like people wondered for the 30-plus years before that if anybody could outdo The Babe's 60 homers. As Aaron Judge, Barry Bonds, Sammy Sosa, and Mark McGwire can tell you, people are still interested in home runs. But the Great Home Run Chase of 1998 feels like a trick now, doesn't it?

There is, of course, an important principle involved—honesty. For many years, as a deterrent, it mattered that a player with the undeniable Hall of Fame achievements of a Shoeless Joe Jackson would be denied the Hall, this ultimate celebration of his career, thanks to the 1919 scandal.

There are still those who look at Jackson's numbers in that Series (.375, the only home run) and make the argument for him; he was illiterate, after all, we're not really sure if the fix was in for all eight games, how much the players received and when the money stopped, exactly how involved he was with all of it.

But we also know from Jackson's grand jury testimony where he admitted there were plays where he helped the Reds score, moments not scored an error but designed to help Cincinnati runners, there were balls that went over his head, at-bats where he didn't deliver—up eight times with runners in scoring position, not a single run driven in until the late-inning home run in that final decisive game, well after that contest had been decided. Baseball historian Jerome Holtzman was never sympathetic to Jackson's cause. Perhaps Jackson couldn't read, he said, "but he could count."

We Can't Turn Our Head

Let's be honest, it's more than a little crazy to have a Baseball Hall of Fame exhibition hall and not include some of the game's most significant players—far more people know about Shoeless Joe Jackson than Freddie Lindstrom—you can't deny history. Why not acknowledge it?

Wouldn't it make more sense to acknowledge what these miscreants did *on* the field and at the same time, point out their serious mistakes off the field for future generations? Yes, these guys *were* great players, but some of their decisions away from the diamond were awful, examples of what *not* to do. They were some of the greatest players we've seen, no question. But there is a right and a wrong way to play the game, to live your life. Wouldn't that be an important and effective message to share?

It's silly to walk into Cooperstown's wonderful Hall of Fame and pretend we never heard of Pete Rose and Roger Clemens and Barry Bonds and the rest, like they didn't matter one bit to the game's history. We can't say that.

These players mattered *a lot*; in some ways, they altered the game's history. Why not just lay out what they did, after all this time and all this publicity, get it out there. We can handle it. So can they.

A recent visit to the Hall revealed an interesting exhibit entitled "In the Shadow of Homers," a large glass display case that displayed game jerseys of Sammy Sosa and Mark McGwire and their instruments of destruction, as well as those Starting Lineup plastic player figures that were a big hit with kids at the time. There was also a "Nobody's Better Than Canseco" fan poster—they did recognize the steroids' whistleblower—and the exhibit also made sure to present the *Sports Illustrated* cover with McGwire and Sosa dressed in togas and laurel crowns as that magazine's "Sportsmen of the Year." Oops! Wonder if those *SI* editors regret that one?

You can understand why those who are already in the Hall say that letting Rose in would cheapen the honor. They didn't do the stupid things he did. Why lower the Hall's standards? It's a valid point, and one that all the commissioners and many of the Hall of Famers stand by to this day.

But could they say Pete Rose didn't earn it? That he didn't meet Hall of Fame standards by what he did on the field? Bonds, Clemens, Sosa, McGwire, and probably others demonstrably benefited by the use of performance-enhancing drugs. The drug use helped separate them from their peers, it was an undeniable advantage, and the record books show the staggering impact steroids had on the game.

What Pete Rose did was selfish, illicit, shameful, crooked. But it cost him way more than whatever he lost at the betting window. That too, is undeniable. Maybe it should have cost him the whole enchilada.

Since then, Major League Baseball has changed its approach to gambling, embracing Draft Kings, promoting gambling on the game, even on individual at-bats. Honestly, it's hard to play "the integrity of the game" card now. There are players who abused steroids, served their penalty, and are now back in the game. An entire team, the Houston Astros, may have gotten to and won a World Series by cheating. There are so many moments we know about where the game's "integrity" was compromised. And what *don't* we know about? What will come out in a few years?

Finding a way to recognize these exiled players will be controversial, sure. But baseball could offer a separate section explaining what they did, why they weren't elected in the normal way, offer a cautionary tale to any potential impressionable youth, and at the same time, offer some recognition of what they did on the field and why it was important. And hell, it *was* important.

Satchel Paige, for example, didn't earn his Hall of Fame berth for what he did pitching as an old man. It was in recognition for all he'd done before. He was an important part of the game's history, even if he didn't get to show it when he was in his prime.

What these miscreants did, as much as many of us hate it, is also a part of the game's history. We shouldn't have to read between the lines. Put it out there, all of it. It's a dark chapter but so what? The game survived.

Nobody in their right mind can defend what Pete Rose did. It was wrong, it'll always be wrong. But if he had a gambling addiction, a sickness that he could not control, something that compelled him to bet, despite what he had to know would be a monumental risk to his career and reputation, doesn't that make his case a little bit different? Whether he admits a gambling addiction or not, hasn't Rose been punished enough? Will keeping him out of the Hall ultimately save or improve baseball in any way?

In a way—pardon my goofy analogy—but it's like having an Impressionist art museum, finding a half-dozen previously undiscovered Van Goghs, but refusing to display them because he chopped off part of his own ear.

You can say—and many do—that Rose earned himself a spot in Cooperstown by what he did on the field and surrendered that spot by what he did off it. Maybe that was fair. Maybe a lifetime ban was deserved and necessary.

When it comes to modern sport, gambling may be a necessary evil. The NBA had an issue with one of its referees and point spreads. A handful of NFL players received lifetime bans for betting on their own games. Some college athletes did the same thing. And that's just what we know now in 2025.

So far, no baseball players have wandered down that path. Pete Rose's ban seems to have served as a deterrent. Players known for sometimes scurrilous behavior were scared off by that lifetime ban. Will the lifetime ban of former Pirates player Tucupita Marcano earlier in 2024 have an impact? It's something worth watching.

"Even Lenny Dykstra told me, 'Boy, I'm glad you got Rose. That stopped me cold,'" baseball's lead prosecutor John Dowd said.

But there is also a lot to be said for forgiveness. People make mistakes, sometimes grave mistakes. Certainly at 84 years of age in 2025, Pete has made more than his share. Baseball fans across America are likely still divided on this guy. But if the response of the crowd in Atlanta at that World Series game with the All-Century Team is representative of how the mass of people feel about Pete Rose—and it may not be—they sounded more than ready to forgive him.

Are you?

PETE AT THE PLATE

Though Pete Rose collected more major-league hits than any batter in history, it's unlikely any modern batting coach would encourage a new pupil to model his swing after the former Cincinnati star, the self-proclaimed "Hit King." Few modern hitting instructors would have recommended Ty Cobb's odd split-handed swing either, but it was right for Cobb's time.

Rose's short, compact swing, and his Popeye-like forearms and strong hands, yanked the bat through the strike zone with little elegance (think the opposite of Ted Williams or Ken Griffey) but with maximum effectiveness.

Rose was also a smart hitter. He explained his philosophy—and then some—to writer Roger Angell in *Game Time*.

"Well, I don't think there's anybody's going to get me out for long," he told Angell. "Nobody's got a book on me. I switch-hit and I hit the ball everywhere. I can hit the fastball and the breaking ball, and I might hit you down the right-field line one time and up the other way the next time. If some pitcher's been getting me out, I'll do one of six things. I might move up in the box or move back. I might move away from the plate or come closer. I might choke up more or choke up less.

"I can usually tell what I'm doing wrong by the flight of the ball. I've seen guys play major-league ball for ten, twelve years, and if they go oh-for-fifteen they want to change their stance, like it's the end of the world. That's ridiculous. The only thing that's rough about this game is that you can't turn it on and off like a faucet. If I'm swinging good, I'll come to the park even on an off day, just to keep it going. This game is mental. There's a lot of thinking in it."

To Rose, and this has certainly proven to be a key element throughout this book about matchups, you have to understand *who* you're facing and *how* he works.

"The pitchers don't change. Tom Seaver don't change," Rose told Angell. "If you're a good hitter, hitting in the majors is easier, 'cause you're facing the same pitchers all the time. I'm particular about that. I have to know the way a guy throws.

"If you don't believe me, look at my Championship Series record, where I got more hits than anybody in the game, and then look at my World Series average. I don't know the pitchers in the World Series, unless they were in my league once, but look at what happens in the fifth and sixth and seventh games, when I begin to see the same guys out there pitching. Look that up."

Following Rose's suggestion, Angell looks up how Pete did. He writes: "In the five World Series in which Rose has played [up to that point] in 1970, 1972, 1975, 1976, and 1980 he has gone hitless at the plate—0 for 16—in the opening games. His second-game average is .157. His third-game average is .285. His fourth-game average is .285. His fifth-game average—he has been in four of them—is .375. His sixth-game average, for three games, is .416. He is 4 for 9 in his two seventh World Series games—.444."

As a switch-hitter, Rose was remarkably consistent on either side of the plate. As a lefty, he had way more turns at plate—10,055 to 3,998 as a righty—and he batted .307. As a right-handed hitter, Rose batted .293, only a 14-point difference which is unusual. Another famous switch-hitter, Mickey Mantle, had a 48-point differential. Mantle hit .282 against right-handers, considerably higher (.330) vs. lefties. Eddie Murray, another switch-hitter, batted .293 as a lefty (lots more at-bats, of course) and just .276 against righties, a 17-point difference. Chipper

Jones was an anomaly in this—he had just a one-point difference between his lefty and righty swings (.303 lefty, .304 righty).

While there may never be anybody trying to copy his style, Rose was tremendously successful, winning three batting titles (.335, 1968; .348, 1969; .338, 1973; the year he was MVP). He had more than 200 hits in a season 10 times, won a couple of Gold Gloves, played infield and outfield, played 162 games—that's all of them—at least seven times and more than 150 games in 17 seasons and in two others he played 148 and 149.

Pete wasn't much of a home-run hitter but here's one for you. What do Don Sutton, Juan Marichal, and Ferguson Jenkins all have in common? Each pitcher surrendered exactly four homers to Pete Rose!

So here's the scoop on Pete. If there was a game somewhere, Pete Rose would be in it, full tilt just about every time, every at-bat, every inning. No wonder he had more at-bats than anybody who ever played the game.

WHO GOT PETE OUT?

As detailed earlier, Rose excelled against the best of the National League starters in part because he knew them so well. But there were pitchers he struggled with. He faced Bob Forsch over 100 times and hit just .198 (20-for-101, seven doubles, one homer, nine RBIs). Randy Jones, the clever lefty who mostly toiled for the San Diego Padres, held Pete to .183 (17-for-93, just a couple of doubles). Andy Messersmith fanned Rose 12 times in 54 at-bats, holding him to .204 (11-for-54, four doubles, one triple). Lefty Al Downing was tough, holding Rose to a .185 average (10-for-54, with one double) and so was Bill Gullickson (Rose hit .192, 10-for-52, with one double, one triple, and one home run,). Rose also did not fare well against Mike Torrez, hitting .171 (7-for-41,with one double, one triple, and one home run) As was the case with many others, it wasn't as if each of these pitchers had one particular pitch that puzzled Rose. Randy Jones was as different from Andy Messersmith as Al Downing was different from Bob Forsch.

And let's say this—nobody was happier to see Sandy Koufax retire than Pete Rose. Koufax held Rose to .175 (10-for-57, one double, 10 strikeouts). Facing another fireballer, Nolan Ryan, Pete was a bit more successful: Rose hit .273 vs. Ryan, (18-for-66, two doubles, 17 walks, and 13 strikeouts). But he once said trying to hit Koufax was like eating soup with a fork.

But there were many pitchers on whom Rose feasted.

Claude Raymond .472 (17-for-36)

Eric Rasmussen .471 (16-for-34)

Ray Culp .450 (18-for-40)

Wayne Twitchell .424 (14-for-33)

Jim Rooker .418 (23-for-55)

Ken Holtzman .409 (18-for-44)

Tommy Sisk .407 (22-for-54)

Bob Welch .400 (22-for-55)

Rose was well known as a needler, calling Philadelphia teammate Von Hayes "Five-for-One" as Hayes came to the Phillies in a trade involving five players going to Cleveland in return. He may not have ever razzed Boston's Carl Yastrzemski, but he could have. For Pete Rose absolutely owned lefty Darold Knowles, collecting 10 hits in 17 trips (.588) with a pair of doubles, unlike poor ol' Yaz.

As we noted elsewhere, Boston's Hall of Famer Yastrzemski hit just .077 (2-for-26) against the well-traveled lefty. Yaz's second ever hit off the guy, a flare single to left field just over shortstop, came after a sorry 0-for-17 stretch against the reliever.

Pete Rose, on the other hand, was one hitter who learned from every trip to the plate. Ask the same Darold Knowles.

Pitching for the Phillies against the Reds, Knowles fanned Rose the first time he faced him in 1966. He surrendered a double to him two days later, then got him to ground out, then fanned him a week after that—all in relief appearances.

It was 11 years before Knowles saw Rose in the right-handed batter's box again, when Knowles had moved on to the Cubs and Rose to the Phillies. Pete had learned, collecting four consecutive hits off the guy on his way to that .588 average, even higher than Pete's .531 against Hall of Famer Warren Spahn.

The last time Pete Rose faced Knowles, he had quite a capper. It was in 1979, when Knowles came on in the ninth, trying to protect a 5–4 Cardinals lead. He retired Larry Bowa and Greg Luzinski and was one out away from a win.

But never-say-die Pete Rose lined a single to left field to start what became a two-out, three-run, game-winning rally. When the dust cleared, the Phillies had three runs, Knowles had a loss, and Darold Knowles was damn happy he didn't have to face Pete Rose any more.

Chapter Thirteen

Left Out of *Last Time Out*

In updating my 2005 book *Last Time Out* in the summer of 2022, the idea was to add some terrific players that weren't among the 25 chosen for edition one. The reason they didn't make the original was sound. Most of 'em were still playing.

It was quite an amendment, adding Yogi Berra, Barry Bonds, David Ortiz, Chipper Jones, Mariano Rivera, Derek Jeter, Reggie Jackson, Mark McGwire, Sammy Sosa, Nolan Ryan, Roger Clemens, and a few more.

Invariably, there were also those magnificent players who, for one reason or another, were left out of *Last Time Out*. In some cases, like the final game of Pittsburgh's great Honus Wagner, there just wasn't much of a story to tell.

For Wagner, his finale came at the end of the 1917 season. At age 43, Wagner came into an extra-inning game for Red Smith and played a couple of innings in the field before being lifted for a pinch-hitter in the 13th. Bill Wagner, no relation, hit for Honus and promptly hit into a double play. I guess the Baseball Gods would have preferred to let the old man hit.

Honus's final major-league at-bat had come a few days earlier on September 11 against Cardinals pitcher Oscar Horstmann, who whiffed him.

Of course, there were some players you had to have in the original *Last Time Out*—Ruth, Gehrig, DiMaggio, Williams, Cobb, Mays—whether they did anything dramatic in their final game or not. But there were still important players that we just weren't able to get to.

So . . . here are a few that didn't make it in either edition. Hope I didn't miss one of your favorites. Here are their final major-league appearances:

Al Kaline, Detroit Tigers—October 2, 1974 vs. Baltimore Orioles—The great Al Kaline left the game quietly, as was his style. He started against lefty Mike Cuellar and batting in the first inning, took a called third strike. He came up in the third and flew out to left field. When his spot in the lineup came up again, Kaline let Ben Oglivie pinch-hit for him. Kaline ended with 399 career home runs.

Paul Molitor, Milwaukee Brewers—September 27, 1998 vs. Cleveland Indians—One of the most stylish right-handed hitters of his time, Molitor reached on an infield single to second base against reliever Doug Jones.

Jim Rice, Boston Red Sox—August 3, 1989 vs. Cleveland Indians—Boston's great slugger saw his career come to a startling halt in early August. Batting against reliever Rod Nichols, Rice flew out to right field in his last at-bat.

Jimmie Foxx, Philadelphia Phillies—September 23, 1945 at Brooklyn Dodgers—Foxx played in both ends of a doubleheader. In the first game against Les Webber, he grounded to short. In the nightcap, he doubled off Tom Seats, then fanned in the fifth. When Foxx's spot came up in the seventh, he let Tony Lupien pinch-hit in his spot.

Frank Robinson, Cleveland Indians—September 18, 1976 vs. Baltimore Orioles—Player-manager Frank Robinson put himself up as a pinch-hitter against lefty Rudy May of the Orioles and singled. Alfredo Griffin pinch-ran for him.

Warren Spahn, San Francisco Giants—October 1, 1965 vs. Cincinnati Reds—The 44-year-old Warren Spahn came on in relief in the seventh inning of a 17–2 Giants loss. After reliever Gaylord Perry had allowed three straight singles, Spahn came on to face Johnny Edwards, who walked, Leo Cardenas reached on an error as Edwards attempted to score and was thrown out at the plate. That was the last out Spahn saw from the mound. Pitcher Sammy Ellis singled to left, scoring Cardenas, chasing Spahn. He went 7–16 that season for the Giants, his 363rd and final win coming on September 12, a complete-game victory over the Cubs. He allowed a pair of homers to John Boccabella in that final game. Spahn allowed 434 homers in his long career, ranking him eighth on the all-time list.

Fred Lynn, San Diego Padres—October 3, 1990 at Los Angeles Dodgers—Facing former reliever Don Aase, a former Red Sox teammate, Lynn lined out to right field.

Joe Mauer, Minnesota Twins—September 30, 2018 vs. Chicago White Sox—Three-time batting champ Joe Mauer doubled to left field off reliever Juan Minaya for his final hit. He also went back behind the plate for the final inning of his career.

Robin Yount, Milwaukee Brewers—October 3, 1993 at Boston Red Sox—One of the greatest of all Brewers, Yount came up for the final time in the 12th inning as a pinch-hitter for Juan Bell. Relief pitcher Cory Bailey wasn't sentimental about Yount's final at-bat at all. He struck him out.

Wade Boggs, Tampa Bay Devil Rays—August 27, 1999 at Cleveland Indians—Coming perilously to close to hitting below .300 in his final major-league season, Boggs fouled out to the catcher in the first, hit into a 4-6-3 double play in the third, and rapped into a 4-to-6 fielder's choice in the sixth against Dave Burba. He walked in the ninth and was able to retire with a .301 lifetime average.

Nomar Garciaparra, Oakland A's—October 4, 2009 vs. Los Angeles Angels of Anaheim—Nomar Garciaparra, such an offensive weapon in the first part of his career with the Boston Red Sox, left the game quietly, striking out against reliever Darren Oliver as a pinch-hitter in the eighth.

Albert Pujols, St. Louis Cardinals—October 8, 2022 vs. Philadelphia Phillies—Returning to the team where he cut his teeth, Pujols had a rejuvenated final season in St. Louis, singling down the third base line off reliever Seranthony Domínguez in the eighth inning of the second and final game of the Cardinals' wild card series loss.

Willie McCovey, San Francisco Giants—July 6, 1980 at Los Angeles Dodgers—Returning to the San Francisco Giants after a brief stint in San Diego, McCovey pinch-hit and lifted a sacrifice fly against reliever Rick Sutcliffe.

Jim Thome, Baltimore Orioles—October 3, 2012 at Tampa Bay Rays—Facing reliever Fernando Rodney, Thome lifted a short flyball to left field to end the ballgame.

Duke Snider, San Francisco Giants—October 3, 1964 vs. Chicago Cubs—Leading off the ninth against reliever Lindy McDaniel, Snider singled to right field. After two more outs, he trotted home on Willie Mays's second homer of the game, his 46th.

Adrián Beltré, Texas Rangers—September 30, 2018 at Seattle Mariners—Adrián Beltré wound up his career with a couple of at-bats in a 3–1 loss at Seattle's Safeco Field. Leading off the second against starter Roenis Elías, Beltré singled to right field, his final career hit, number 3,166. He led off the fifth against Elías and flied out to right and came out of the game.

Todd Helton, Colorado Rockies—September 29, 2013 at Los Angeles Dodgers—Todd Helton bowed out in a 2–1 Rockies win that included his final hit, a first-inning single off Hyun-Jin Ryu, his 2,519th career hit. After a foulout and a walk, Kenley Jansen whiffed him in the ninth in his final major-league at-bat.

Harmon Killebrew, Kansas City Royals—September 26, 1975 at Texas Rangers—Pinch-hitting for Tony Solaita in the eighth against reliever

Clyde Wright, Killebrew reached first on Rangers shortstop Toby Harrah's error. Rodney Scott pinch-ran for him.

Rickey Henderson, Los Angeles Dodgers—September 19, 2003 vs. San Francisco Giants—Pinch-hitting, Rickey Henderson was hit by a pitch from reliever Jason Christiansen and came around to score his 2,295th run in his final game.

Mel Ott, New York Giants—July 11, 1947 vs. St. Louis Cardinals—In the first game of a doubleheader, player-manager Mel Ott stepped up as a pinch-hitter in the eighth inning for pitcher Larry Jansen and facing reliever Ken Burkhart, bounced out to first base unassisted. And that was it.

Johnny Bench, Cincinnati Reds—September 29, 1983 vs. San Francisco Giants—Pinch-hitting in the fifth inning for Ted Power against the Giants' Mark Calvert, Bench ripped a two-run single to left. Gary Redus came in to pinch-run for Bench.

Hank Greenberg, Pittsburgh Pirates—September 18, 1947 vs. Brooklyn Dodgers—Facing reliever Clyde King in a 7–7 tie in the ninth inning, Greenberg popped out to second base. But Hank went home happy when teammate Wally Westlake followed with a walkoff homer to win the game for the Bucs.

Eddie Mathews, Detroit Tigers—October 6, 1968 vs. St. Louis Cardinals—Facing the electric Bob Gibson of the St. Louis Cardinals in Game 4 of the 1968 World Series, Mathews drew a seventh-inning walk. Gibson was a 10–1 winner, throwing a five-hitter, fanning 10. Earlier, Mathews got one of the hits, a second-inning single.

Manny Ramírez, Tampa Bay Rays—April 6, 2011 vs. Los Angeles Angels of Anaheim—Pinch-hitting for catcher John Jaso in the bottom of the eighth, Ramírez flew out to right field against reliever Kevin Jepsen. That was the last time we got to see Manny Being Manny. A second failed drug test ended Ramírez's major-league career.

Al Simmons, Philadelphia A's—July 1, 1944 vs. Detroit Tigers—Simmons collected two hits in his first three trips but batting against reliever Boom-Boom Beck in the bottom of the eighth, he bounced into a fielder's choice. Finally, after hanging around for season after season, trying to get to 3,000 hits, Simmons hung 'em up.

Rod Carew, Los Angeles Angels—October 5, 1985 at Texas Rangers—Carew got on base in his final at-bat, reaching on an error when pitcher Matt Williams fumbled his bunt attempt. Earlier, he walked, struck out, and grounded out.

Mike Piazza, Oakland A's—September 30, 2007 vs. Los Angeles Angels of Anaheim—Piazza singled to right field in his final major-league at-bat against reliever Chris Bootcheck.

Dick Allen, Oakland A's—June 19, 1977 at Chicago White Sox—Allen pinch-hit for Tony Armas in the second game of a Sunday doubleheader against reliever Francisco Barrios in the seventh and struck out. After grounding out and hitting into a double play in the first game, he got a pair of singles to right for his last major-league hits.

Ralph Kiner, Cleveland Indians—September 25, 1955 at Detroit Tigers—Kiner pinch-hit for pitcher Bud Daley in the top of the seventh inning against Bob Miller and was called out on strikes.

Jim Palmer, Baltimore Orioles—May 12, 1984 vs. Oakland A's—Palmer took over for Sammy Stewart in the eighth with the Orioles trailing 8–1 and gave up a three-run homer to Davey Lopes. In the ninth, he allowed a triple to Mike Davis and an RBI single to Tony Phillips. Palmer then announced his retirement.

Willie Stargell, Pittsburgh Pirates—October 3, 1982 vs. Montreal Expos—You'll never guess who the Pirates chose to lead off in this final game. That's right, Wilver Dornell Stargell! He lined a single off starter Steve Rogers, then left the game for a pinch-runner. Stargell only started three games that season, appearing in 74 games with just 85 at-bats. His 475th and final home run was a game-winner off Tom Hume in the eighth inning of a June 21 game in Cincinnati.

Frank Thomas, Oakland A's—August 29, 2008 vs. Minnesota Twins— Though the hulking Thomas collected a pair of singles as a DH for the A's on this day, reliever Craig Breslow struck him out in his final major-league at-bat.

Vladimir Guerrero, Baltimore Orioles—September 28, 2011 vs. Boston Red Sox—Guerrero wound down his career with the Baltimore Orioles as a DH and finished with an 0-for-4, flying out to center field against reliever Daniel Bard in the eighth.

Ryne Sandberg, Chicago Cubs—September 28, 1997 at St. Louis Cardinals—Sandberg, one of the greatest of all Cubs, had just a pair of at-bats in the season finale against the St. Louis Cardinals. He grounded to short and flied to center against Manny Aybar.

Ichiro Suzuki, Seattle Mariners—March 21, 2019 vs. Oakland A's— Ichiro went 0–4 in his major-league finale in a game played at the Tokyo Dome. Reliever Lou Trivino got him to ground out to short in the eighth inning in his final at-bat. He popped out to second and walked in the season opener the day before against Mike Fiers.

Ernie Banks, Chicago Cubs—September 26, 1971 vs. Philadelphia Phillies—Ernie Banks only got to play one in a 5–1 loss in the Cubs' last home game of the season. He singled in his first at-bat, walked, grounded to short and in his final major-league at-bat, popped out to third against Ken Reynolds.

Dennis Eckersley, Boston Red Sox—October 2, 1998 vs. Cleveland Indians—Eck's last regular-season appearance came six days earlier, working the final inning of a 5–2 loss to Scott Erickson and the Baltimore Orioles. He had just one more appearance in the postseason, throwing the ninth inning of Boston's 4–3 loss to the Cleveland Indians in Game 3 of the ALDS. Boston went on to lose the series, 3–1. Future Red Sox star Manny Ramírez hit Eck's third pitch into the left field seats, he fanned Jim Thome, got Travis Fryman to fly out, and Brian Giles to foul out to end the inning and Eck's Hall of Fame career.

Tom Glavine, Atlanta Braves—August 14, 2008 vs. Chicago Cubs— One of the finest lefties in history, Glavine's final major-league start didn't go very well. He took the loss in an 11–7 thumping by the Cubs, throwing four innings, allowing seven hits and seven runs, allowing home runs to Aramis Ramírez and Alfonso Soriano. Glavine lost his final five starts but wound up with a 305–203 won-loss record.

Greg Maddux, Los Angeles Dodgers—October 15, 2008 vs. Philadel- phia Phillies—After closing out the regular season with a 2–1 win over the San Francisco Giants, breaking a personal three-game losing streak, Maddux went to the bullpen for the Dodgers' postseason run, working three times in relief in the NLDS and NLCS. His final appearance came against the Philadelphia Phillies in the fifth and final game of the NLDS, working two innings in relief of starter Chad Billingsley. Maddux tossed a clean fourth inning but the Phils reached him for two runs in the fifth thanks to singles to Jayson Werth and Ryan Howard and a pair of errors by shortstop Rafael Furcal as Philadelphia won the NLCS, four games to one. The final major-league batter Maddux faced—a nice trivia ques- tion—was Phillies pitcher Cole Hamels, whom he got to ground out to first base. Maddux wound up 8–13 that year for the Dodgers, winding up a Hall of Fame career at 355–227.

John Smoltz, St. Louis Cardinals—October 10, 2009 vs. Los Angeles Dodgers—Smoltz's final major-league appearance came in Game 3 of the Dodgers' sweep of St. Louis in the NLDS after he wound up his reg- ular season with a loss to the Cincinnati Reds, dropping his season mark to 3–8. Against the Dodgers, Smoltz threw two innings in relief of starter Joel Pinero. He had the strikeout pitch working, fanning the side after a Casey Blake single leading off the sixth, adding Rafael Furcal and Matt

Kemp to lead off the seventh. But Andre Ethier ripped a triple to deep center and Manny Ramírez singled him home. James Loney followed with a single but Smoltz got Blake to fly out, ending the inning and his major-league career. Smoltz finished with a won-loss record of 213–155, earning election to the Baseball Hall of Fame in 2015.

Lefty Grove, Boston Red Sox—September 28, 1941 at Philadelphia A's—The 41-year-old Grove lasted just one inning, allowing four hits and three runs in dropping his record to 7–7. He won his 300th game on August 16 and made two unsuccessful starts after that, working just two-thirds of an inning, allowing four runs and five hits in an 11–9 loss to the St. Louis Browns, then worked just a third of an inning, retiring Tuck Stainback on a flyout, then giving way to Jack Wilson who went on to take the loss. Grove wound up with a 300–141 lifetime record.

Don Mattingly, New York Yankees—October 8, 1995 at Seattle Mariners—Don Mattingly's fine career came to a halt after an 11-inning loss to the Seattle Mariners, who defeated Jack McDowell thanks to a walkoff double by future Hall of Famer Edgar Martínez in the fifth and deciding game of the ALCS. The win advanced the Mariners to the ALCS. Mattingly's final five games for the Yanks were impressive; he batted .417 with a homer and six RBIs. But in this finale, Mattingly was 1-for-5, his hit a two-run double off Andy Benes in the sixth. He flied out and in the 10th, faced Hall of Famer Randy Johnson, on in relief, who sent Mattingly into retirement with a called third strike.

Boog Powell, Los Angeles Dodgers—August 24, 1977 at Pittsburgh Pirates—Big Boog Powell made his final major-league appearance in the 10th inning of a game vs. the Pittsburgh Pirates. Reliever Rich "Goose" Gossage got Powell to bounce out to second base. He finished with 339 home runs.

Early Wynn, Cleveland Indians—September 13, 1963 at Los Angeles Angels—It took a while but burly right-hander Early Wynn got his 300th career win, working five innings in a 7–4 win over the Kansas City

A's on July 13. His final pitching appearance was in relief against the Angels where he faced two batters, allowing an RBI single to Jim Fregosi before getting Charlie Dees to line out to short. Wynn wound up with a 300–244 lifetime record.

Brooks Robinson, Baltimore Orioles—August 13, 1977 vs. Oakland A's—In an unusual move, the immensely popular Brooks Robinson was announced as a pinch-hitter with two outs in the bottom of the ninth for Al Bumbry in a game the Orioles trailed 9–6. But he didn't take a swing. After a standing ovation, Tony Muser stepped in for him—a pinch-hitter for the pinch-hitter—and fanned against reliever Doug Bair to end the game.

Miguel Cabrera, Detroit Tigers—October 1, 2023 vs. Cleveland Guardians—Miguel Cabrera, who won the Triple Crown in 2012, brought a halt to a wonderful career with an eighth-inning walk against reliever Enyel de los Santos. Cabrera's final career hit—his 3,174th—came on September 30, a fourth-inning double down the line against Guardians starter Triston McKenzie. Cabrera played 98 games in 2023, hitting .257 with four home runs and 34 RBIs. He wound up with a .306 career average, 511 home runs, and 1,881 RBIs.

Nelson Cruz, San Diego Padres—July 3, 2023 vs. Los Angeles Angels—Nelson Cruz wound up his 19-year major-league career with an 0-for-2, popping out to shortstop against reliever Sam Bachman in his final at-bat. His final major-league hit came two days earlier, a single to center off Cincinnati Reds reliever Alec Mills. Cruz played in 49 games for the Padres, batting .245 with five home runs and 23 RBIs. He wound up his career with 464 lifetime homers, a .274 career mark with 1,325 RBIs.

John Nogowski, Pittsburgh Pirates—August 15, 2021 vs. Milwaukee Brewers—Nogo wound up his major-league run with a pinch-hit at-bat against reliever Brent Suter, who got him swinging in the fifth inning. Two nights earlier, Nogo collected his final major-league hit, a pinch-hit RBI single in the fourth inning off Brett Anderson. He played 53 major-league games for the St. Louis Cardinals and Pirates in 2020 and 2021 and hit .452 (19-for-42) in his first 10 games for the Bucs, a rookie record. He homered off Arizona's Taylor Widener on July 20, a two-run shot. He also made three pitching appearances for the Pirates, including a shutout ninth inning against the Braves in his third game for Pittsburgh, also collecting four hits.

Chapter Fourteen

Ranking the Middle of the Order

It seems likely that the first time anybody really paid attention to the actual batting order of a baseball team was in 1929 when the New York Yankees decided to put a #3 on the broad back of George Herman Ruth and a #4 on the equally imposing broad shoulders of Henry Louis Gehrig. The two of them were about halfway through their unprecedented stomp through the American League when the Yankees decided to use uniform numbers. Like anybody could confuse the two.

For a decade, Ruth and Gehrig dominated the American League as nobody else ever would. From 1925 to 1934, Babe hit third, Lou fourth, and over that stretch, they swatted 772 home runs, homered in the same inning 19 times, and 72 times hit home runs in the same game. Between them they drove in 2,762 runs, hit 633 doubles, ran out 183 triples, collected 3,558 hits, leading the Yankees to four AL pennants and three World Series titles. In the process, Ruth and Gehrig transformed the game and what those number three and four spots in the order ought to do for a ballclub.

The two of them also had a flair for the dramatic—Ruth, especially. First home run in an All-Star Game, first home run in Yankee Stadium, etc. You may remember reading about Ruth's famous "called shot" in Game 3 of the 1932 World Series against the Chicago Cubs. Well, what happened was Ruth and Gehrig had already homered in the game and were feeling chipper.

When Ruth came up in the fifth, he seemed to be gesturing and bantering with the Cubs dugout from the batter's box. Reportedly, the Cubs had voted former Ruth teammate Mark Koenig only a half share of the World Series money and the Babe was sticking up for his pal. After a lot of chatter, probably a lot of it unprintable, Ruth looked up and had two strikes on him. He then either pointed to the bleachers or pointed to the dugout, saying "it only takes one" or something a little more colorful and promptly launched Charlie Root's next pitch into the center field seats, exactly where some say he pointed. Talk about a legend.

History seems to have forgotten that Gehrig followed with his own homer to right field, knocking Root out of the game. Nobody remembers Gehrig's blast or that they went back-to-back.

Gehrig turned out to be a most worthy successor to the Babe. Lou joined the team straight off the Columbia campus at age 22. Ruth at 30 was at the peak of his game. It had to be something to see. But they were quite different players.

Both were left-handed hitters, but Gehrig had a little more speed. One season, he actually hit more triples (20) than home runs. In fact, it doesn't show in the history books but in a 1934 game against the Senators, Gehrig tripled to left, to center, and to right. That 1934 game was washed out so Lou lost credit for the triples.

For fans who love their milestones, it was also tough to see Gehrig wind up at 493 homers, so close to 500. Actually, it should be 494. In a 1931 game against Washington, Gehrig smoked one over the center field fence that bounced back into the field of play so quickly, center fielder Harry Rice snared it. Yankees teammate Lyn Lary only saw the last part—Rice snaring the ball—so he ran to the dugout, thinking it was the third out. Gehrig was called out for passing the runner.

When comparing the career numbers for Ruth and Gehrig, there were differences there, too. Gehrig generally struck out a lot less (790 times in 17 seasons, to Ruth's 1,330 in 22) while Ruth drew more walks (2,062 to Lou's 1,508).

Gehrig hit a little better vs. righties (.356 to .354) but Ruth had the edge vs. left-handers (.320 to .302). According to Baseball Reference data, Babe hit 484 homers off right-handed pitchers, 210 vs. lefties; Lou had 342 vs. righties, 136 against lefties. That leaves Babe with 22 homers *not* accounted for. Maybe they haven't landed yet.

Lou Gehrig   Babe Ruth

Lou Gehrig	Overall Stats	Babe Ruth
113.7	WAR	182.6
2164	G	2503
9665	PA	10627
2721	H	2873
493	HR	714
1995	RBI	2214
102	SB	123
.340	BA	.342
.447	OBP	.474
.632	SLG	.690
1.080	OPS	1.164
179	OPS+	206
	Awards & Honors	
✓	Hall of Fame	✓
8	Championships	7
7	All-Star	2
2	MVP	1
1	Batting Title	1
	ERA Title	1
1	Triple Crown	

Ruth, not a player who kept himself in top shape as he got older, played only a few months into his 40th year, struggling with the Boston Braves in just 28 games (.181). Of course, he did have a dramatic three-homer game in Pittsburgh, his 714th and final home run being the first ball hit out of Forbes Field. He wanted to halt his career right there; he knew he was done.

Reportedly, after Ruth's third home run of the game, he headed for the Pirates dugout to sit down and rest because it was closer to his left field position. He knew it was time to go but Braves management told Ruth that opposing National League teams—Babe had been an American League player, of course—had sold tickets in all their home ballparks to see him so they talked him out of retiring. Unfortunately, he played just five more games, leaving a Memorial Day doubleheader after a single at-bat (a groundout to first). Not much of a grand finale for game's greatest player.

Gehrig's career, of course, was cut short by the disease that now bears his name, playing only eight games into the 1939 season, retiring at age 36. He was 0-for-4 in his final game, hitting three flyouts and a groundball.

His final at-bat was a flyball to center against Pete Appleton of the Washington Senators. If only he could have played another season or two, he would have had 500 home runs and maybe 3,000 hits.

So, when it comes to rating the game's best three-four combinations, you start with them. No three-four combination will ever last as long or come close to matching what those two did. But there were some who were really formidable, even if they didn't last as long as Babe and Lou. Here are a few worth taking a look at.

"BATTING THIRD AND FOURTH . . ."
Manny Ramírez and David Ortiz—Boston Red Sox, 2003 to 2007
It was a job for superheroes. Surely there were many times over the empty years when devoted denizens of Fenway Park would wobble home after another disheartening loss, staring up into the Boston sky for the bat signal. If this wasn't a job for Batman and Robin, it might be too much for one man, even Superman. They needed help. How many times would

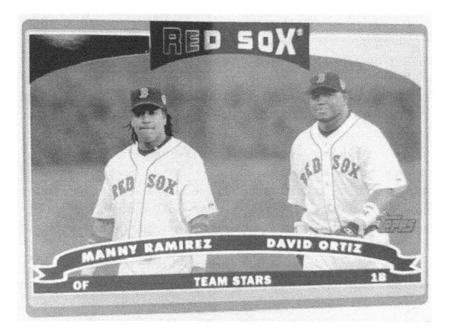

the cruel and inconsiderate hand of Fate extend a middle finger to Red Sox Nation?

Whether it was Bucky "Bleeping" Dent's horrid screen shot on a haunted October afternoon or a little bleeping groundball that, of course, took a "bleep you" hop over the cursed and extended glove of Billy Buckner in a World Series or a Tim Wakefield knuckleball hit deep into the night to knock the Sox out of a World Series berth . . . there were so many other near-misses ever since Red Sox ownership dispatched that Ruth fella to the Bronx. It seemed the curse of the Bambino could not and would not be lifted. But then, magically, suddenly, it was.

As the year 2000 opened, help was on the way from unexpected places; first, from Cleveland with the arrival of Manny Ramírez, one of the game's most gifted—if truly eccentric—right-handed sluggers. Manny could not wait to plant his cleats in a Fenway Park right-handed batter's box a cozy 315 feet away from a 30-foot wall and sure enough, he homered on the very first pitch he saw.

It would be a couple of years before he was joined by a hulking castoff from the Minnesota Twins organization, who, like Bruce Wayne, began his operations under an alias. Arias, to be specific.

By the time he arrived in Boston a couple of years after the arrival of Manny, he was calling himself David Ortiz. No one could have predicted what the two of them would do in the regular season and the postseason. Not many duos could change the tide of history. They did.

As incredible as it seemed at the time, Boston's dynamic duo, Manny Ramírez and David "Big Papi" Ortiz, went on to lead the Boston Red Sox to world championships in 2004 and 2007 and the momentum of those two wins may have led to two more in 2013 (Manny was gone by then) and 2018 (David was gone, too). They changed the face of the Red Sox, each with their own distinctive style and style of play.

If you average Ramírez's and Ortiz's collective home run totals for their five-year run together, it ends up being 0.4 percent higher than Ruth-Gehrig's numbers.

Their longball average was also higher than the annual home run totals for the Braves' pair of Eddie Mathews and Hank Aaron, the Willies, both Mays and McCovey for the San Francisco Giants, or even Yankee heroes Roger Maris and Mickey Mantle, a remarkable achievement in the days of the bullpen guy with a 95-mile-per-hour fastball, defensive shifts, relentless coast-to-coast travel, and all sorts of other modern challenges.

Remember that when Babe retired in 1935 with 714 home runs, the next guy closest to him, Gehrig, had about half as many (378). Next was Jimmie Foxx with 302. That's how far Babe was ahead of the pack.

Though Manny and David tormented AL hurlers only half the length of the Ruth-Gehrig era—five years—what a five-year-run it was! Unless you were an enemy pitcher, they were a joy to watch.

Stationed in left field, where three previous successive Hall of Famers had torn up the grass (Ted Williams, Carl Yastrzemski, Jim Rice), the free-spirited Ramírez was really an 11-year-old in an adult's body. Nobody ever had more fun walking up to the plate, swinging the bat, savoring the trouble he caused enemy pitchers.

Manny Ramírez   David Ortiz

	Overall Stats	
69.3	WAR	55.3
2302	G	2408
9774	PA	10091
2574	H	2472
555	HR	541
1831	RBI	1768
38	SB	17
.312	BA	.286
.411	OBP	.380
.585	SLG	.552
.996	OPS	.931
154	OPS+	141
	Awards & Honors	
	Hall of Fame	✓
2	Championships	3
12	All-Star	10
1	Batting Title	
9	Silver Slugger	7
1	WS MVP	1
	LCS MVP	1

He lived in a million-dollar penthouse at the Ritz-Carlton that some said cost $1,000 a day. Fenway fans learned you might see Manny do anything, like make a great leaping catch at the left field fence, high-five a fan, and throw a strike to first base to double off the runner.

You might see him duck into the ancient scoreboard built into Fenway's Green Monster and come out with a sign—another episode of "Manny Being Manny." You might see him reluctantly sent up as a pinch-hitter in a key spot at Yankee Stadium and watch him take three strikes straight down the middle. You might see him come dashing out of the Red Sox dugout, holding a tiny American flag, celebrating his first day as an American citizen.

You might see him hit a baseball on top of the roof of a center field restaurant at Tropicana Field a mind-blowing distance away (I was there!). You might see him ignore other pitches to sit on a curveball, then hit it 450 feet into the right field stands. You might even see him cut off a throw from a fellow outfielder (Johnny Damon)—a cutoff before the cutoff—and return it to the infield posthaste. Nobody understood that one, probably not even Manny.

Though he had his pouty, difficult, inexplicable moments with the Red Sox travel secretary and many others, and often played a lousy, disinterested left field, when it came to being on offense, it was a different story. Manny stepped into the batter's box with an ineffable joy, a sense of discovery, a light and happy spirit that you could see in his bouncy, jubilant trots around the bases after each of his 555 career home runs or his spontaneous celebrations at whatever base he stopped at. He was just like a kid. And proud of it.

Though his departure from Boston was difficult and there were hard feelings on both sides and multiple end-of-the-season trade talks throughout the tail end of his stay, his 500-plus home runs, .312 career average, and more clutch moments than anybody could imagine established him as a sure Hall of Famer, one of the greatest right-handed batters in history.

Except Manny Being Manny, his numbers fading as he aged, was caught using performance-enhancing drugs in the form of human chorionic gonadotropin—a woman's fertility drug. Worse, he was caught twice and, understandably, shown the door, ending a remarkable career. Well, one in MLB anyway. Ramírez later took his bat to Taiwan, Australia, and all over. Not the finish he should have had.

Though his extraordinary numbers certainly should have warranted a berth in Cooperstown, the Baseball Hall of Fame, his off-the-field actions have taken that away, likely forever.

Two years after Manny arrived at Fenway, the powerful Ortiz came to Boston and occupied that number four spot for the Red Sox. The American League saw right away how formidable the two would be. Manny had won the batting crown at .349 the year before and with David hitting behind him, Manny batted .325 with 37 home runs and 104 RBIs. Ortiz batted .288 with 31 homers and 101 RBIs and all of a sudden, the Red Sox were in contention for the AL crown.

The Red Sox came close in 2003, losing in seven games in the ALCS to the hated Yankees on Aaron Boone's extra-inning walkoff homer off a Tim Wakefield knuckler. Would the curse ever end?

Thankfully, it did end in 2004, though the Red Sox famously had to dig out of a 0–3 hole against the damn Yankees to do it. The Sox prevailed thanks in large part to some improbable Ortiz heroics, hits and homers that seemed to come at just the right dramatic moment. The bigger the spot, the more Big Papi seemed to command the stage. And Manny, well, he kept on being Manny and he led the Red Sox to the world title in 2004, sweeping the St. Louis Cardinals, Ramírez winning the World Series MVP. That season, Manny led the American League in round-trippers with 43, hitting .308 with 130 RBIs. Ortiz hit over .300, too (.301) with 41 homers and 139 RBIs. What a dynamic duo!

In 2005, they again turned in sensational seasons—Ramírez .292, 45, 144; Ortiz .300, 47, and a league-leading 148 RBIs—but somehow, things fell apart by the end of the season. The Bosox were swept by the White Sox in the postseason.

In 2006, they both put up stinging numbers—Ramírez .321, 35, 102; Ortiz .287, with league-leading totals of 54 home runs and 137 RBIs, but a five-game sweep by the Yankees in August ruined the season. The Yankees got revenge for that 2004 flop, dominating the Sox (9–21). Injuries to several players flattened the spirit of the club and knocked them out of the postseason.

Boston found a way to bounce back in 2007, winning the World Series with another sweep, sparked by two more strong seasons from Manny and David. Ramírez hit .296 with 20 homers and 88 RBIs, while Ortiz batted a career high .332, and clubbed 35 home runs with 117 RBIs as the Red Sox rolled over the Colorado Rockies in four straight games.

The dream pairing came to an end in 2008. Whining, complaining, acting generally discontented with everything and everyone, Ramírez played just 100 games for the Red Sox that season (.299, 20, 68) before management had to make a move. By now, the Manny Being Manny act had worn thin and Red Sox dealt him away as far across the continent as they could—Los Angeles. Manny wound up with good numbers for the year—.332, 37, 121—but the Dynamic Duo era in Boston was over.

Somehow, the increased responsibility seemed to inspire Ortiz, who then seemed to become a singular figure, a larger-than-life force who was able to change the fortunes of an entire team. Manny's departure didn't impact the Red Sox as it might have.

Over the next eight seasons, David "Big Papi" Ortiz emerged as the guy the other team did not want to face with the game on the line.

And of course, who could forget his impassioned speech after the Boston Marathon bombing, "This is our fucking city." If Ortiz didn't have the beating heart of Red Sox Nation under his sleeve before that, well, that did it.

From then on, there seemed to be so many moments when the game came around to his particularly decisive at-bat, that hulking frame relishing these white-knuckle moments, delivering again and again over these eight seasons for the Red Sox, winning another World Series in 2013 and carving out a Hall of Fame resume.

While stat-driven analysts like Bill James have insisted for years that there is no way to determine a hitter's "clutch" numbers, claiming there are too many variables, it's too difficult, blah, blah, blah, nobody who watched the whole of Ortiz's career would doubt him in the clutch. He came through way more often than you could imagine—or so it felt.

Serving as a designated hitter—we rarely saw him in the field—all of Fenway would erupt when big #34 would step out of the Red Sox dugout. He approached the plate as if he felt every eye in the stadium on him—which, of course, it was. He'd spit into each hand, rub them together, step into the batter's box, left foot first, looking out at the pitcher, swinging his bat, his expression full of confidence, that of someone who had done his homework. And he had.

The famous grand slam off Detroit's Joaquin Benoit, for example, in the 2013 ALCS, saw Ortiz walk to the plate, Boston trailing 5–1 in the eighth inning after being one-hit in the series opener, his instincts telling him to look for one pitch, a changeup. To forget all else. Look for that changeup and pounce.

When you're facing a pitcher in that spot, a guy with 95 miles per hour in his arm, to forget that sizzling velocity, the mounting pressure of the moment—if the Red Sox lose *this* game, they're cooked. To push all that aside, to single-mindedly look for that one particular pitch in that moment, well, to use a technical term, that took balls.

Earlier in the year, months earlier, Benoit had gotten him out with that pitch. Ortiz remembered that. Big Papi filed that away, a moment from months earlier, after hundreds of at-bats all leading up to this moment. Considering the Detroit pitching staff and what they'd be bringing to the hill (Max Scherzer, Justin Verlander, etc.), they'd be done.

Ortiz trusted his instincts, looked for that one pitch—and got it. And he didn't miss it. He launched a high, soaring drive toward the Red Sox bullpen, the roars of the crowd rising as that little white ball, carrying the hopes and hearts of all New England with it, headed for paydirt. Bam!

The next thing the Fenway Faithful saw were the legs of Detroit's Torii Hunter, diving into the Red Sox bullpen to try to snare the ball—but he couldn't. A famous *Boston Globe* photo capturing Boston police officer Steve Horgan, his hands in the air in a touchdown-like celebration, the mirror opposite of Hunter's extended legs, diving for the ball, was an image emblazoned in Red Sox lore for all time.

If he wasn't a legend already, that blow might have sealed it. Ortiz went on to hit .688 in the subsequent 2013 World Series, the kind of Series that goes down in history.

While his Red Sox didn't reach another Series during his run, Ortiz played on for three more solid seasons, leaving the game at age 40 after a superb final season. Ortiz, despite hitting into a shift, batted .315 and led the league in doubles (48) and RBIs (127). Wow.

No, he didn't get to leave Fenway like Ted Williams with a dramatic home run or even like Carl Yastrzemski with a watery-eyed jog around the ancient ballpark. He got a walk.

Much of Fenway refused to leave, standing, applauding their baseball hero. After a while, the applause unrelenting, still echoing through the park, David Ortiz walked back out to the top of the mound and tipped his cap. He didn't say a word. He didn't have to.

Hank Aaron and Eddie Mathews—Milwaukee/Atlanta Braves, 1954 to 1966

For at least half of his Hall of Fame career, Hank Aaron wasn't really thought of as a home-run hitter. He may have hit in the number four spot behind slugging third baseman Eddie Mathews, but Hank didn't hit tape-measure shots.

Not only that, Hank couldn't, didn't or wouldn't hit more than 44 home runs (his uniform number!) in a season. He did it four separate times!

(We're kidding here. Hank did hit 45 in 1962 and 47 in 1971. He must have lost count.)

As great as he was, Aaron wasn't ever the kind of player who seemed to call attention to himself. The only noise you heard from Hank was when he swung the bat.

When his pursuit of Babe Ruth's lifetime home run total of 714 became national news, it was as if someone finally remembered to invite Hank to the party.

His predecessor in the Braves lineup most of the time in those years was Eddie Mathews, a power-hitting lefty slugger who led the league in home runs twice and drove in over 100 runs five times. Mathews played a solid third base for the Braves and was a nine-time All-Star with a career average of .271.

But playing in Milwaukee, not exactly a media center, he was largely overlooked, even more than Aaron. That carried over to the Hall of Fame voting. It took Mathews a while to earn the Cooperstown honor that should have been obvious and immediate. Not many hitters club over 500 home runs, and even fewer were third basemen. He had to wait until 1978, 10 years after he retired. It was ridiculous.

Mathews was an MVP runner-up in '53 and '59. The only time he was on a national stage—the '57 and '58 World Series against the Yankees—other than a 10th-inning walkoff homer against Bob Grim in 1957—he wasn't much of a factor in either Series, hitting .233 in the Braves' win in '57 and .160 in their seven-game loss in '58.

You might say Hank was overlooked, too. He was NL MVP in 1957 and finished third four separate times, in the top ten a dozen times—talk about consistency! But neither he nor Mathews could get the Braves back to the Series.

During the regular season, Mathews and Aaron were the topic of discussion in every opposing pregame clubhouse and were a formidable pair in the Braves lineup, homering in the same inning 17 times and in the same game 75 times.

Eddie Mathews		Henry Aaron
	Overall Stats	
95.9	**WAR**	143.1
2391	**G**	3298
10101	**PA**	13941
2315	**H**	3771
512	**HR**	755
1453	**RBI**	2297
68	**SB**	240
.271	**BA**	.305
.376	**OBP**	.374
.509	**SLG**	.555
.885	**OPS**	.928
143	**OPS+**	155
	Awards & Honors	
✓	**Hall of Fame**	✓
2	**Championships**	1
12	**All-Star**	25
	MVP	1
	Batting Title	2
	Gold Glove	3

Across the National League, they were a well-kept secret, the scourge of visiting pitchers, but not national headliners. Neither Aaron nor Mathews got the kind of notoriety that perhaps they were due, their attendance dwindling in Milwaukee, the Braves taking their show to Atlanta in 1966.

After the terrific 1957 and '58 seasons, those two straight trips to the World Series, winning in seven games over the Yankees in 1957, losing in seven games to the Yankees in 1958, the Braves never really threatened to return to the Series. They were always pretty good and did win 80-plus games every year. But they didn't quite ever get there. Had they been more successful on a national stage, had there been a National League Championship Series back then, there might have been a lot more noise about the duo of Eddie Mathews and Hank Aaron as one of history's best all-time three-four combos. But we can say this: National League pitchers knew who they were, that's for sure. And so did outfielders, watching balls sail over their heads.

Mickey Mantle and Roger Maris—*New York Yankees, 1960 to 1966*

If there ever was an example of the far-ranging, long-lasting impact of the New York media, it might well be the saga of the M&M Boys, Mickey Mantle and Roger Maris. You've likely heard way more about them than any other combo other than Ruth and Gehrig. Their fame was such that in 1962, Hollywood even grabbed the two of them for a cameo role in a really lame movie called *Safe at Home*. (I bought an 8mm version of this Castle Films movie as a kid.) They were on the covers of magazines, and everybody was talking about them. It was almost against the law to pick up a newspaper's sports page *without* reading about the home-run chase between Mantle and Maris.

Were they the greatest slugging duo since Babe and Lou? Not quite. Not when you take a really close look at their numbers.

Sure, the combination of the two Yankees chasing down Yankees predecessor Babe Ruth's 1927 60-home-run mark caught America's attention throughout that summer. It was the precursor of the fabled Mark McGwire vs. Sammy Sosa home-run duel that would light up America some 37 years later. With baseball games played every day, a

Mantle-Maris watch was perfect for the media, who love that kind of thing.

Mickey and Roger got boatloads of media attention, something Maris, in particular, detested. Time and again, he'd come into the locker room after a game, speak plainly and directly about what had happened in the game, then he'd read what he had said in the newspapers, and complain about it. Even though they quoted him *exactly*.

As noted in my book *Last Time Out*, taking an excerpt from Roger Kahn's article "The Press and Roger Maris," you could see Roger didn't understand how things worked.

Mickey Mantle | | Roger Maris

	Overall Stats	
110.2	WAR	38.3
2401	G	1463
9910	PA	5847
2415	H	1325
536	HR	275
1509	RBI	850
153	SB	21
.298	BA	.260
.421	OBP	.345
.557	SLG	.476
.977	OPS	.822
172	OPS+	127
	Awards & Honors	
✓	Hall of Fame	
7	Championships	3
20	All-Star	7
3	MVP	2
1	Batting Title	
1	Gold Glove	1
1	Triple Crown	

"Maris came to bat four times and hit no homers," Kahn wrote. "Reporters asked if he'd had good pitches to hit. 'I didn't get too many strikes,' Maris said. 'But they were called strikes. (Umpire Hank) Soar had me swinging in self-defense.'"

"Now, this is a standard baseball player bitch," I wrote. "This is not surprising in any way. Every ballplayer since the beginning of the game has complained about the umpiring. (Ten years of phone conversations with my baseball-playing son confirm this!) But when this quote was shared with the nation's readers, there was backlash.

"'The next day's newspapers headlined that casual, typical ball player's gripe,'" Kahn wrote. "Maris was shocked. Until that moment he had not fully realized the impact his sentences now carried. He had not fully realized the price one pays for being a hero. He was disturbed, upset, withdrawn. Tortured would be too strong a word, but only slightly. He showed his hurt by saying little; his mouth appeared permanently set in its hard line. . . . "

In other words, he pouted.

Later, Kahn recounts this line as he saw the outfielder dig himself in deeper. "When asked about the fans in right field—these are Yankee fans—Maris said 'Terrible. Maybe the worst in the league.' He recounted remarks that had been shouted at him and, under consistent prodding, ran down the stadium customers for ten or fifteen minutes.

"The next day, after reading the papers, he said to me 'That's it. I been trying to be a good guy to the writers, but I quit. . . . From now on I'll tell the writers what pitch I hit but no more big spiels. . . . '"

Now, the writers quoted exactly what he said. But evidently, it never occurred to Maris how it would look in print. After this many seasons in the major leagues—he played in Kansas City and Cleveland before coming to New York—he was no rookie.

Apparently, nobody in the Yankees PR office thought to explain to Maris that the media wasn't necessarily confrontational, you simply had to think that what you were *saying was going in the newspaper*. Maris never really figured that out. Sorry, Roger. You should have had "no comment."

As much as you may have read and heard about the two of them, it seems surprising upon looking at the record that their run was for just six seasons. Generally speaking, Roger and Mickey batted in the three and four spots for just those seven seasons from 1960 to 1966, after which Maris was dealt away to St. Louis to finish his career.

Evaluating those Mantle-Maris years now, you'd have to say Mantle had maybe three great seasons, the same for Maris. They were not in Ruth-Gehrig territory. Not even close.

If you'll recall, the 1961 season was a time of expansion. The American League added the second-generation Washington Senators and the Los Angeles Angels, which led some people to suggest that the move watered down pitching staffs. That may be a reach, but there were some very strange hitting events that occurred that season and never again.

Detroit's Norm Cash led the American League with a .361 average, some 90 points higher than his career mark. It was the *only* time he batted over .300 in 17 major-league seasons.

Cleveland's Jimmy Piersall, whom we know for other reasons, was third in the batting race that year at .322, 50 points higher than *his* career numbers and the only time *he* batted .300 over a full season in a 17-year career.

The same goes for Minnesota Twins catcher Earl Battey, who hit .302, his only season over .300., and Baltimore's Jim Gentile hit .301, *his* only season over .300. Now, we do see players' numbers rise and fall over the seasons, and maybe it was just a fluke that so many players seemed to turn in record years. But it was odd.

Understandably, the Mantle-Maris home-run chase got everyone excited. Maris, that left-handed dead-pull swing seemingly perfect for Yankee Stadium's short right field porch, turned in an amazing season—61 home runs with 30 of them hit at the Stadium, 31 on the road. (Ruth had 28 at home, 32 on the road in 1927.)

And it was quite a race between the M&M Boys throughout the summer. Mantle hung right with Maris until the final week when an odd hip abscess, reportedly thanks to a shot from a quack doctor, forced Mickey to miss the last few games of the regular season, ending his chase of Ruth. Mickey was not much of a factor in the World Series. But nevertheless, Mickey finished the 1961 season, one of his finest, with a .317 average, 54 homers, and 128 RBIs.

In the 1961 MVP vote, Maris barely edged out Mantle for his second straight MVP. To some fans, the fact that Roger won two MVPs qualifies him for the Baseball Hall of Fame. Well, if you take a look at the rest of his career, his numbers aren't there.

In 1962, as a follow-up to his 61-homer year, Maris hit 33 homers with 100 RBIs. And from 1963 on, his numbers fell, some might even say plummeted. He hit .269-23-53 in '63, .281-26-71 in '64, .239-8-27 in just 46 games in '65, and a sad .233-13-43 in '66, his last year in New York. Those aren't Hall of Fame numbers.

Going back over those numbers now, the really odd thing that jumps out at you, besides the declining nhome-run totals—remember Roger and Mickey were playing in a 296-foot "hit-me-a-popup" right field bandbox—is the lack of doubles for the two of them. It's stunning.

For most home-run hitters, doubles have always been a key part of their games. Ted Williams, Joe DiMaggio, Babe Ruth, Lou Gehrig, go on down the list, almost all these guys hit lots of doubles. Not Mantle or Maris.

Look at Mickey's totals in two-base hits for those six years: 1960–1966: 17, 16, 15, 8, 25, 12, 12. Are we talking about Chuck Schilling here? Weird. This is *Mickey Mantle*.

How to explain it? Well, one rationale was that Mantle's oft-injured legs made him reluctant to try for two, unless it was of the stand-up sort. Another was defenses played him so deep, it would have been almost impossible to go for a double. Who knows? Contrast Mantle's double totals with another AL All-Star over the same stretch. Detroit's Al Kaline's two-base hit totals for those seven seasons were 29, 41, 16 (in 100 games), 24, 31, 18 (in 125 games), and 29. Comparing their double totals for those seasons: Kaline 188, Mantle 105.

It wasn't like other Yankees didn't hit doubles, they did. In 1961, Mantle's teammate Tony Kubek hit 38 doubles, twice as many as Mickey. Bill Skowron had 23. In 1962, Bobby Richardson had 38 two-baggers, Clete Boyer 26, Tom Tresh 24, Elston Howard 23. Mantle? Just 15 in 123 games.

Maris's double totals at Yankee Stadium were unusually low, too. Except for 1962 when he had 34 two-base hits, Maris's double numbers were 18, 16, 14, 12, 9, and 7. Makes you wonder if they were so disappointed—or shocked—that they *didn't* hit it out with every swing, they just hung out at first base.

Willie Mays and Willie McCovey—San Francisco Giants, 1959 to 1971

They were well named. San Francisco Giants stars Willie Mays and Willie McCovey gave National League pitchers the willies. Between the two of them, while playing together from 1959 to 1971, the Willies slammed exactly 800 home runs, terrorizing NL pitchers across the league for 13 years.

Mays, a muscular right-handed hitter whose graceful swing, arms fully extended, seemed to magically sweep across the entire zone, the mighty McCovey, whose hammering left-handed swing seemed awkward but deadly, the two of them were the perfect yin-yang counterpoint in the middle of the Giants' order.

And they were a truly dynamic duo, too. Mays won a batting title (.345), led the league in home runs four times, drove in over 100 runs 11 times, including eight in a row. McCovey led the league in home runs three times, in RBIs twice, and had over 100 RBIs four times. Their career numbers are simply staggering. Mays stayed a Giant until a 1972 trade back to where he started, back to New York with the Mets. McCovey left San Francisco for a bit, returned and finished his career as a Giant. Between them, Mays and McCovey clobbered 1,095 home runs, drove in 3,702 runs, hit 949 doubles, and 182 triples. Mighty.

Yet as unarguably great as those two were—and they had some formidable teammates—Orlando Cepeda, a Hall of Famer, Felipe Alou, Bobby Bonds, Matty Alou, Jim Davenport, Jim Ray Hart, etc.—they made it to just one World Series. It was a puzzle. Their ace was Juan Marichal, a Hall of Famer, their number two was Gaylord Perry, also a Hall of Famer.

Thanks to some terrific Dodgers teams and that unstoppable Sandy Koufax / Don Drysdale combination, the Giants' seasons always ended in disappointment. Similarly, the great Marichal never won a Cy Young Award, thanks to Koufax, Drysdale, Bob Gibson, Tom Seaver, Steve Carlton, etc. He was consistently great but always a runner-up. Like the San Francisco Giants.

Willie Mays		Willie McCovey
	Overall Stats	
156.2	WAR	64.4
3005	G	2588
12545	PA	9692
3293	H	2211
660	HR	521
1909	RBI	1555
339	SB	26
.301	BA	.270
.384	OBP	.374
.557	SLG	.515
.940	OPS	.889
155	OPS+	147
	Awards & Honors	
✓	Hall of Fame	✓
1	Championships	
24	All-Star	6
2	MVP	1
1	Batting Title	
12	Gold Glove	

RANKING THE THREE-FOUR COMBOS

1. David Ortiz and Manny Ramírez—2003 to 2007
   HR: Ortiz 208, Ramírez 180–388 total (Avg. 77.6 per season)

2. Babe Ruth and Lou Gehrig 1925 to 1934
   HR: Ruth 424, Gehrig 348–772 total (77.2)

3. Hank Aaron and Eddie Mathews—1954 to 1966
   HR: Aaron 442, Mathews 415–857 total (71.4)

4. Mickey Mantle and Roger Maris—1960 to 1966
   HR: Mantle 216, Maris 203–419 total (69.8)

5. Willie Mays and Willie McCovey—1959 to 1971
   HR: Mays, 430, McCovey 370–800 total (67)

The job description for the three and four spots in the order might be this: the number three hitter is the one guy you want up at the plate with two outs, and the number four hitter is the guy you want up with men on base to drive in runs.

When you look back at the historic three-four combos through baseball history—and here are five of the greatest—there are some surprises. Wouldn't you think managers would rather hit Hank Aaron (.305) third ahead of Eddie Mathews (.271), trying to get Hank a few more at-bats? Same for Mickey Mantle (.298) and Roger Maris (.260): Wouldn't you want the higher-average hitter (Mantle) up a little more often?

Of course, there are many other worthy three-four combos throughout the game's history—Ken Griffey Jr. and Edgar Martínez with Seattle, Jeff Kent and Barry Bonds with the Giants, Roberto Clemente and Willie Stargell with the Pirates, and many others.

But in the end, you go back to Ruth and Gehrig, who started all this number three hitter, number four hitter stuff. And it's a good bet that if you could have asked the Babe, it made perfect sense for him to hit third with Lou fourth. After all, Ruth did have a higher career average of .342 to Gehrig's .340 (wink).

CHAPTER FIFTEEN

The Outliers: Great Hitters, Obscure Pitchers

ONE OF THE ENDURING CHARMS OF THE SPORT OF BASEBALL IS ITS unpredictability. Not only does this play out on a daily basis—how many of you have gone to a game, seen something, and thought to yourself, "I've never seen *that* before"?—it carries over to just about every other element of the game, including—maybe especially—the postseason.

How many times have regular-season dynamos like the 1954 Cleveland Indians (111–43) or the 2001 Seattle Mariners (116–46), teams that clearly seemed better than their peers, faltered at the end of year in the playoffs? Neither team won a World Series.

When it comes to the matter of major-league hitters vs. major-league pitchers, there have been and will be many more inexplicable happenings. Logically speaking, these are things that cannot be explained, even by technology.

Let's agree that by the time a player has established himself as a .300 hitter at the major-league level, he's proved he can hit against the best arms in the world, right? You would naturally assume he's going to keep *on* hitting, no matter who's on that mound. But as *College GameDay's* Lee Corso so often says in another sport, not so fast, my friend.

Regardless of how great a hitter was—and what hitters were better than the foursome of Stan Musial, Rogers Hornsby, Ted Williams, and Joe DiMaggio?—there is always, *always* some pitcher they just couldn't hit. Why? It's one of the game's unsolved mysteries. Now, sure, there had to be *something* about the pitcher's delivery that was good enough to get him to the majors. And it had to be good enough for him to stay in the bigs. Since hitting a baseball is about as intricate and inexplicable an athletic task as there is, there may not *be* a reasonable explanation for why these great hitters can't hit *everybody*. But they can't. And won't.

Boston's Carl Yastrzemski, for example, a personal hero of mine growing up in New Hampshire, had 13,992 plate appearances over a 23-year career. Or just about more times up than anybody but Pete Rose or Hank Aaron. Yet in 3,015 at-bats against left-handed pitching over the course of his 23-year run, Yaz wasn't any closer to solving lefties at the end of his career than he was at the start.

Lifetime, Yaz batted .299 against right-handers, .244 vs. lefties, a considerable 50-point swing. It certainly wasn't like he didn't have enough practice. And against some lefties, he had no chance. For Yaz, as mentioned earlier, it was crafty Darold Knowles. Facing Knowles over a 12-year run, Yaz was a brutal 2-for-26 (.077), about as close to an automatic out as there was. And Carl Yastrzemski was, inarguably, a first-ballot Hall of Famer.

A fellow star of Polish extraction, Stan "The Man" Musial, for example, was perhaps the most consistent of all major-league hitters, not only winding up with a .331 career average, but Musial collected two hits in his final home game to give him a perfect home/away breakdown of his 3,630 hits—1,815 hits in each location. Now that's consistency.

Yet, facing an old Negro Leagues veteran pitcher named Sam "Toothpick" Jones, who rode a nasty curveball to a 103–104 lifetime mark, Musial might as well have sent up the batboy. Stepping in against Sad Sam Jones, Musial hit like a pitcher and we don't mean Babe Ruth. In 49 at-bats against the guy, Musial collected just six hits, five singles, and a lone double for a .122 average, fanning 11 times. Go figure.

As also noted in the introduction, another famous St. Louis Cardinal named Rogers Hornsby—generally recognized as the greatest right-handed hitter in the history of the game—could not figure out a skinny righty slop thrower named Ben Cantwell, a pitcher who had gone 4–25 in one awful season (1935).

Offering a bewildering assortment of curveballs, changeups, and knuckleballs, Cantwell held Hornsby to a .130 average with just one extra-base hit in 33 trips to the plate. Hornsby retired with a .358 lifetime average. Cantwell retired with a lifetime record of 76–108. How did that happen? It's baseball!

Boston's indomitable Ted Williams had his own nemesis, too. Jim Wilson, a former teammate of Williams with the Red Sox, had himself a journeyman career as a right-handed starter for several teams, posting a career mark of 86–89. Yet facing Ted Williams, he was dominant. Ted did homer off Wilson the first time he faced him in 1949. But after that, Wilson took over and in 36 career at-bats stretching over nine years, Williams managed just five more hits (.167). He could hit Bob Feller and Jim Bunning, both Hall of Famers. But Wilson?

In 1957, when Williams nearly batted .400 again (a stunning .388) Wilson, then pitching for the White Sox, played his part in keeping Ted under .400 by holding him to a 3-for-17 (.177) that year. You might say nobody else was getting Ted out but Wilson. If you took away his at-bats against Wilson, Williams's mark for the 1957 season would have been .397, just three measly points—maybe one hit—from another .400 season. As a 40-year-old.

[Insert 15.1_Jim_Wilson here.]

Wilson's success against Ted continued into most of 1958, when Williams won himself a second straight batting title. Through the first four months of the season, Wilson held Ted hitless until an August 20 start against the Red Sox. After getting Williams to hit into a double play in the first inning and walking him in the third, Wilson faced #9 with two on, up 7–1 in the fifth. Uh oh. Finally, here Ted swung and connected, launching a three-run homer. It was the last time Ted would face him. It turned out that Wilson's major-league career ended after just three more starts.

Another all-time great, Joltin' Joe DiMaggio, a right-handed batter, had his troubles with clever lefty Billy Pierce (4-for-30, .133, one home run). Hal White, a stumpy right-hander for the Detroit Tigers and St. Louis Browns, gave up a hit to DiMaggio in his third at-bat against him in 1942, the first time he faced him. But after that he was able to

JIM WILSON
pitcher MILWAUKEE BRAVES

hold Joe to one hit—a measly single—through the rest of DiMaggio's career. From there through the end of DiMaggio's career, he held Joe to 0-for-20! Had you ever heard of him?

These numbers certainly are fascinating and revealing, aren't they? There certainly wasn't any particular reason teams *didn't* keep track of those sorts of things back in the day, but the fact is, they didn't. If they had, you wonder how that might have changed their thinking, their in-game strategies.

If, for example, with the game on the line, it was Yaz coming up against Knowles, would Red Sox manager Dick Williams have pinch-hit for a sure Hall of Famer?

Let's say a similar situation happened for Hall of Famer Frank Thomas, "The Big Hurt." What if it came down to a crucial at-bat for him against Boston's ace Pedro Martínez, also a Hall of Famer. What if the White Sox manager looked down and saw Thomas was on his way to a 2-for-24 (.083) with a lone homer in all those at-bats against Pedro, would he still let him hit in that spot?

Try and think of this chapter—"The Outliers"—as a look at those generally unsung pitchers who, for one reason or another, were able to handle some of the game's greatest hitters. As you read about how these hitters struggled, remember that you also have to consider how the game has changed. As noted in the introduction, rarely will a current hitter get that third, fourth at-bat against a starter. Back in Babe Ruth's and even in Ted Williams's day, they generally did. The more you see a pitcher, you would think, the better your chances of success. With the modern game, you just don't get that many at-bats against a particular pitcher. Managers are always going to the bullpen.

Babe and Lou and Mickey Struggled, Too

If you go back and look at things back in the day, even the great Babe Ruth had guys who got him out. Babe struggled with Detroit's tough Tommy Bridges. As Ruth's career was winding down, Bridges was able to hold Babe to 7-for-39 (.180) with four homers allowed. Another hurler who had Ruth's number was lefty Ed Wells, who held The Babe to a .204 average, fanning him 14 times.

For Ruth's batting partner Lou Gehrig, his problem pitcher was Washington's Ken Chase, who gave Lou fits, holding Gehrig to 3-for-22 (.136) with only a couple of doubles. Gehrig made up for his struggles with Chase by pounding the aging Senators star Walter Johnson at almost a .500 clip (10-for-21, .476 with four homers).

Another all-time great Yankee, Mickey Mantle, a switch-hitter, had the advantage of never seeing the breaking ball going away from him. Yet Gaylord's older brother, Jim Perry, a righty, gave him a rough time (8-for-60, .133 with 10 strikeouts). But the Mick did reach him for five homers.

Two other pitchers gave Mickey trouble. Mantle did smack a couple of homers off knuckleballer Hoyt Wilhelm but not much else. Wilhelm held Mantle to 10-for-52, a .192 average, with two homers, 11 strikeouts, and 14 walks. Boston's Earl Wilson had an either-or relationship with the Mantle swing. He held Mick to 9-for-47, .192 and fanned him 14 times. He also walked him 14 times and allowed six home runs.

As it turned out, where Mickey was concerned, the king of whiffs was the veteran Early Wynn. While Mantle did reach him for 13 home runs, the most he ever hit off any pitcher, batting .242 (39-for-161). But Wynn got him back—48 whiffs.

WHIFFS VS. A PITCHER—MICK OR REGGIE?

You've probably read the famously funny Mantle quote about the mighty whiff.

"During my 18 years I came to bat almost 10,000 times," he said once. "I struck out about 1,700 times and walked maybe 1,800 times. You figure a ballplayer will average about 500 at-bats a season. That means I played seven years without ever hitting the ball."

When it came down to one player striking out against a particular pitcher in a career, Mickey Mantle and Reggie Jackson ended up having a ferocious competition that neither one likely ever knew about. You may know that Reggie is the all-time major-league strikeout leader with 2,597, almost 900 more than Mickey's 1,710.

But individually, when it came to striking out against a single pitcher, Reggie was a narrow winner. Jackson fanned 49 times against the curveballing Bert Blyleven in 131 at-bats. (He hit six homers.) Mickey had one fewer—48 strikeouts—against Early Wynn in his 161 at-bats.

Chances are you'll be surprised by who's third on the strikeout list, Hank Aaron! Aaron faced Don Drysdale 221 times and Drysdale got him 47 times. But Aaron got him 17 times for round-trippers.

The next highest whiff total by a hitter against a single pitcher was The Babe. Though he batted .311 against the great Lefty Grove, Grove got him on strikes 45 times. Another big strikeout guy was Ruth's contemporary Jimmie Foxx, who fanned 39 times against Yankees star Red Ruffing.

The only other player we could find with more than 40 whiffs vs. a pitcher was Pittsburgh's great Willie Stargell. Though he batted .290 against St. Louis's great Bob Gibson with five home runs, Gibby got him on strikes 41 times. Tom Seaver got Stargell 38 times, and Steve Carlton got him on 33 visits to the plate. But Willie had some success; he hit eight dingers off Seaver, five off Carlton.

You might think Nolan Ryan, the strikeout king, would have a lot of whiffers against him. Tops on his individual list was Claudell Washington, who fanned 39 times in 90 at-bats (.144). There wasn't any other hitter he fanned 40 times.

The same goes for the Dodgers' great Sandy Koufax, who was a strikeout king, too. Koufax's biggest strikeout victim was Cincinnati's Vada Pinson, who batted .288 against him with a pair of homers, but Koufax fanned him 34 times, tops among all National League hitters he faced.

There were a few other hitter-pitcher combos with strikeout totals that wound up in the mid-30s; Dave Kingman fanned 36 times against Steve Carlton (eight home runs), while Mike Schmidt fanned 35 times against Montreal's Steve Rogers and 35 times against Seaver. Schmidt hit seven home runs off Rogers and just a pair against Seaver.

Boston's Carl Yastrzemski played 23 seasons, had the third most all-time at-bats, and he faced Detroit's Mickey Lolich enough to strike out 35 times against the pudgy lefty. Yaz homered off him seven times.

Two of the other great strikeout pitchers of all time, Bob Feller and Roger Clemens, each had themselves a 30-whiff guy. Feller got slugger

Rudy York 36 times (.128, 2 homers) and Clemens got lefty hitter Chili Davis 30 times (.262, three homers).

To close out the strikeout talk, if you were starting a game facing Rickey Henderson, you'd certainly want big Randy Johnson. Henderson led off a game 85 times against Randy, whiffed 30 times, drew 26 walks, but collected only seven hits, a .119 average. Pretty awful for the game's greatest leadoff hitter.

AARON, PUJOLS, MAYS, AND MORE

Continuing to look at what pitchers gave the great hitters issues, there were more surprises. The great Hank Aaron had some less-than-famous arms who gave him fits. Reliever Jim Brosnan, who might have been more famous as an author (*The Long Season, Pennant Race*) than a pitcher, held Aaron to 8-for-50 (.160) with only a pair of doubles and four whiffs. Houston's flame-throwing Don Wilson held Aaron to 5-for-34 (.147) with 12 whiffs in 34 at-bats. Ouch! Bill Stoneman held Hank to 6-for-31 (.194) with a pair of homers allowed and no strikeouts. That's odd. Tommy John, pre- or post-surgery, was also a puzzle for Hank—2-for-17 (.118) with three strikeouts.

Don't however, bring in reliever former Dodgers reliever Ron Perranoski to face Hank. In 18 at-bats against the lefty, Hank collected 13 hits (.722) including a pair of doubles and homers.

You just never know. Willie Mays, for instance, struggled with Ken Johnson, a veteran righty (91–106 career mark). Johnson held him to 13-for-81, .161, fanning him 14 times. Willie did touch him up for five homers. He struggled, like many did, with Steve Carlton (11-for-62, .177 with 15 strikeouts) and Jim Maloney (10-for-58, .172). But Max Surkont? He held Willie to a .121 average, 4-for-33 with a double and triple. Nobody would have called that one.

The slender fireballer Chris Sale had no trouble with a fading Albert Pujols when he played for the Angels later in his career, holding him to 2-for-24, .083 with eight whiffs, and so did Sean Manaea (1-for-22, .046) and Corey Kluber (1-for-20, .050). But of the pitchers he had 50 or more at-bats against, you'd never guess the two who did the best job of getting him out. That would be Seattle's Hisashi Iwakuma (9-for-60,

.150, 10 strikeouts) and veteran hurler Francisco Liriano, who worked for six different teams and held Pujols to 4-for-26, .154.

The home-run heroes of the 1998 season and after—Mark McGwire, Sammy Sosa, Ken Griffey Jr., and Barry Bonds—each had their own nemesis. McGwire, for example, could not handle the hard, darting sinker of the nasty Kevin Brown. Brown held the slugger to just seven hits in 49 at-bats (.143) with only one home run, that in his fifth at-bat against the guy. He did even worse against the powerful Roger Clemens, who must have chuckled when he saw McGwire come up. He faced Clemens 53 times, walked six, hit one single, one double, hit two solo homers, and whiffed 14 times. That's right—4 for 47, .085.

Facing the great Orel Hershiser, McGwire was a force, collecting 11 hits in 24 at-bats, including five homers for a .458 average. Funny, huh?

For Sosa, the late Darryl Kile was a complete mystery. He was 8-for-60 (.133) against him with three homers but 23 strikeouts. John Smoltz, a Hall of Famer, was also a puzzle for Sammy (4-for-38, .105 with one of the four hits a triple!). Oddly, unlike McGwire, Sosa hit Kevin Brown pretty well (12-for-38, .316 with four homers and only 10 whiffs). He also murdered Hershiser, too—13-for-27, .482, with four home runs.

Like a lot of lefty hitters, Ken Griffey Jr. had some trouble with southpaw hurlers. Chuck Finley was a particular challenge for him (12-for-73, .164, four doubles, two homers, 18 whiffs) and somebody named Omar Olivares held Griffey Jr. to 3-for-28 (.107) with one homer. "Everyday Eddie" Guardado, the estimable Twins reliever was a mystery, too (2-for-21 or .095, one homer, 11 whiffs). Griffey's numbers against some of his era's finest starters wasn't as good as you might expect from a Hall of Famer. American League starters like Kevin Appier (11-for-59, .186), Mike Mussina (8-for-50, .160, 13 strikeouts) Tim Belcher (5-for-35, .143, one solo shot), Alex Fernandez (6-for-34, .177, two HR), and Pedro Martínez (1-for-15, .067) all gave Griffey trouble.

But my old New Hampshire pal Mike Flanagan of the Baltimore Orioles was easy pickings for him. Griffey collected eight hits in 17 at-bats, .471 against the 1979 Cy Young winner. I had personal experience with the lefty Flanagan, who once pitched three innings against my Milford, New Hampshire, American Legion team, fanning nine. I hit a dying quail foul down the right field line off a changeup. Flanagan was a legend in the Granite State, once fanning 21 hitters and hitting three homers in an American Legion game vs. Nashua's Coffey Post. He didn't need a designated hitter.

Looking at the record of Barry Bonds, who eclipsed the two home-run kings in subsequent seasons (never mind *how* he might have done so) was pretty consistent against virtually all the starters of his time; the guy could flat-out hit. But here's our man Tim Belcher again, that well-traveled righty who pitched for a bunch of teams and found ways to get Barry out. Like Griffey Jr., Bonds was stumped against Belcher.

He faced him 49 times, collected just six hits (.143), one home run, two doubles—and fanned 11 times. He homered off him in his eighth at-bat against the guy, back when his career was just starting and he was a Pirate in 1989. He never homered off him again.

David Cone was also tough for Bonds (7-for-40, .175, one homer) but well-traveled righty Mike Bielecki has to take the top prize. Surprise, surprise! Another righty hurler who was on the move (70–73, five teams in 13 seasons), Bielecki handled Bonds (a Pirates teammate during Barry's first two seasons in the majors) like a baby (3-for-35, .086, one homer, one double, eight whiffs), finally allowing an opposite-field home run to him in April 1996, his 34th at-bat against him. You can bet Bonds wasn't bragging about that one.

Looking back through all these pitcher-hitter matchups was endlessly entertaining. And to close, there are a number of internet regulars who always seem to want to put up Sandy Koufax's career numbers vs. those of say, Bob Gibson or Tom Seaver. It's a great discussion and let's just say all three of those guys made hitters' lives miserable. Take a glance at the remarkable records of these three aces.

Facing Sandy Koufax

Willie Stargell .083 (2-for-23), 1 3B, 2 RBIs, 10 K

Harvey Kuenn .118 (8-for-70), 3 RBIs, 12 K

Willie McCovey .143 (6-for-42), 1 HR, 2 RBIs, 15 K

Ernie Banks .173 (23-for-133), 7 HR, 19 RBIs, 31 K

Pete Rose .175 (10-for-57), 1 2B, 2 RBIs, 10 K

Lou Brock .185 (12-for-65), 4 2B, 1 HR, 28 K

Tony Pérez .200 (5-for-25), 8 K

Dick Allen .229 (8-for-35), 1 3B, 1 HR, 1 RBI, 13 K

Joe Morgan .241 (7-for-29), 2 HR, 4 RBIs, 7 K

FACING TOM SEAVER

Bobby Bonds .118 (6-for-51), 4 HR, 10 RBIs, 24 K

Johnny Bench .156 (12-for-72), 5 HR, 5 RBIs, 26 K

Greg Luzinski .175 (14-for-75), 3 HR, 9 RBIs, 31 K

Mike Schmidt .188 (16-for-85), 2 HR, 5 RBIs, 35 K

Hank Aaron .205 (16-for-78), 4 HR, 8 RBIs, 14 K

Dick Allen .208 (11-for-53), 4 HR, 9 RBIs, 22 K

Roberto Clemente .242 (15-for-62), 2 HR, 6 RBIs, 21 K

FACING BOB GIBSON

Willie Mays .196 (18-for-92), 3 HR, 9 RBIs, 30 K

Donn Clendenon .203 (15-for-74), 6 HR, 6 RBIs, 37 K

Roberto Clemente .208 (26-for-125), 4 HR, 16 RBIs, 32 K

Dick Allen .211 (12-for-57), 1 HR, 7 RBIs, 27 K

Hank Aaron .215 (35-for-163), 8 HR, 26 RBIs, 32 K

Ernie Banks .229 (24-for-105), 3 HR, 13 RBIs, 24 K

Frank Robinson .229 (19-for-83), 4 HR, 19 RBIs, 12 K

Bobby Bonds .240 (18-for-75), 4 HR, 10 RBIs, 20 K

CHAPTER SIXTEEN

Lefty Grove vs. Sandy Koufax: Best of All Time?

WHAT IF. IF YOU'RE A BASEBALL FAN—AND IF YOU'RE NOT, WHY ARE YOU here? (wink)—you've heard that phrase more times than you can count.

"What if Ted Williams hadn't lost all that time to military service?" Or "What if Babe Ruth was playing in today's game?" Or "What if Willie Mays hadn't played the bulk of his career in that glorified wind tunnel called Candlestick Park?"

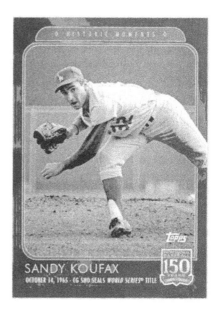

Or "What if Red Sox manager John McNamara had sent defensive replacement Dave Stapleton out to play first base in the 10th inning of the 1986 World Series instead of sticking with Billy Buckner?" Or "What if Sandy Koufax could have played past age 30?" There are many more.

Let's add another: "What if Lefty Grove made the big leagues when he should have, at age 20 or 21, instead of age 25? What sorts of all-time records might he have set?"

As it stands, "the terrible tempered Mr. Grove" as *New York Times* columnist Red Smith once referred to him, owns one of the game's finest lifetime marks, winning 300 games, losing just 141, leading the American League in earned run average nine times, in strikeouts seven years in a row, a 30-game winner once (31 in 1931), a 20-game winner seven other times. Truly exceptional work. But it says here, Lefty's numbers could have been even better.

Philadelphia A's owner-manager Connie Mack, who was thought to throw nickels around like manhole covers, laid out $100,600 for the lefty (called "Groves" in an October 11, 1924 *New York Times* story reporting the major purchase) from the Baltimore Orioles of the International League, which translates into almost $1.8 million in today's terms.

As it turned out, the hard-throwing Grove didn't get to compete in his first major-league game until April 14, 1925, a little over a month past his 25th birthday. Baltimore owner Jack Dunn was notorious for hanging onto to what-should-have-been-big-league talent until he got the price where he wanted it. If you were going to sign the best pitcher he ever had, you were going to pay for it. Connie Mack did, just after Grove had turned 25 and thrown 1,184 innings for Dunn's minor-league Orioles for five seasons, going 108–36. *What if* he had gotten an earlier start?

When you consider that Koufax, a bonus baby who had a major-league roster spot without necessarily earning it for several years, was into his *seventh* big-league season by age 25, you can see where we're going with this. What might have Lefty Grove done with that extra time in the major leagues?

For Koufax, those early years were just a holding pattern. He was just starting to develop into the brilliant Dodgers ace he would become over the next six seasons. But Koufax also had multiple opportunities to

Sandy Koufax   Lefty Grove

Sandy Koufax	Overall Stats	Lefty Grove
48.9	WAR	106.8
397	G	616
314	GS	457
2324.1	IP	3940.2
165-87	W-L	300-141
9	SV	54
2.76	ERA	3.06
131	ERA+	148
2396	SO	2266
25.2	K%	13.6
817	BB	1187
8.6	BB%	7.1
	Awards & Honors	
✓	Hall of Fame	✓
4	Championships	2
7	All-Star	6
1	MVP	1
3	Cy Young	
5	ERA Title	9
2	WS MVP	
3	Triple Crown	2

learn the game and learn how to pitch and how *not* to. Which turned out to be the key. Once he decided to *not* try to strike everyone out, to take the oft-offered advice of catcher Norm Sherry telling him to take the grunt out of his fastball, his mound work improved radically. Brilliantly. Historically.

For Grove, as you might expect, his first major-league season showed a learning curve. He was 10–12 in 1925, his only losing season, and while he led the American League in strikeouts (116) he also led it in walks (131) and wild pitches (nine). Once he had that year behind him, Grove went 185–54 over the next seven seasons.

Imagine that Grove made the majors at age 20—got that learning curve season out of the way—then began to dominate the way he did. Could you add, say, at least 22 wins for another five seasons—and there were years he won 31, 28, 25 and 24. We're adding at least 100 more wins, which would put him at 400–420 wins.

Yeah, Cy Young won 511 games in a time when guys could pitch both ends of a doubleheader. We're talking a different game once baseball moved into the 1920s. The question here is this: Would Grove have been a better investment than Sandy Koufax? Can you make a case for him being the greatest left-hander of all-time?

THE BEST OF ALL TIME?

Happily, there are film clips of Grove available on YouTube. You can see him standing on the mound, tall and slim, that left arm easily drifting back as the right leg easily kicks halfway between first and home, every pitch seems effortless, natural, something that looked like it was supposed to happen.

The great Red Smith described his delivery this way: "On the mound he was poetry," Smith wrote. "He would rock back until the knuckles of his left hand-almost brushed the earth behind him, then come up and over with the perfect follow-through. He was the only 300-game winner between Grover Alexander and Warren Spahn, a span of 37 years. He had the lowest earned-run average in the league nine different years, and nobody else ever did that more than five times. If the old records can be trusted, Alexander, Christy Mathewson, Johnson and Sandy Koufax each won five ERA titles. Some men would say these were the best pitchers that ever lived. Are the records trying to tell us Old Man Mose was twice as good as any of them?"

Grove's first major-league start went about like you'd expect from a rookie fireballer. Pitching at Philadelphia's Shibe Park against the Red Sox on April 14, 1925, Boston's leadoff batter Ira Flagstead dumped the game's first pitch into right field for a single. Doc Prothro followed with a single to center. Grove got Ike Boone to hit into a double play and Bobby Veach to foul out. Hooray! He had a scoreless first. There was more trouble ahead. Leading off the second, Joe Harris walked, Ewell Gross was hit by a pitch, and when first baseman Jim Poole fouled up Billy Rogell's sacrifice bunt, the bases were loaded. Val Picinich hit a sac fly to score Boston's first run off Grove. After an out, Flagstead slapped one up the middle for an infield hit to make it 2–0, Boston. After enduring an Ike Boone single and an Ewell Gross walk and escaping with a scoreless third, the Red Sox pounced on the rookie for three more runs in the fourth, chasing him from his first start.

Picinich opened the inning with a double down the right field line, Alex Ferguson walked, Flagstead bunted them up, Prothro walked (remember Grove led the league in walks!), a Boone groundout scored one run, and Veach's line-drive single to left scored two more runs, bringing Grove's debut to a halt.

He left the game trailing 5–0, but Mack's A's rallied against the Red Sox and pulled out a 9–8 extra-inning win so Grove escaped his first loss. That didn't happen until his third start on April 21, a 6–2 loss to the Senators where Grove threw eight innings, allowing seven hits, walked six, fanned four. But he was 0–1.

In his fifth outing, Grove gave up the first home run of the 162 he would allow (to the Yankees' Aaron Ward), but in working four innings in relief, he earned his first big-league victory. He didn't face Babe Ruth or Lou Gehrig in that game and got his second loss the very next day, starting and going four innings, allowing eight hits, six runs with four walks.

But Grove was learning. On the Fourth of July, the hard-throwing rookie finally got to face Ruth and Gehrig in a memorable duel at Yankee Stadium, his true major-league baptism, throwing 14 brilliant shutout innings, ultimately losing on a two-out Steve O'Neill RBI single in the bottom of the 15th. Grove, a rookie, remember, hooked up with the Yanks' Herb Pennock, who also went all 15 innings, allowing just four A's hits. Talk about making an impression!

Against the Yankees' big guns, the first-year hurler did well. Ruth reached him for a single to right in his first at-bat and again in the 13th inning. In between, Grove got him to hit into a double play and a popout to second.

As for Gehrig, Grove fanned him the first time he faced him and got him twice more that game, allowing a two-out single in the sixth. In the ninth—with the game still scoreless—the Yankees had Gehrig sacrifice Bob Meusel over after a single, trying to set up the win, but Grove worked out of it.

In the 10th, Grove fanned Earl Combs and Ruth, then struck out Gehrig for a second time in the 11th. As this was going on, A's manager Connie Mack—and the Yankees—were finding out what kind of pitcher this rookie was going to be.

Still scoreless in the 13th inning, the Yankees made a real bid to win it. Ruth led off with a single and Meusel doubled to right, chasing Babe to third, the winning run just 90 feet away. Grove walked Gehrig intentionally to load the bases but with high heat, his best pitch, Grove got O'Neill and Ward to foul out to first, then induced Ernie Johnson to ground out to first to end the threat.

Years later, Grove reflected on his "out pitch." "My high hard one was my best pitch," Grove told the *New York Times'* Arthur Daley. "Connie Mack used to tell all the pitchers that they should pitch low to the outside or high to inside when in doubt. But he always said to me, 'Not you, Robert, because you'll pitch your own way anyway.' I would say 'Yes, Mister Mack, my high hard one is my best pitch.'"

Grove fanned Joe Dugan and Combs in the 14th, giving him nine on the day. The scoreboard was still blank.

In the top of the 15th, the A's Jimmy Dykes made a bid to give Grove the lead, lining a triple to right field for the fourth hit off Pennock. But a great relay throw from Ruth to Dugan to O'Neill nabbed Dykes at the plate in a close play, keeping the game scoreless.

In the bottom of that inning, the Yankees finally won it when Bobby Veach singled, Meusel sacrificed him to second, and after Grove fanned Gehrig for a third time, O'Neill lined an RBI single to center and the Yankees and Pennock had the 1–0 win.

Famous for a volcanic temper, no doubt Grove probably wanted to destroy the visiting clubhouse at Yankee Stadium. But after 15 innings of pitching, he might have been a tad tired. As far as we know, the Yankee Stadium visiting clubhouse and the Stadium itself was still standing the next day.

By the way, that 15-inning game took two hours and 50 minutes.

After that 10–12 first season, Grove went 13–13 in year two, then took off with seven 20-plus win seasons in a row, including an extraordinary 1931 season when he won 31 games, was named the American League's Most Valuable Player, and led the league in wins, ERA, strikeouts, complete games (27!) and shutouts (four). Just for a contemporary reference, Justin Verlander, a pretty fair country pitcher, *has 26 complete games for a 19-year career!*

GROVE SOLD TO BOSTON

Though Grove's career took off, the A's weren't drawing. Mack's A's won three straight pennants (1929–1931) but Philadelphians seemed to be losing interest in the club. That, plus the impact of the Great Depression, made things tough at Shibe Park. As attendance sank, Mack decided he had no choice but to start selling off his players. He sold Al Simmons, Mule Haas, and Jimmy Dykes to the Chicago White Sox in 1932 for $150,000 and in December of 1933, he dealt Grove to the Boston Red Sox.

A sore arm hampered Grove that 1934 season, posting an 8–8 record in just 109 innings and at first, it looked as if Mack had dumped the cantankerous Grove at just the right time.

But Lefty's left wing came back. And he would go on to win 97 games over the next seven seasons for the Red Sox, maintaining his spot among the American League's elite pitchers.

There were a few hiccups. On July 14, 1938, there was an alarming item in the *New York Times*. "Grove, Unable to Grip Ball, May Be Near

End of Career." An AP writer with a flair for the dramatic wrote the following: "The once-mighty fireball arm of lanky Bob (Lefty) Grove lay limp tonight—and the career of one of baseball's greatest pitchers depended on a doctor's diagnosis of a strange ailment that struck him on the mound today. Dr. Edward J. O'Brien, team physician, said long diagnosis and extensive X-rays were needed to determine whether the Red Sox would lose their thirty-eight-year-old star hurler. 'There is no pulse in Grove's left arm and he is unable to grip firmly with his hand,' Dr. O'Brien said. 'I have never encountered a similar case but I judged from my initial examination that it was not a recurrence of the bicep muscle trouble he had back in 1934. The fact that Grove has circulation in his arm and is not suffering any pain is encouraging. But we will not know just how serious the injury is until tomorrow at least. He is being held at the hospital for observation.'"

Four days later, Grove was back on a mound, raising his seasonal record to 11–1 by throwing 12—yes, a *dozen*—innings to beat the White Sox's future Hall of Famer Ted Lyons, 4–3. Evidently, Lefty was a quick healer.

He had not, however, calmed down. Playing for Joe Cronin, Boston's player-manager, Lefty carried the Sox into a scoreless tie in the ninth. And somehow, Cronin booted the ball, it rolled to the fence, and the Red Sox—and Grove—lost 1–0. The story goes that Cronin, knowing what lay ahead, darted into his office and locked the door. However, there was a wire netting above the office and Grove climbed up onto a chair so his head was above the netting and Cronin was in sight. And Lefty let him know in terms that were not exactly considerate how disappointed he was in his shortstop and his manager and the results of that day's ballgame. This was Lefty Grove.

He continued pitching well for the Red Sox, was 97–54 and heading into the 1941 season, he had 293 career wins, just seven shy of the magical 300-win total.

No pitcher since Walter Johnson had won 300 games. Lefty's goal at the start of the 1941 season was clear. It took him a few tries but on July 25 against the Cleveland Indians, Grove finally got number 300, but again, it was not easy. Grove pitched a complete game, surrendered a dozen hits, and in the fifth inning, found himself trailing 4–2. But then Ted Williams hit a two-run homer to tie the score.

When Cleveland countered with a Boudreau home run in the seventh and a Williams error on Gee Walker's triple, the Tribe had a 6–4 lead and it looked like Lefty would have to wait for number 300.

But the Red Sox rallied and a two-run Jim Tabor homer in the seventh tied it, and in the eighth, a Jimmie Foxx triple and another Tabor homer clinched the landmark win for Grove. When Grove induced Boudreau to fly out to Dom DiMaggio in center, that closed out win number 300.

Grove made just six more appearances, including a couple of starts, for the rest of the 1941 season, tossing just 23 innings. It turned out Lefty's career would end on that 300th victory. The Red Sox gave him his release at the end of the season.

SANDY'S BRILLIANT RUN

There are those who look at Koufax's modest lifetime win totals—165–87, a little more than half of Grove's totals—and understandably wonder why the Hall came a callin'. Generally speaking, pitchers need to have 250–300 wins to even be considered for Cooperstown status.

But when the magnificent Koufax was forced into retirement at age 30 thanks to an unrelenting arthritic elbow, the Dodger great was at the absolute peak of his powers. *What if* he'd been healthy and, like Grove, pitched into his 40s?

While Koufax's brilliance was confined to six seasons, if you take a thoughtful look at every single major-league hurler over the long history of the game, it's difficult to find anyone who put together a six-year run like Koufax. Except, maybe, for Lefty Grove.

On the mound, Koufax exuded confidence, poise, almost an elegance. Koufax was exceptionally limber and as writer Roger Angell once suggested, "[T]here was a bow and arrow feeling about the way he used his body." What he meant was Koufax had a bit of a rhythmic lean back, his shoulders truly tilting up as he stretched out his leg to full extension, then reached his arm so far back it almost touched the dirt, then delivered the ball over the top as he stepped toward the plate. It was fierce but somehow graceful.

Blessed with extraordinarily long fingers, a blistering fastball, and a 12–6 curveball that, because of the change in his delivery, hitters could identify but still couldn't hit, he became such a dominating pitcher, there were few dissenters when he was elected to the Hall of Fame in his first year of eligibility, the youngest player (at 36) to ever earn that honor. And there was no doubting his talent.

Speaking on the *Colin Cowherd Show*, Pete Rose was, as usual, blunt. "I hit .175 off Sandy Koufax," he said. "He was unbelievable. I got 10-for-57 off him. Get your calculator out, that's .175. He had a great fastball, (Rose picks up a round ball off the table) and he had a curveball that broke (he drops the ball on the floor) like that. How in the hell are you going to hit that curveball?"

Talking to Jane Leavy for her book on Koufax, Yankee Bobby Richardson had the same sentiments.

"The report comes in and says 'His fastball really takes off,'" he said. "You think 'I've seen lots of fastballs.' When you see it for the first time, I couldn't believe it. I had not seen stuff like that before. By the third time up, I was honestly just trying to hit the first pitch because I didn't want to strike out again."

So, if you think of the home plate area as a sort of box, you had his 90-plus fastball soaring up and out of the box (it may not actually have risen, it just didn't sink as fast as a normal pitcher's ball) and a curveball that broke from one corner of the box to the other swiftly, relentlessly, on the kind of downward plane that made it difficult to square up.

Across the league, pitchers and hitters knew when they were in a game against him, this would not be, in the old phrase, "a walk in the park."

Phillies manager Gene Mauch told Leavy about watching Koufax warm up before a no-hitter in 1964.

"The man threw a hundred and fourteen pitches! Warming up! One hundred and fourteen pitches! For about eighty-five or ninety or close to a hundred of those pitches, he was scowling and grimacing and shaking his head, just really down. He couldn't find anything. He couldn't find his release point or his rhythm. Something was bothering the hell out of him. But he was gonna stay out there until he got things the way he wanted it.

"So after about ninety-five or so pitches, he started nodding his head and smiling. Sandy Koufax didn't smile. But now he's smiling at his catcher, who had his back to me. He started nodding his head, and I said, 'Oh my God, I'm in for it.'"

And the Phils were. Koufax fanned a dozen in that June 4 no-no, including four of the final five hitters, allowing just four balls hit out of the infield.

Not everyone remembers the Koufax years as fondly. As St. Louis Cardinals great Bob Gibson explained to author Jane Leavy, "They are not fond memories. People come and ask how it was to pitch against Sandy Koufax. Sandy Koufax was a pain in the ass. You pitched against him and you knew the score was going be two to one, one to zero. Normally, two to one, one to zero, *I* won."

But there was a physical price to pay for such dominance. Koufax tried everything to cope with the pain in his arthritic elbow: cortisone shots, steroids into the joint, codeine, nothing worked. Somehow, Koufax pitched through it. But he had his skeptics.

"When my back hurts," the Pirates' great Roberto Clemente groused, "they call me a goldbrick. Koufax says his elbow hurts and they make him a national hero. Sore arm my foot. He threw as hard tonight as he ever has. He can't have a sore elbow and throw like that . . . What does he think the National League is, a joke? Last year, he wins twenty-six games and this year he wins twenty four, and all I hear about it how much pain he has in his elbow. What does he want people to believe> That he could win fifty games a year if his elbow wasn't sore?"

And here's another "what if" for Sandy. What if the Dodgers were a bit more judicious in how many times they handed him the baseball? From 1962 to 1966, Koufax threw 1,631 innings, including three of his last four years over 300 innings and was 97–27 over that span, fanning more than 300 batters three times, including a record 382 in 335 2/3 innings in 1965.

As Leavy noted in her book *Koufax*, "Pitching a complete game in spring training is unthinkable, even without an arthritic arm. On March 30, 1965, Koufax did just that. The next morning, his roommate, (Dick) Tracewski, was at the sink shaving when Koufax walked in. "He says, 'Look at this.' And he had this elbow. The elbow was black. And it was swollen. There was muscles that were pulled and there was hemorrhaging. From the elbow to the armpit, it looked like a bruise. It was a black, angry hemorrhage. It was an angry arm, an angry elbow. And all he says is, 'Roomie, look at this.'"

Sandy and Lefty vs. Their Leagues

You might think that since the National League from 1960 to 1980 was just stocked with Hall of Fame pitchers like Sandy Koufax, Bob Gibson, Juan Marichal, and others, there were dozens of duels between these aces modeled after the Muhammad Ali vs. Joe Frazier trilogy or the Ali-Norton three-fight duel. But there weren't.

Koufax and Gibson went up against one another just five times, Koufax throwing three shutouts. In two of those games, the score was 1–0, with home runs by Tommy Davis off Gibson deciding each game. (Which perhaps explains Gibson's grouchy response.)

Though the Giants were certainly the Dodgers' archrival through the length of their careers, Koufax and Marichal only dueled each other four times. You would think there would be more.

The last time Koufax squared off against Bob Gibson was April 26, 1966, Koufax's final season. Sandy won 4–2 but allowed 13 hits, three by Flood, two by Brock, Charley Smith, and Julián Javier. He fanned eight.

Gibson allowed four runs in the first, singles by Willie Davis, Ron Fairly, a Jim Lefebvre double and singles by John Roseboro, Nate Oliver, and John Kennedy—six hits! He only allowed one more hit over the next seven innings, a Roseboro double in the third.

Against Marichal, the last time Koufax pitched against him was the infamous Marichal-Roseboro game in August 1965, and after the incident where Marichal hit Roseboro on the dome with a bat, Koufax walked McCovey and Jim Davenport, then allowed a three-run homer— and the lead—to Willie Mays.

In examining Koufax's career numbers against the National League, there are surprises. Could Koufax possibly have a career losing record against any team? Yup, the Reds had a 20–19 edge over him.

But the New York Mets and Houston Colt .45s/Astros were an easy mark. He was 17–2 against New York, 14–2 against Houston.

Perhaps not surprisingly, the team batting averages against Koufax were rough, four teams under .200 (Mets .170, Cubs .177, Astros .184, Phillies .185). The Braves had the highest team average (.227) and even though the Giants lineup had three Hall of Famers—Mays, McCovey, and Cepeda—it was the Atlanta Braves who actually hit the most home runs against him—36. Hank Aaron hit seven, Orlando Cepeda five, Felipe Alou (three, who also hit four off Koufax as a Giant), Willie McCovey only one. (Koufax held him to .143.)

For Lefty Grove, playing in an era when team batting averages were generally higher, his numbers pale in comparison to Koufax's. Strikeouts were fewer, players were taught to take that two-strike swing and as a result, collected more hits.

The best Grove could do was hold the Red Sox to a .241 team mark, while the Indians and Yankees were a point apart, hitting .265 and .264 against the lefty. Grove allowed the most home runs to the Yankees (41 in 92 games) and 37 to the Tigers in 102 games. Grove's won-loss record was 35–8 against the Red Sox, no doubt a reason they wanted him. He was 60–19 against the Tigers, 44–23 against the Tribe, 42–17 against the St. Louis Browns, and 41–18 against the White Sox. Somewhat surprisingly, his record against the Yankees and Senators weren't quite as convincing—34–26 vs. New York, which is understandable because that includes some mighty Yankees teams and 31–25 against Washington, which isn't.

WHO DO YOU PICK—SANDY OR LEFTY?

The obvious answer to this question depends on what you're looking for. If you're looking for longevity, Grove is a clear winner over Koufax. Sandy's six seasons were extraordinary but still, it was just six seasons. As grouchy Bob Gibson noted—correctly—Koufax might have won the Pitcher of the Decade honors, but a decade is 10 years, not six.

Lefty Grove was a franchise arm and Connie Mack's mighty deal was well worth it.

He pitched through sore arms, temper tantrums, pretty lousy salaries, and always seemed to find ways to be up on the hill, even four days after a deeply concerning hospital stay—no pulse in his pitching arm?—winning 20 or more games seven times, including 20 at age 35 with only 121 strikeouts in 273 innings. He found a way to get guys out. Nobody was ever more competitive.

"I might have won 500 games if I'd have pitched forty years ago," he told Arthur Daley once. "Consider all the things those guys had going for 'em that I didn't. First of all, they had the dead ball. Guys used to lead the league with a half-dozen home runs. Second, a ball hardly was ever thrown out of play. You could pitch with a discolored ball or a scuffed one. The dirty baseball was hard to follow and the scuffed one sailed, which made it harder to hit. Third, they had the privilege if throwing trick deliveries like the shine ball, the emory ball and the spitter."

Grove continued to find ways to win, even when his strikeout totals came down. Despite pitching lots and lots of innings, he only allowed as many as 20 home runs one time and that was at age 40 in 1940, his next-to-last season. He had 10 different seasons with single-digit home runs allowed and halved his walks, generally walking no more than 60–70 batters per season.

What's tricky is you have to remember that Lefty pitched in an era when strikeouts weren't as common and you could lead the league with fewer than 200 whiffs. Grove only surpassed 200 strikeouts in a year once. That says a lot about the state of the game and the environment he worked in.

If he was pitching in an era like Koufax where strikeouts *did* happen by the bundle—Sandy whiffed 382 one season—you'd have to think Grove would have plenty of his own.

What we don't know—two more what ifs—is how Grove would adjust to modern swing-and-miss hitters. The high pitch, an element that has returned to the modern game, seems like something he'd use to his great advantage.

The *other* what if would be if modern medical technology could have helped Sandy Koufax deal with his arthritic elbow. Reading the mind-bending things that Koufax went through to try to pitch, injecting steroids into the joint, throwing complete games in spring training, wearing out his skin with ice or Capsolin, what if there was a way, medically speaking, that he could have pitched without pain?

The idea of the opener wasn't introduced into the game in his time, but what if the Dodgers decided to use Koufax as an opener? Instead of logging all those innings, the number of pitches mounting as the year went on, what if the club had him throwing two or three innings to get the club off to a rip-snortin' start every few days, something to keep the pitch count down? Imagine a modern hitter having to face Koufax two or three times a week?

Now, if you've seen Koufax in action—there are films out there if you missed him live on TV—you know what a challenge National League hitters faced. There isn't a lot of film of Grove, but his numbers, leading the league in ERA nine different years with good teams and bad, throwing over 250 innings 11 times and winning, that says a lot, too.

Was Lefty Grove the greatest lefty in the history of the game? Was Sandy Koufax? What if—we picked them both?

TOP HITTERS VS. LEFTY GROVE

Tris Speaker .444 (12-for-27), 5 2B, 1 3B, 0 HR, 7 RBIs, 10 BB, 3 K

Al Simmons .436 (24-for-55), 6 2B, 1 3B, 2 HR, 14 RBIs, 3 BB, 6 K

Harry Heilmann .425 (34-for-80), 6 2B, 1 3B, 4 HR, 14 RBIs, 5 BB, 8 K

Jimmie Foxx .385 (10-for-26), 4 2B, 0 3B, 1 HR, 4 RBIs, 2 BB, 6K

Joe DiMaggio .361 (26-for-72),. 7 2B, 1 3B, 2 HR, 10 RBIs, 6 BB, 5 K

Ty Cobb .333 (5-for-15), 1 2B, 0 3B, 0 HR, 4 RBIs, 6 BB, 2 K

Babe Ruth .311 (42-for-135), 2 2B, 0 3B, 9 HR, 33 RBIs, 13 BB, 45 K

Lou Gehrig .306 (66-for-216), 12 2B, 7 3B, 9 HR, 45 RBIs, 26 BB, 47 K

Hank Greenberg .289 (33-for-114), 7 2B, 1 3B, 9 HR, 33 RBIs, 19 BB, 16 K

Struggling Hitters vs. Lefty Grove

Bill Dickey .217 (18-for-83), 5 2B, 0 3B, 2 HR, 11 RBIs, 11 BB, 5 K

Tony Lazzeri .231 (37-for-160), 6 2B, 0 3B, 4 HR, 21 RBIs, 13 BB, 39 K

Goose Goslin .225 (38-for-169), 6 2B, 3 3B, 1 HR, 17 RBIs, 8 BB, 23 K

Billy Rogell .228 (36-for-158), 13 2B, 0 3B, 0 HR, 8 RBIs, 6 BB, 23 K

Top Hitters vs. Sandy Koufax

Bill Virdon .404 (21-for-52), 4 2B, 0 3B, 0 HR, 3 RBIs, 7 BB, 8 K

Gene Oliver .392 (20-for-51), 1 2B, 0 3B, 4 HR, 9 RBIs, 3 BB, 4 K

Hank Aaron .362 (42-for-116), 6 2B, 3 3B, 7 HR, 16 RBIs, 14 BB, 12 K

Jesús Alou .353 (12-for-34), 1 2B, 0 3B, 1 HR, 4 RBIs, 2 BB, 7 K

Stan Musial .342 (13-for-38), 13 2B, 2 3B, 2 HR, 7 RBIs, 6 BB, 5 K

Roberto Clemente .297 (33-for-111), 6 2B, 2 3B, 6 HR, 16 RBIs, 10 BB, 20 K

Curt Flood .296 (32-for-108), 6 2B, 1 3B, 2 HR, 7 RBIs, 7 BB, 6 K

Vada Pinson .288 (34-for-118), 7 2B, 2 3B, 2 HR, 10 RBIs, 6 BB, 34 K

Orlando Cepeda .288 (23-for- 80), 4 2B, 0 3B, 5 HR, 15 RBIs, 3 BB, 18 K

Dick Stuart .286 (18-for-63),. 2 2B, 0 3B, 5 HR, 12 RBIs, 5 BB, 7 K

Eddie Mathews .281 (25-for-89), 3 2B, 0 3B, 3 HR, 7 RBIs, 13 BB, 22 K

Willie Mays .278 (27-for-97), 8 2B, 1 3B, 5 HR, 14 RBIs, 25 BB, 20 K

STRUGGLING HITTERS VS. SANDY KOUFAX

Rico Carty .000 (0-for-18), 0 2B, 0 3B, 0 HR, 0 RBI, 1 BB, 8 K

Willie Stargell .087 (2-for-23), 0 2B, 1 3B, 0 HR, 2 RBIs, 1 BB, 10 K

Ernie Banks .173 (23-for-133), 1 2B, 2 3B, 7 HR, 19 RBIs, 10 BB, 31 K

Bill White .176 (18-for-102), 4 2B, 0 3B, 1 HR, 6 RBIs, 9 BB, 28 K

Lou Brock .185 (12-for-65), 4 2B, 0 3B, 0 HR, 1 RBI, 3 BB, 28 K

Frank Robinson .233 (24-for-103), 7 2B, 0 3B, 7 HR, 23 RBIs, 16 BB, 20 K

CHAPTER SEVENTEEN

Carew, Boggs, Gwynn, Brett: Who Got Them Out?

THE GAME OF BASEBALL WAS MADE FOR LEFT-HANDERS. LEFT-HANDED batters have an extra step advantage heading to first base, they generally have an edge at the plate, since the majority of pitchers they'll ever face are right-handed, so their breaking balls will always curve in toward them instead of away, and left-handed pitchers with half or maybe 25 percent of the stuff of their righty counterparts can go on and have a long, successful career (right, Jamie Moyer?).

And finally, for whatever bizarre reason, most stadiums—in the major leagues and on the way there, offer a shorter right field fence for those poor beleaguered left-handed hitters. What a bunch of crap!

Forget Yankee Stadium's bandbox 314-foot right field (296 at the original ballpark)—which many American League hurlers would like to do. You can go all the way back to the Polo Grounds, where the clever lefty Mel Ott—remember, the guy who lifted his right leg up before he swung?—found a way to yank 323 of his 511 home runs down the right field line, a cozy 256 feet away.

The rationale for this architectural windfall for lefties, of course, is most hitters are naturally right-handed. It would be against the law to have a left field as close as right field in Yankee Stadium or the Polo Grounds. Oh no, that wouldn't be fair. Ridiculous.

Think of the game's greatest hitters. Babe Ruth, Ted Williams, Stan Musial, Lou Gehrig, Barry Bonds, Ty Cobb, Ken Griffey Jr., Tris Speaker,

Duke Snider, Eddie Mathews, Joe Jackson, Reggie Jackson, Bo Jackson (just kidding, Bo was right-handed). They're all lefties.

Now maybe you noticed that I'm leaving out four terrific hitters who are going to be the subject of this chapter—Rod Carew, Wade Boggs, Tony Gwynn, and George Brett. Yes, they were all lefties, too.

Between these four hitters there are 23 batting titles, 12,358 hits, and enough groans from major-league pitching coaches to drown out a stadium. Being left-handed might have been the only thing these four had in common. As hitters, they were all quite different.

The slender Carew was able to slice the ball to left, rip it down the right field line, and he also used the bunt and his great speed. Carew, for

	Tony Gwynn	George Brett	Wade Boggs	Rod Carew
Overall Stats				
WAR	69.2	88.6	**91.4**	81.2
G	2440	**2707**	2439	2469
PA	10232	**11625**	10740	10550
H	3141	**3154**	3010	3053
HR	135	**317**	118	92
RBI	1138	**1596**	1014	1015
SB	319	201	24	**353**
BA	**.338**	.305	.328	.328
OBP	.388	.369	**.415**	.393
SLG	.459	**.487**	.443	.429
OPS	.847	.857	**.858**	.822
OPS+	132	**135**	131	131
Awards & Honors				
Hall of Fame	✓	✓	✓	✓
Championships		1	1	
All-Star	15	13	12	**18**
MVP		1		1
Batting Title	8	3	5	7
Gold Glove	5	1	2	
Silver Slugger	7	3	8	
LCS MVP		1		

example, had 91 bunt hits in his career total of 3,053 and won himself seven batting titles.

The highly disciplined Boggs, like Gwynn, also had incredible bat-to-ball skills and would go through entire seasons without a single popup. Boggs hit over .360 four times, won five batting titles, and collected as many as 240 hits in a single season.

Gwynn, too, had amazing bat control, rarely struck out, and was uncannily able to find holes in the infield wherever they chose to play him. He won an amazing eight NL batting titles and had nine different full seasons with fewer than 20 strikeouts (a good couple weeks for Reggie Jackson).

Finally, George Brett settled in at third base in Kansas City and was a phenomenon for 21 years, showing power to all fields, leading the league in doubles twice and triples three times. He also won batting titles in three different decades.

So yeah, these guys could really swing it. But it wasn't like they batted .500. *Somebody* got these guys out. Let's take a look at each one of these Hall of Famers and see what pitchers *didn't* hiccup when they saw these guys step into the left-hand batter's box. We'll also look at who they *did* hit in their Hall of Fame careers. You'll be surprised.

ROD CAREW (TWINS, ANGELS—1967–1985)

One of the first things we learned about sweet-swinging Rod Carew was he was born on a train in Panama. The next thing we learned was that this slender lefty had a knack for hitting the ball through the infield, no matter where they were playing him. And Carew was unique in that he was maybe even more dangerous *after* he left the batter's box. In a game against the Detroit Tigers in 1969, Carew stole second, third, and home—in the same inning!

That year, he stole home seven times, five times in the very first inning, 17 times for his career. Ty Cobb was the all-time leader with 54 steals of home.

Carew was strategic about it.

"Pitchers don't expect you to take a risk so early and kill off a potential rally," Carew said, explaining his larceny.

Carew has remained involved in the game and admits he doesn't like how the game has shifted away from that little chess game between hitter and pitcher.

"In today's game, a lot of kids don't know themselves," Carew said. "They don't know what kind of hitters they are, and the more that baseball allows them to keep trying to hit home runs, the worse a lot of them are going to be up there. They're not going to learn anything about hitting.

"For a guy that can hit five or six home runs a year, why is he up there trying to hit home runs? They give you foul line to foul line to hit, to use the whole field. That's what the game is supposed to be based on, but guys aren't doing that today. That's why you see a lot of strikeouts and I'm disgusted with the strikeouts and disgusted that they think that walking back to the bench is fun after striking out three or four times a game. That's no fun at all for hitters. Either they're going to have to change and allow hitters to be the type of hitters that they were [back in the day] or not. If you don't, then it's going to keep getting worse."

Contrary to a hitting scientist like Ted Williams, who could lecture on the Bernoulli Principle at the drop of a ballcap, Carew trusted his quick hands and always tried to keep things simple.

"I always looked for the fastball. I didn't look for the breaking ball," he said. "I could get out on my front foot and still put the breaking ball in play, but I never wanted to miss a fastball. I stayed on the fastball from strike one all the way through the at-bat. If he threw me a breaking ball with two strikes, I fought it off, and I could get out on my front foot just enough to flick at it and put it in play. But I never, ever wanted anyone to throw a fastball by me with two strikes."

The one lefty who seemed to be able to do just that was Louisiana Lightning, the Yankees' Ron Guidry. Carew was just 4-for-34 (.118) against Guidry, far and away the worst hitting stats Carew posted against anybody. In 1977, the first time he faced him, Carew was a 10-year vet and a perennial All-Star. He got Carew out the first four times he faced him, gave up an RBI single in his fifth at-bat, and then didn't allow Carew another hit against him for three years. In September of 1980, Carew slashed a triple against him. Carew's final hit against Guidry came three years later, a first-inning single. Then he got him out four more times.

There were other AL starters who gave Carew a hard time; the Indians' fireballing lefty Sam McDowell (5-for-28, .179), Toronto's dominating righty Dave Stieb (10-for-46, .217), and the Orioles' clever lefty Scott McGregor (9-for-44, .205). And like a lot of other AL hitters, Carew struggled against Hall of Fame relievers Rollie Fingers (6-for-32, .188) and Rich Gossage (7-for-37, .189).

With his ability to bunt and his speed on the bases, there were those—including Ted Williams—who thought Carew might be the next .400 hitter. Rod didn't get there but he did manage a superb .388 season in 1977, collecting 239 hits. Carew did manage to hit .400 or better against a raft of AL hurlers like Don Kirkwood (*.611!*) Bart Johnson (.548), Dan Spillner (.531), Doug Bird (.515), Dick Drago (.494), Len Barker (.463), Jim Beattie (.455), Dennis Leonard (.449), Ed Figueroa (.429), Pat Dobson (.424), Lary Sorensen (.407), and Glenn Abbott (.407).

Though Carew wasn't a home-run hitter, just 92 in his career, he was able to show some power against Jim "Catfish" Hunter, slamming seven home runs and seven doubles against the Hall of Fame righty. His line against Luis Tiant, whom he faced more than any other hurler was interesting—103 at-bats, 37 hits (.359) with three doubles, four triples, and three home runs.

WADE BOGGS (RED SOX, YANKEES, DEVIL RAYS—1982–1999)
Unlike Carew, Gwynn, and Brett, all of whom made The Show at a young age, Wade Boggs's path to the big leagues wasn't immediate. It almost didn't happen.

"I was told in the minor leagues that I'll never play third in the big leagues," Boggs once said. "That I don't hit for power so I'm not going to play in the big leagues. I'm not fast enough. I was told so many different things. The only thing I ever wanted to do was play professional baseball and, in the minors, I was getting paid to play so I didn't get discouraged."

When Boggs did make the Red Sox out of spring training in 1982, he still hadn't convinced manager Ralph Houk he could play. Through the end of June in his rookie year, the 24-year-old Boggs only appeared in 15 of the team's first 66 games and was hardly Boggs-esque, hitting just .258.

An injury to batting champion Carney Lansford gave Boggs his chance. For the rest of that season, he hit .358 and a career was born.

Before long, as Boggs started winning batting titles, we heard all about his quirks: eating chicken until further notice for every meal, doing his pregame running at 7:17 every single night, waking up at exactly the same time every day. He not only refused to strike out, he never tried to hit home runs. And he never would, sometimes to the frustration of his coaches. Noted baseball writer Tom Boswell, who'd closely followed Boggs's career, lent an ear to one of those coaches in a 1982 column.

"There's no question that Boggs hits the ball farther and harder than Jim Rice or Dwight Evans or Don Baylor," says the old pitching coach Bill Fischer," Boswell wrote then. "He has titanic power that he hasn't shown yet. But he will. He regularly hits the ball onto the roof in Chicago and into the waterfalls in Kansas City. He'll hit 10 home runs in one round of batting practice. He'd win any home run contest he ever entered."

Boswell was entranced. "How many homers could Boggs hit?" he asked. "As many as he wants," Fischer told him. Baylor agreed.

"He outdistances any of us," says Baylor, who slammed 330 career homers. "It's not close. He has great arm extension and he finishes very high—just like a golfer who hits it 300 yards. Look above his locker. Two pictures. One of extension, one of a high finish. Until you see it every day, you don't realize how strong he is. It seems like he can hit it as far as he wants to. Yet he never loses his form. His head isn't flying out like a pull hitter."

But Boggs never did come around as a home-run hitter. He finished with only 118 homers for his 18-year career, even though he did hit 24 home runs in the 1987 season, when he won the third of his four consecutive batting titles with a .363 average. He only hit double figures one more time, whacking 11 in the strike-shortened year of 1994 when he played in the New York Yankees' bandbox. With the current emphasis on power vs. strikeouts, you even wonder how much a team would value a Wade Boggs, even with a .328 career average.

Boggs was a fanatic about how he hit, even in batting practice. He had given a lot of thought to what happens once you get into that batter's box, a sacred place for him, and wasn't going to change, no matter what sorts of displays he showed in batting practice.

"Nobody can take a batting title away from me," he told Boswell in that column. "You don't vote for that. There are no (front-office) politics," Boggs says, tight-lipped under his red mustache. "You have to work hard for everything you get in this life, but you don't always get what you deserve. . . . If I'm obsessed with being the best, then it's because I don't want anybody to take anything away from me."

"Don't say luck doesn't matter," he told Boswell. "No matter how much you prepare, you can't eliminate luck. A perfect swing can be a line drive right at somebody and an imperfect swing can be a bloop hit. I had 12 diving catches made against me in one week early this year. Daryl Boston dove four rows into the seats to take a home run away from me. They're never even out—not even close. You lose far more hits than you get."

One thing Boggs could not do, for all his consistency, was hit Matt Young. A 6-foot-3 lefty with a career mark of 55–95, 4.40 for the Seattle Mariners and several other teams, hardly numbers that would trouble any major-league hitter, Boggs was hopeless against the guy.

He faced him 25 times over his career, managing just two hits (.080). In their first meeting in 1983 in the first inning of a Wednesday night game in Seattle, Young got Boggs to bounce to third. It was three years later in late April when Boggs ended an 0-for-10 streak off Young with an infield hit. It was another three years before he got his only other hit off Young, an RBI single to left in September. He had one last at-bat against Young the following year and was caught looking at a called third strike.

There were a few other AL starters from his time who were able to hold Boggs down. Bob Welch (5-for-36) held him to .139 and the trio of Chris Bosio (9-for-48), Scott Sanderson (6-for-32) and Greg Swindell (6-for-32) held him to .188. Hall of Famer Don Sutton, a noted curveballer, held Boggs (7-for-34) to .206. He hit just about every-body else.

He hit .450 against Cy Young winner Bret Saberhagen and batted over .400 against a slew of different arms—Jim Clancy (.450), Walt Ter-rell (.433), Scott Bankhead (.429), Mike Flanagan (.424), Charlie Lei-brandt (.418), Tim Belcher (.410), and Kenny Rogers (.405). In batting .366 against Oakland's ace Dave Stewart, he also reached him for four homers, the most Boggs hit off any pitcher.

Boggs got his 3,000th hit in a manner that would have pleased his old coach Bill Fischer. Playing for the Tampa Bay Devil Rays, Boggs slugged a home run off Cleveland's Chris Haney and when he reached home plate, Boggs bent down and gave it a kiss.

He played just 10 more major-league games, had 10 more hits, and retired at the end of August.

Interestingly, Boggs's seasonal average had dipped to .294 in late August. But a 3-for-3 performance on August 25 got him back over .300. He got two more hits the next day but closed out his career on August 27 with an 0-for-3, walking in his final at-bat. It was a close call but his final numbers for his final season—.301.

TONY GWYNN (PADRES, 1982–2001)

"Sometimes hitters can pick up differences in spin," Hall of Fame hurler Greg Maddux explained one day. "They can identify pitches if there are different release points or if a curveball starts with an upward hump as it leaves the pitcher's hand. But if a pitcher can change speeds, every hitter is helpless, limited by human vision."

Then, thinking of some particularly difficult moments in an other-wise extraordinary career, he thought of one exception. With an adjectival expletive, which will be justified momentarily.

"Except," Maddux said, "for that (expletive) Tony Gwynn."

Maddux, the winner of 355 major-league games earning four consec-utive Cy Young Awards and 18 Gold Gloves, a pitcher who established himself as the winningest pitcher in the modern era after Warren Spahn's 363 victories, had one batter that was his Rubik's Cube. That was San Diego's Tony Gwynn.

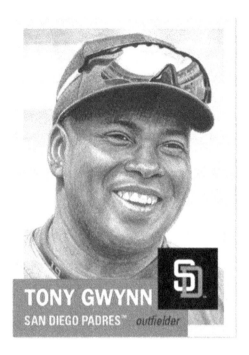

TONY GWYNN
SAN DIEGO PADRES™ *outfielder*

Gwynn faced Maddux more than any other pitcher in Gwynn's 20-year career, 103 plate appearances. And Gwynn didn't mind those at-bats one bit, batting .429 against this pitcher who seemed to be able to bring the rest of baseball to its knees. Facing Maddux, Gwynn went 39-for-91 with eight doubles and one triple. And if that wasn't humiliating enough for the masterful Maddux, check this out. The great Maddux, who collected 3,371 whiffs in his career, could not strike Gwynn out even once. Not one time. No wonder he resorted to profanity.

In an odd way, Tony Gwynn was not threatening in the same way Luis Tiant, on the pitching side of things, wasn't difficult to face. Reggie Jackson once called Tiant "the Fred Astaire of baseball. It's a comfortable 0-for-4." Gwynn was the kind of hitter that went 3-for-4 and you didn't worry about it later on. That's just who he was.

Gwynn, a husky left-handed hitter who grew even huskier as his career continued, just had that quick bat, shooting baseballs through holes where infielders couldn't reach or where they used to be. You didn't worry about him hitting a home run, even all that many extra-base hits.

But he was always on base, always finding a way to get the ball by those poor infielders.

Witnessing a Gwynn 5-for-5 was a master class in Wee Willie Keeler's old dictum, "Hit 'em where they ain't." Except when Wee Willie said it, they had gloves about the size of an individual pepperoni pizza or smaller and had no idea of what a shift was. He probably had plenty of places to shoot for.

In the modern era, shifts were just pointless to stop Gwynn. He somehow found a way to get the ball through the infield better than any other National Leaguer, going all the way back to Stan Musial.

But even so, there were six pitchers who were able to handle him. Omar Olivares held him to a .120 average (3-for-25). Lefties Denny Neagle (7-for-36, .194) and Shane Rawley (4-for-22, .182) were tough on him. He had minimal success against José DeLeón (7-for-35, .200), John Smiley (8-for-39, .205), and Mario Soto (7-for-33, .212).

His biggest challenge, though, was saved for someone you likely haven't heard of, unless you were a member of his immediate family.

A hard-throwing, diminutive lefty named Frank DiPino allowed the great Tony Gwynn but one hit. One. Tony faced him 23 times, earned one walk, one sac fly, and one sac bunt (Gwynn sac bunting??). He was 1-for-20, .050. Imagine that.

DiPino was with the Cubs in 1988 and brought in from the bullpen to face Gwynn. He got Tony to hit a weak flyout to left. He faced him again two nights later with two outs and a runner on, but he got him to fly out again. He even got a win against the Padres that year, whiffing Gwynn in an extra-inning game. DiPino pitched for three different teams: Houston, where he held Gwynn to 0-for-5, then 1-for-8 as a Cub, and 0-for-7 for the Cardinals. Just amazing.

Now, keep in mind that Gwynn hit .343 at home, .334 in other ballparks, .342 before the All-Star break, .334 afterwards, .375 when he swung at the first pitch, .351 with a full count on him. With two strikes, he batted .302. Yes, .302 with two strikes on him. Wow.

One thing about modern pitching staffs: Collectively they almost always can find a way to slow a guy down, especially with two strikes on a hitter. You don't see guys winning multiple batting titles anymore.

Gwynn's extraordinary success was something to see. They couldn't figure a way to get him out.

After winning his first batting title in 1984 (.351), Tony ran off three batting crowns in a row—'87-'88-'89—(.370, .313, .336). After four interlopers captured the next four NL crowns—Willie McGee rapped out a .335 average for the Cardinals in 1990 before being traded to Oakland late in the season, switch-hitting Terry Pendleton's .319 won the 1991 title, Gary Sheffield's quick bat took the 1992 title with a .330 and Andres Galarraga took advantage of the thin Colorado air to bat .370 in 1993—Gwynn took over.

For the next four seasons, 1994 to 1997, Gwynn set the pace for NL batters with batting averages that were impressive—.394, .368, .353, and .372.

As terrific as those achievements were, Gwynn's strikeouts—or lack of them—were astonishing. Imagine playing *an entire season* with whiff numbers like these: 19, 16, 19, 19, 15, 17, 28 (Tony's one slip-up), 18, 14. These were Gwynn's numbers from 1991 to 1999. Now that's bat control.

In an era where the strikeout is increasingly and discouragingly common, Gwynn was not that guy. He just didn't whiff very often. Nolan Ryan got him the most of any pitcher with 9 strikeouts, but he still hit .300 against him.

One more thing. Other than General William Tecumseh Sherman, Gwynn might have been the most unpopular individual in the history of Atlanta, as he terrorized what the rest of baseball considered as the finest pitching staff assembled in modern times. Gwynn rapped around three Hall of Famers—John Smoltz, Tom Glavine, and Maddux—like they were also-rans. He hit .462 against Smoltz, .312 against Glavine, .429 against Maddux, .357 against Steve Avery, hitting .352 for his overall career against the best pitching staff of modern times, a full 24 points above his career average of .328. That's impressive.

Gwynn hit even better against the Houston Astros (.355), the Mets (.356), and the good ol' Colorado Rockies (.379!).

Besides manhandling Braves pitchers, some of the other guys who felt Maddux's pain were Jeff Brantley (.571), Don Carman (.485), Doug

Drabek (.469), Mark Gardner (.444), Ron Darling (.441), Bobby Jones (.426), Ted Power (.424), and Pete Schourek (.412).

Against other Hall of Famers, Gwynn faced seven of them aside from the Braves. He batted over .300 against Ryan (.302) and Pedro Martínez (.314) and in minimal at-bats, did great against Dennis Eckersley (6-for-14, .429)

Gwynn did show some signs of respect for his elders, catching some Hall of Famers at the end of their careers—Tom Seaver (3-for-14, .214), Phil Niekro (3-for-15, .200), Steve Carlton (5-for-21, .238), and Don Sutton (2-for-12, .167). Gwynn's consistency with everyone else was unshakeable.

Oddly enough, as good as he was, his older brother Mike did a much better job holding Gwynn down. Mike Maddux held Gwynn to a .250 (4-for-16) average. But before the older Maddux gets too carried away, keep in mind that in his last seven at-bats, Gwynn managed three walks, a bunt single, a double, and a home run against just one groundout. It might be a good thing that he stopped pitching to Gwynn when he did.

And for Greg Maddux, well, there were signs that he, too, was finally figuring the guy out, long after the damage had been done. Facing Gwynn at the end of his career, Maddux got him on a groundout and two flyballs the final three times he faced him. He might have said something to him—we don't know for sure. What we do know is those three consecutive outs lowered Gwynn's career average against the Hall of Famer from .438 to a more respectable .429. You can bet Greg Maddux is still ticked off about it.

GEORGE BRETT (ROYALS, 1973–1993)

As we have seen, even the greatest of hitters have one or two or three pitchers that they cannot—for whatever reason—hit. At the same time, we recognize the difficulty for even the finest major-league hitters to put up magisterial, outrageous batting averages against *any* big-league hurler. After all, there are four infielders and three outfielders ready to track down any ball hit their way. Consequently, it's rare but you might see someone hit .400 or so; in a fluke circumstance, you might even see them approach .500.

Then we come to the case of former New York Yankee Ed Figueroa, a former 20-game and 19-game winner with a 80–67 lifetime record, a successful, established major-league hurler. Except when he faced George Howard Brett.

The sweet-swinging Brett stepped into the left-handed batter's box 45 times against Figueroa, probably with a smile on his face. In 41 at-bats, Brett collected—get this—25 hits! Yes, math whizzes, that's a .610 batting average. Higher than any mano-a-mano stat we've run across in our unofficial survey. And incredibly, almost half of those hits came in his first 14 at-bats against the guy in 1975! Yes, 12 hits in his first 14 at-bats—an .857 average. Wow.

Over the next four years, Figueroa calmed things down a bit, holding Brett to 6-for-18, a .333 average when he won 19, 16, and 20 games for the Yankees. But in his final year against Figueroa (1980), Brett's at-bats went like this: single, walk, single, flyout, double, single, single, home run, groundout, double.

Brett's older brother Ken, a fine hitter himself, had himself a decent major-league career as a much-traveled left-handed pitcher. His little brother, well, he was a Hall of Famer. He could flat-out hit.

"Lots of hitters look to swing in zones, but I just look for the ball," George Brett said once. "My home runs come as a result of good fundamentals, not because I'm trying to hit a home run. I just try to hit the ball hard, not far. If you try to hit it far, you take a long swing that messes you up. But if you just try to hit it hard, your swing's got to be quick. And that's what you want, a quick swing."

Brett was a disciple of a hitting guru named Charley Lau, who was not worth a damn as a player himself but became a much-lauded hitting instructor. Brett bought in.

As Dave Anderson of the *New York Times* noted while interviewing Brett, Lau's advice was never far away.

"On the shelf in his locker is a videotape entitled 'The Art of Hitting .300,' a visual adaptation of Charlie Lau's book on batting technique. Charlie Lau was the Royals' batting coach during George Brett's first few seasons, then he was hired by the Yankees and later the Chicago White Sox before he died early last year of cancer.

"I look at the tape every so often,' George Brett said. 'It refreshes your memory about certain things, certain fundamentals. You see Charlie and his smiling face, and it just reminds me of all the times we were together. The last time I looked at it was back in August, when I wasn't swinging right. It straightened me out.'"

Compared with the three other lefty Hall of Famers, it's fair to say Brett was the most dangerous. He hit 317 home runs, as many as 30 in a season. He hit 665 doubles, as many as 45 in a season. He hit 137 triples, as many as 20 in a season (1979), the most in baseball in decades (excepting Willie Wilson's 21 in 1985). As noted earlier, Brett won batting titles in three separate decades, had a .305 lifetime average, won a Gold Glove and an MVP, one of baseball's greatest all-time third basemen.

But as with everyone else, Brett had some pitchers who he struggled with. And perhaps surprisingly, they weren't all lefties. In fact, the pitchers who put up the best numbers against him were righties Mike Mussina (3-for-24, .125), Allan Anderson (4-for-28, .143), Steve Hargan (4–27, .148), and Eric Plunk (3–20, .150). Next were Kevin Tapani (4–26, .154) and Mike Norris (6–38, .158), both righties.

Some lefties, naturally, were in there—John Cerutti (4–26, .154), Geoff Zahn (10–53, .189), and Mark Langston (9–47, .191). Three other AL starters did a good job with him, Greg Swindell (6–29, .207), Scott McGregor (12–54, .222), and Dave Stieb (16–71, .225).

But there were plenty of top-line pitchers that Brett wore out: Mike Smithson (.553), Jim Abbott (.531), Jon Matlack (.455), Kevin Brown (.455), Bill Singer (.438), Jim Clancy (.436), Matt Young (.429), Dave Goltz (.419), Lary Sorensen (.419), and Danny Darwin (.406).

He hit six homers off Dan Petry, five homers off Jack Morris (.330), Frank Tanana (.302), Jim Clancy, Floyd Bannister (.348), and Ron Guidry (.321). Playing at a time when the crop of starting pitchers was perhaps the finest in baseball history, Brett faced 15 different Hall of Famers. His numbers were pretty impressive against them, too.

Brett vs. Hall of Famers

Tom Seaver .389

Jim Kaat .344

Jim Palmer .342

Jack Morris .330

Dennis Eckersley .328

Phil Niekro .304

Don Sutton .296

Gaylord Perry .293

Nolan Ryan .287

Roger Clemens .284

Rollie Fingers .273

Catfish Hunter .271

Ferguson Jenkins .268

Bert Blyleven .231

Mike Mussina .125

When you think about George Brett these days, the moment that everybody seems to remember is the Pine Tar Game. It happened on July 24, 1983. There were two outs in the ninth, the Yankees holding a 4–3 lead, when tempestuous manager Billy Martin called in Rich "Goose" Gossage to try to get that last out—George Brett.

Gossage threw, Brett swung, and the ball soared over the 353 marker midway into the right field seats to give the Royals a 5–4 lead. Within seconds, Martin charged out from the dugout, charging at home plate umpire Tim McClelland, claiming that Brett had too much pine tar above the trademark on his bat, claiming that the home run shouldn't count. The umpires gathered, examining the bat, even measuring the bat on home plate before McClelland turned to the Royals dugout and called Brett out.

Brett came charging out of the dugout as if launched from a cannon, immediately got into McClelland's face, and both benches emptied. It was the kind of thing Billy Martin would go to bed dreaming about.

But it was a pyrrhic victory for the Yankees. American League president Lee MacPhail ruled that the home run counted, that the game would be resumed. Martin, of course, protested, even sent an assortment of players out in unfamiliar positions (Ron Guidry in center field?) and the resumption lasted just 10 minutes. The Royals won, 5–4.

What nobody remembers—except maybe Gossage and Brett—is the *next* time he faced Gossage, April 8, 1992—nine years later, Gossage pitching for the A's, trying to protect a 3–2 lead. George Brett homered again.

This time, nobody said a word about pine tar. Or if they did, they said it with a smile.

CHAPTER EIGHTEEN

Two You Might Not Know:
Al Simmons and Harry Heilmann

IN THE PROCESS OF RESEARCHING THIS BOOK AND WANDERING BACK through box scores from the early days of the game, the lifetime numbers of a couple of players kept popping up—Al Simmons and Harry Heilmann—players you've heard of but honestly, probably didn't know a lot about.

Both are Hall of Fame players, and both certainly made their mark on the game. But it's also fair to say that compared with their peers from their playing days, they aren't talked about at all.

One of them won four batting titles, one more than George Brett, including one that he won with a six-hit performance in an end-of-the-season doubleheader, just like Ted Williams did to much more acclaim years later. In another end-of-the-season doubleheader, he had *seven* hits to win *another* batting title and come within one at-bat of hitting .400 again. But you've hardly ever heard of the guy.

The other won two batting titles, contended for several, and left the game fifth on the game's all-time home-run list after stubbornly refusing to officially, completely, utterly retire. You almost had to laugh when you looked at Simmons's record—a remarkable five-year span where this guy played in 102 games, then 37, then only nine, then 40, then took a year off then played four more games. No other player had as long a goodbye as Al Simmons.

There seems to be a connection between Simmons and Heilmann. They even competed against one another in the American League batting race, and each one entered the Hall of Fame long after they should have.

Fame is a funny thing. Some players, extraordinary in their time, just aren't noticed. Al Simmons and Harry Heilmann both played in a time of high batting averages, true. They were stars at the same time there were other players you couldn't ignore, like Babe Ruth and Ty Cobb and Lou Gehrig. No matter how well they did, somehow, *their* stories were mostly forgotten, overlooked, lost in time. It seemed like a good idea to take a look at the twists and turns of their careers, how they compared to some of the all-time greats. Perhaps in doing that, we'll see Al Simmons and Harry Heilmann in a more accurate light and understand why, unlike some of their contemporaries, nobody ever said much about them, then or now.

AL SIMMONS (ATHLETICS, TIGERS, RED SOX, SENATORS, 1924–1944)

There is no particular reason that being able to strike a baseball with unusual consistency should have a negative impact on your personality. One of the game's greatest hitters, Stan Musial of the St. Louis Cardinals, was as warm and as heartening a soul as ever suited up. The same goes for heroes like Babe Ruth and Lou Gehrig and Hank Aaron, men who seemed as genuine and approachable as any all-time great. Even Willie Mays, before he got old and grouchy, seemed to bubble with enthusiasm and joy as long as you caught him in a baseball uniform.

There were also those irascible ones, guys who could really swing it but weren't exactly known for their diplomacy—guys like Ty Cobb, Ted Williams, Rogers Hornsby, Barry Bonds, Albert Belle, Dick Allen . . . we could go on. And there is another guy who always seems to be forgotten in either category—that of being a great hitter and also of being a legendarily disagreeable sort. Al "Bucketfoot" Simmons ought to make the cut in both cases.

A career .334 hitter, those final numbers were dimmed by diminishing returns on his five seasons hanging on as a part-time coach / pinch-hitter (he hit just .230 during that time). Simmons finished with 2,927 hits,

307 homers, 539 doubles, and spent the 14 years of his after-game life (he died of a heart attack at age 56) grousing about many things, including not collecting 3,000 hits, something he felt—maybe correctly—would have given him the notoriety and acclaim he never received.

When he finally hung them up, Simmons ranked high in most of the major career records for right-handed batters, third in RBIs with 1,825 behind Rogers Hornsby and Cap Anson, second with 307 home runs behind former teammate Jimmie Foxx.

As he left the game, he trailed only Babe Ruth (714), Jimmie Foxx (527), Mel Ott (510), and Lou Gehrig (493) on the all-time home-run list. With his 307 round-trippers, he was six home runs ahead of Rogers Hornsby (301). Chances are you've heard of all of those other guys. Not Al.

If you *have* heard about Simmons, the one thing you probably know is how he strayed from traditionally taught baseball hitting techniques at the plate. On the pitch, Simmons's left or front leg would take a step in the direction of third base, or "bailing out" in hardball terminology. Just as Mel Ott had that very unusual style of lifting his right leg (he was a left-handed hitter) before the pitch, Simmons defied orthodoxy. Amazingly, coaches at that time were either smart enough—or fearful enough—to avoid suggesting any change. They let Al and Mel swing away and were glad they did. As Hall of Fame hurler Ted Lyons said, "When Simmons was at his peak, you couldn't do anything with him. If you tried to waste a ball on him, he would reach out and hit it for two bases."

With all his success, he was never pleasant about it. Any of it. Years after one of his retirements, Simmons and former teammate Jimmy Dykes sat down with the *New York Times'* Arthur Daley and the conversation drifted to their former manager Connie Mack, who had some unusual strategies for motivating his hitters, including him. Daley, who was really good at this sort of thing, listens and then relates the conversation in his column.

Daley wrote: "How about the time you were in a slump," said Dykes, "and every guy on the team was pulling for you so hard the whole club goes to pot? So Mister Mack asks you—politely of course,—if you'd

Al Simmons
WIKIMEDIA COMMONS

object if he has us ride you for a change. So every time you go up to the plate, we holler 'Strike out, yah bum.'"

"It worked, didn't it?" asked Simmons, proudly. "But I'll never forget the time I came back to the bench grumbling. I hadn't gotten a loud foul and I'm screaming about the lousy background. 'How can a guy be expected to hit against that sort of background," I yelled.

"'By golly, Al,' Mister Mack says to me, very stern-like. 'Don't ever say a thing like that as long as you live. If you're going to react that way about the background, and you're a .350 hitter, what do you think the effect is going to be on the .275 and .250 hitters?' Do you know what? I never forgot that. When I'm coaching on third base and hitter begins to beef about the background I just holler 'shuddup.'"

Sportswriters of the time must have taken a liking to the guy and vice versa. You could see that from an earlier column where the *New York Times*' John Kieran caught up with Simmons when he was struggling. Al opened up immediately.

"Me? I'm just a bowl of applesauce right now, said Al," Kieran wrote, probably chuckling as he typed it. "But I'll get going. I won't be satisfied until I'm hitting .350 at least. Say, those scorers have taken away a dozen blows from me. On the level! Just when I needed 'em, too, for the first time in eight years. Gr-r-umph."

Early on, Simmons got some expert instruction from a guy who knew a little bit about hitting—Ty Cobb. Connie Mack actually asked Cobb to room with Simmons on the road. Imagine what those conversations must have been like. But Simmons did learn.

A's infielder Jimmy Dykes remembered listening in on one of those sessions. "Cobb is showing him how to hit lefthanders. He's telling Al to get up on the plate against them. So Al is telling me 'The next day, we're facing a lefty and I get up on the plate and go three for four. After the game, I'm sitting in front of my locker all smiles. Cobb comes by, looks at me, and says 'Well, rockhead, you're finally learning, aren't you?'"

Don't those little excerpts give you a fair idea of what daily life was like within earshot of Al Simmons? Imagine sitting next to him on the bench after a lineout?

Simmons once explained his hitting philosophy this way to Kieran. "There's no reason to be friendly with a pitcher who's trying to take your bread and butter away from you. You're going to get paid off on what you hit, and those pitchers are trying to give you the works all the time. I never had any sympathy for a pitcher." The pitcher, he explained, always had the edge. "He always knows what he's going to throw, and you don't. All you have is a round bat that you're supposed to hit with. They give you that big herky-jerky motion and stall around and try to get you off stride and play you for a chump. How are you going to feel friendly toward guys like that?"

Simmons was the quickest player ever to achieve 2,000 hits, doing it in 1,390 games. But he fell just short of 3,000. Even though he hung around, served as a player-coach off and on for five seasons—Connie Mack brought him back to the Athletics in 1940 with the express purpose of giving him a chance to get to 3,000—it never worked out. He was 73 hits short when he died, just a few days past his 54th birthday.

"If I'd ever imagined I could get as close as this," he told the *Times'* Red Smith. "3,000 hits would have been easy. When I think of the days I goofed off, the times I played sick or something and took myself out of the lineup because the game didn't mean anything, I could cut my throat. When I finally decided I had it made, I was never again the ballplayer I was when I was hungry. The only man I ever knew who never lost his fire when he got rich was Ty Cobb." Simmons was voted into the Baseball Hall of Fame in 1953. He died three years later.

After Simmons had passed, Daley described what it was like to watch him take that awkward but irrepressible swing. "Unquestionably, Simmons was the worst looking of all the top hitters," Daley wrote. "His style was atrocious. He hit with his 'foot-in-the-bucket.' That meant he didn't step into the pitch with his forward foot, the left one. Instead, he stabbed his foot toward third base. Although this violated every proper concept of the batting art, big Al somehow contrived to level off beautifully over the plate with wrists, arms and shoulders."

He grounded into a fielder's choice against Detroit's Boom Boom Beck in his final major-league at-bat on July 1, 1944, after collecting a pair of infield hits earlier, leaving him 73 short of that magical 3,000.

Could the guy hit? You bet: .458 vs. Ed Walsh, .425 vs. Hank Johnson, .414 vs. Rube Walberg, .408 vs. Urban Shocker, .407 vs. Earl Whitehill, .404 vs. Sad Sam Jones, .422 vs. Sam Gray. Facing some Hall of Famers, Simmons showed his mettle, batting .436 vs. Lefty Grove, .367 against Ted Lyons, .336 against Lefty Gomez, and .324 against Walter Johnson.

While Simmons wasn't a huge home-run guy, never hitting more than 36 in a season and only hitting over 30 three times in his career, he did spread his homers around, clearing the bases eight times against Whitehill and Hank Johnson, hitting seven homers against Willis Hudlin, General Crowder, Milt Gaston, George Blaeholder, and George Pipgras.

For his career, Simmons hit .369 against lefties, .325 against right-handers, and his career average hitting in the cleanup spot was .350; with two outs, he hit .329, with two outs and runners in scoring position, he hit .345. The guy won two batting titles, collected over 200 hits in a season six times. And get this, imagine getting 253 hits in a season, you hit .387 and you finish *third!*

The winner of the title that year, well, that is the other guy we're talking about in this chapter, Detroit's amazing Harry Heilmann, who hit .393 to win that 1925 batting crown.

Harry Heilmann (Tigers, Reds 1914–1932)

The most famous end-of-the-season doubleheader batting performance belongs, of course, to Boston's great Ted Williams, closing out the 1941 season. Williams came into that final twinbill against the Philadelphia A's with a .3995 average, which would have rounded up to an even .400 had Williams chosen to sit it out. He did not, collected six hits in eight at-bats, and wound up with a .406 average, the last major leaguer to bat .400 for a season.

Another infamous final-day doubleheader involved someone who didn't play, someone who did, and some hanky-panky that has become legendary over the years. In 1910, Cleveland's Napoleon Lajoie, one of the AL's top hitters, seemed well on his way to a batting title, leading Detroit's Ty Cobb by 30 points at midseason. Lajoie had his eyes on a brand-new car, the Chalmers 30, which the Detroit auto maker had promised to award to the league's leading batter that season.

Cobb, chasing a fourth straight title, found a way to catch up to Lajoie as the year wound down. Heading into the final day, Cobb led .383 to .376. Thinking he had the car in hand, Cobb chose to sit out the final games. Lajoie was in St. Louis, facing the lowly Browns in a doubleheader, trailing by seven points. That's a lot of points to make up in a couple of games.

But the players all knew about the car, about Cobb's lead, and some believe there was a plot to help Lajoie. As the doubleheader began, Lajoie tripled in his first at-bat and when he got to third, something seemed to change. When he came up for his second at-bat, Browns third baseman Red Corriden, following manager Jack O'Connor's directions, played back, almost in left field. It was suggested (wink) to Lajoie that he simply bunt toward third for an easy hit. He did. Then he did it again. And again. And again. Six more times in all.

With eight hits in his final eight at-bats in the twinbill (check the box score!), Lajoie's batting average climbed to .3841, ahead of Cobb's .383 which *should* have given him the car and the batting crown. It didn't.

The controversy drew the interest of the American League office and ultimately, the batting crown was awarded to Cobb by AL president Ban Johnson. It was later suggested that Cobb had a game counted twice, giving him a narrow edge over Lajoie. In any event, the Chalmers company awarded cars to both men. And nobody has ever suggested that Lajoie's hits shouldn't count. Should they?

Which brings us to a third end-of-the-season doubleheader batting race controversy, one you likely *haven't* heard of. It was October 4, 1925, and four individuals went into the final day with designs on the American League batting crown.

Back on August 20, Cleveland's Hall of Fame player-manager Tris Speaker had a 15-point lead over runner-up Detroit's Harry Heilmann .391 to .376. But as the season wound down, Heilmann caught fire, batting .541 from September 13 on, lifting himself into batting title contention.

With his eyes on a second AL batting crown, Speaker pretty much took himself out of his lineup, only taking seven at-bats down the stretch. That dipped him to .389. He decided to sit out the season finale in Chicago just as Cobb had done in 1910, freezing his average.

The day before, Philadelphia's Al Simmons had three hits in his first three at-bats to climb up to .389, a flat-footed tie with Speaker. But then

Simmons fouled out and hit into a double play in his next two at-bats, winding up his season at .387.

As the final day began, Speaker was still ahead, .389 to Simmons's .387. Heilmann was in between, starting the day at .388.

In game one of the Browns-Tigers doubleheader on October 4, Harry Heilmann went 3-for-6, lifting him to .389, tying him with Speaker for the batting race lead. Ty Cobb, also in striking distance, went 4-for-6 in that game, raising his average to .377. And Cobb did have a shot—if he went 6-for-6 in both games, Cobb would have hit .390 and won himself a 13th batting title.

In game two, like Ted Williams would 16 years later, Heilmann would step up, going 3-for-3 to raise his season average to .392, two points ahead of Speaker and three ahead of Simmons to clinch his third batting title. Cobb wound up at .378.

There's hardly a baseball fan out there who *doesn't* know about Ted Williams collecting six hits on the final day to hit .400. Harry Heilmann did the same damn thing to win a batting title, just seven points from what would have been his second .400 season. In 1927, he did it again, coming into the end-of-the-season twinbill at .391, a point behind Philadelphia's Al Simmons.

Heilmann went 7-for-9 that day, raising his average to .398, rapping into a double play in his final at-bat of the season. A hit would have brought him to an even .400. Simmons, by the way, went 2-for-5 and wound up at .392. Another near-miss for Al on the final day.

Heilmann, like Simmons a right-handed hitter, was remarkably consistent, hitting .350 against righties, .353 against lefties, a line-drive hitter who took advantage of gaps to hit lots of doubles and triples. Look at these numbers against some of the game's great Hall of Famers—Lefty Grove (.425), Walter Johnson (.327), Waite Hoyt (.397), Ted Lyons (.338).

Against some of his other contemporaries, Heilmann was a tough out. Look at these averages: vs. Bump Hadley (.500), Dutch Ruether (.472), Rollie Naylor (. 467), Guy Morton (.465), Dickie Kerr (.429), Jim Bagby (.429), Hollis Thurston (.413), and Howard Ehmke (.405).

He wound up with 542 career doubles, more than Rogers Hornsby, Ted Williams, Frank Robinson, Willie Mays, Ken Griffey Jr., and Lou

Harry Heilmann
WIKIMEDIA COMMONS

Gehrig. He hit 151 triples, more than Mays, Pete Rose, Joe DiMaggio, and Jimmie Foxx. He hit 13 doubles off George Uhle (.393) and Stan Coveleski (.394) and seven triples off Sad Sam Jones (.324.)

Some years later, Heilmann told a remarkable story about how his baseball career began. H. G. Salsinger did a series for the *Detroit News* and included Heilmann's tale.

"If I had not forgotten my topcoat one Saturday noon I would never have become a ballplayer and would probably still be earning my living as a bookkeeper out in California . . . I flunked badly in mathematics and failed to make the varsity baseball team, although I finally got on the roster as a sub," Heilmann wrote.

"After leaving school, I got a job as a bookkeeper with the Mutual Biscuit Co. of San Francisco in 1913. The plant closed at noon on Saturdays and employees were given a half-holiday. On the particular Saturday noon that I mention, I hurried away at the stroke of 12, but after walking a few blocks, remembered that I had left my topcoat in the office and returned to get it. Just as I was leaving the office a second time, carrying my topcoat, I bumped into Jim Riordan, who had been varsity catcher at Sacred Heart college and who was now managing the Hanford team in the San Joaquin Valley League. He told me: 'I was just coming in to see you. I want you to play third base for Hanford. Our third sacker was taken suddenly ill this morning and we've got a game with Bakersfield tomorrow and there's no substitute.'

"I told him that I had never played third base in my life, but he brushed this aside . . . Riordan got me a uniform, told me he would pay me $10 and expenses and I made my debut as a third sacker.

"Luck was with me. The game went 11 innings and I didn't have a fielding chance. I came to bat in the eleventh with two runners on the bases and the score 2-all. I knocked the ball between the left and center fielders, drove in two runs and won the game for Hanford, 4–2.

"The Hanford rooters tossed bills and coins onto to the field and after I got through collecting the contributions, I counted $150. That, along with the $10 that Riordan handed me was more money than I could have made in a month by keeping books.

"Jim Richardson . . . attended the game, scouting for Portland. The next day he called at our house and offered me a contract. He talked me into signing it and rewarded me with a spaghetti dinner as a bonus. I have often thought of that spaghetti dinner in recent years reading about sandlotters and high school boys being paid anywhere from $15,000 to $75,000 for signing contracts."

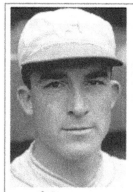

Al Simmons   Harry Heilmann

	Overall Stats	
68.3	WAR	72.2
2215	G	2147
9520	PA	8972
2927	H	2660
307	HR	183
1828	RBI	1543
88	SB	113
.334	BA	.342
.380	OBP	.410
.535	SLG	.520
.915	OPS	.930
133	OPS+	148
	Awards & Honors	
✓	Hall of Fame	✓
2	Championships	
3	All-Star	
2	Batting Title	4

Two years later, he was in the major leagues with the Detroit Tigers and was a mainstay for those Tigers through 1929, consistently batting over .300 and winning four different batting crowns. But as his career wound down, he began to have trouble with arthritis in his wrists. In 1930, the Tigers sold him to the Cincinnati Reds and after playing one fine season with Cincinnati (.333, 19 HR, 91 RBIs) battling wrist injuries, he retired.

After a year off, Heilmann tried to come back in 1932 but his comeback lasted just 15 games. His final at-bat was a popout to first in the eighth inning against Pittsburgh's Larry French in a 4–1 Memorial Day loss to the Pittsburgh Pirates.

In 1934, he took a turn in the broadcast booth, one of the first former players to do so and became a popular broadcaster, doing Detroit Tiger games. Nicknamed "Slug" for his hitting ability *and* his lack of speed, Heilmann made a name for himself as a broadcaster. He was nominated for the Ford Frick Award for his baseball announcing in 2019 and was a finalist but didn't win.

Sadly, the guy who always seemed to be overlooked got the same treatment when it came to Cooperstown. He was elected to the Baseball Hall of Fame in 1952, a year before Al Simmons. It was also a year *after* his death.

Chapter Nineteen

A Former Big Leaguer
Takes a Long Look Back

Just called up from Triple-A Minneapolis after a couple of seasons in the minors, Boston Red Sox outfielder Jim Gosger was set to lead off the second inning at Boston's Fenway Park in the season's final game on October 3, 1965. On the mound was New York Yankees starter Whitey Ford, a future Hall of Famer. As any rookie might, Gosger turned to Boston's number seven hitter, veteran Eddie Bressoud, in the manner of a professional consultation.

"What should I look for, Eddie?" Gosger asked, hoping the vet would offer some helpful advice, as the rookie stepped in to face one of the game's great pitchers.

"Look for the ball, Jimmy," was the only tip Bressoud was able to offer. To some degree, comparatively speaking, that was the extent of pregame preparations for big-league batters in that era of baseball.

Jim Gosger, a journeyman outfielder for a half-dozen teams between 1963 and 1972, was one of the most colorful characters in Jim Bouton's wonderful *Ball Four*, which documented the initial season of the Seattle Pilots, a baseball expansion team. I read the entire book on Christmas Eve the year the book came out. I remember my parents rapping on the ceiling to get me to stop laughing and go to sleep. The book is that good. Gosger is one of the more entertaining participants.

Like the character in Woody Allen's film *Zelig* who always seemed to pop up in places you wouldn't expect, Gosger found himself in the middle of some notable baseball moments.

In 1968, he was stationed out in left field when Willie Horton hit a ball over his head to help Denny McLain win his 30th game of the season on national TV. He was the last man to face the great Satchel Paige, who was summoned to pitch for the Kansas City A's against the Red Sox at age 59. Gosger faced him twice and went 0-for-2.

As mentioned earlier, Gosger got to spend a rollicking season with the Seattle Pilots, a baseball expansion team immortalized in *Ball Four*. In that book, a genuine inside look at the life of a professional baseball player, Gosger had some of the most colorful moments. Here he was, hiding in a closet watching his roommate frolic with a stewardess. When he heard the stewardess say "Oh, I've never done it that way before," Gosger couldn't help himself. He stuck his head out of the closet and drawled a line that was to become a watchword around the clubhouse—"Yeah, surrrrrrre." (I later found out from Gosger the teammate was Tony Conigliaro.)

Gosger also had a tart response to author Bouton himself after getting one of the two hits he managed off the Yankee right-hander. After a line single, Gosger was standing on first base whereupon Bouton, clearly annoyed, looked over at him and said "Why are you hitting me? You're not good enough." Gosger's snappy response was perfect. "I don't know how you get anybody out with that shit you throw."

Later in that season, upon learning he was being sent back to the minors, it was Gosger's lamentable phrase in the clubhouse that rang true. "You know, I didn't think I was that bad a ballplayer," he said, "but they're making a believer out of me."

With great humor, a crackling memory, and a career that took him into major-league batter's boxes against 14 different Hall of Fame pitchers, a chat with Gosger seemed a good way to close out *Diamond Duels* and also, by looking back, a fun way to sum up the way the game has changed in the years since.

I met Gosger during my days as the executive sports editor of the *Port Huron Times Herald*. When baseball ended, he returned to his hometown, worked for the city, and spent a lot of off-hours officiating high school sports. After some cajoling, I was able to bring him to his first major-league game in more than a decade at Tiger Stadium. He was bitter about the game after the New York Mets had cut him loose years earlier.

You might remember Gosger briefly made the news a couple years ago when the Mets, celebrating members of their championship 1969 team, goofed and announced that he was dead. Like Mark Twain, news of Gosger's death was greatly exaggerated, too.

Back when we were headed to Tiger Stadium, he was apprehensive. He hadn't seen a big-league game in person since he had played in one. He was fairly quiet on the ride down, thinking about all the brutal twists and turns of the professional game, all the travel, the trades, the releases, the abrupt ending of it all.

But the moment we set foot inside Tiger Stadium, Gosger left my side and dashed toward the right field rail. "I've gotta see the field," he said, leaving me behind. In a matter of moments when I caught up with him, here was Tom Seaver, broadcasting the game for the Yankees, calling up to his old teammate as he stood next to the Yankees bullpen, chatting with bullpen coach Billy Connors. All of a sudden, Jim Gosger was back in the game.

As the previous chapters I hope have made clear, the game has evolved in a way that nobody could have imagined. Not only is there now video available of every single pitch that night's starter or reliever has ever thrown, there are sites—one of them called "Baseball Savant"—where the actual movement of each pitcher's individual pitch is graphed, sort of like a radar tracking device. Yes, every pitch is monitored. Over a pitcher's entire career.

It is a staggering amount of detail. While it is true the actual number of pitches a hurler will throw in a particular game has been reduced—nobody throws complete games anymore—the scrutiny that goes into every delivery is almost beyond comprehension. Every single pitch—every last one—is charted, graphed, and dissected in a way that would make old Cy Young blow several gaskets. Imagine trying to chart *all* of Young's tosses in 1892 when he threw 453 innings! Even the strongest-fingered CPA would wince.

A Scientific Hitter

Ted Williams, for example, was called "a scientific hitter" because, among other things, he could explain the Bernoulli Principle, had an unusual grasp of the strike zone, a photographic memory of how every pitcher he ever faced worked him, an insatiable desire for knowledge to the point where Ted would pump the umpires—and anyone else he could—for updates on how Bob Feller was throwing and who had the best curveball and who was coming up he hadn't seen yet and on and on.

There are those—my son included—who believe that nowadays, there is no way the slow-footed Williams would have batted .344 for his career or managed even one .400 season. Perhaps. But when you consider the absolutely almost unmanageable amount of information available to the modern hitter, I'm not so certain Ted wouldn't have found a way to use it to his advantage, not to mention stirring developments in physical conditioning, nutrition, bat improvements, livelier baseballs, smaller parks, and, as Ted would put it, dumber pitchers.

Why do I say that? Well, it may not be a matter of hurler intelligence. Look at it this way. If you are simply taught to go as hard as you can for as long as you can—wow, a whole five innings—you're facing batters only twice and chances are you can get by with your "best stuff" until you can't. Here it is, hit it if you can. That's my strategy, hit my 97 on the black.

There's no need to pace yourself the way Christy Mathewson was famous for, only reaching back for that key strikeout at a decisive moment. Or, if you happened to be a reliever and you come in for your particular inning, what sort of strategy is necessary? There isn't much, to be honest. Just throw your killer pitch—a sweeper, a slider, a sinker—until further notice and let someone else take over.

In witnessing my son's decade-long run through professional baseball, all the way up to the majors and back, more than ever, it has become a game of specialists now.

Those with overpowering stuff like, say, Tyler Glasnow of the Los Angeles Dodgers, a 6-foot-8 giant with a blistering fastball and an off-the-table breaking ball that gets a 53 percent swing-and-miss rate, well, if he can give you five or six or maybe seven innings, that's fantastic.

Is he worrying about facing Bryce Harper for a third or fourth time when he's tired and two men are on? Nope, that's some other pitcher's problem.

Because of the emphasis on the strikeout—which, let's face it involves only two defensive players, maybe three in the event of one in the dirt—the idea of a team collecting three, four, five hits in a row—you know, we used to call them rallies—has largely gone by the boards. In its place is the home run. Solo, three-on, whatever. Just hit it out.

Look at the Phillies' Kyle Schwarber in 2023. Schwarber hit 48 singles and 47 home runs, batted leadoff, and his average was *under* .200. His 215 strikeouts? No problem. Just hit me some home runs. There used to be shame involved in striking out. No more.

When my son John was coming up in the Oakland organization, they released him at the end of spring training after a year in which he batted .285, hit eight home runs, drove in 37 runs, sharing time at first base and was given the Gold Glove for being the organization's best defensive first baseman (this with Matt Olson ahead of him in Triple-A!).

The player they kept in his place was a Big Papi lookalike who made and sold grilled cheese sandwiches on the bus; he could not run, play defense, or get a hit with runners on base. A left-handed hitter, he batted barely over .200, hit 12 home runs with a 302-foot right field fence (and an off-shore prevailing wind), 10 of them with nobody on, almost all of the homers struck in one-sided games (the team was terrible) that had no bearing on the outcome of the game. He did not advance past High-A the following year.

John's exit interview with the A's Grady Fuson went something like this, "Well . . . if you want to keep playing." You wonder if Fuson had to be thinking about that when, a few years later, the St. Louis Cardinals called John up to the major leagues and Grady's pick was long out of baseball.

So why did they keep him? The only answer could be he *might* hit a home run from time to time. The hell with the rest of the game.

Technology, as it has in many other aspects of our life, has taken over. How many people do you see on their phones at a ballgame? *There is a game going on!*

When you hear baseball people talk analytics, that is what they're talking about. They are breaking the game down to the point where you almost need an engineering degree to study the charts and graphs and percentages before you dare walk to the plate with a bat in hand. The wonderful surprises of each and every game, those "where did that come from" moments seem to be fewer and fewer. There's an element of severe calculation that, to me, just takes away from the spontaneity of the game.

For example, if you wanted to see how Justin Verlander's fastball moves through the strike zone and how different his fastball was than say Clayton Kershaw's, there are graphs of every single pitch he has ever thrown for you to check out. But studying a graph and watching a video clip aren't the same thing. Remember how Bobby Richardson talked about facing Sandy Koufax's fastball for the first time? Yeah, he read scouting reports that he had a great fastball but he had to *see* it for himself to be able to deal with it.

There are also numbers galore; percentages of how often he throws the pitch, how often it's called a strike, how much it moves through the strike zone, how it has changed over his career, how it changes in a day game vs. night, more details than you could possibly imagine.

Whereas a hitter like Frank Robinson, back in the day, would have to rush to get the morning papers to see who he was going to face that evening or afternoon, pitching rotations, in most cases, are planned so far in advance that Robinson could have found out he was facing Sandy Koufax next Tuesday. Not only that but his manager could have run the numbers: "Hey, let's see how Frank Robinson *did* against Sandy Koufax? Do we hit him third or fifth? How has he done lately against him? How has Koufax done against right-handed power hitters this month?"

Watching the game through the eyes of my son, when I compare what he's seen to how I grew up in the game, baseball has become so specialized, so technical, each individual pitch and every single at-bat scrutinized to an almost surgical degree, hell, it takes a lot of the fun out of it.

If you haven't taken a deep dive into where our game is now, please do. It's a long way past "Look for the ball, Jimmy."

BEGINNER'S LUCK

Getting back to Gosger's first at-bat against the Yankee Hall of Famer on that Fenway night, he had beginner's luck.

"I knew he was a spot pitcher, he had to spot the ball," recalled Gosger, now 80, from his home in Port Huron in 2023. "I had just come up from Toronto and when I got to Boston, Billy Herman called me into his office and said 'You're my centerfielder.'

"So I'm leading off the second, got in there against Whitey Ford, worked the count to 2–2 and he threw me a high slider that I hit into the net in left field. A home run! Geez, I'm running around the bases, looking into the dugout, in awe. I mean, this is Whitey Ford."

As noted earlier in these pages, Ford tended to struggle on the few occasions he was permitted to pitch in Fenway Park. Sure enough, Carl Yastrzemski, on his way to a three-hit game, homered in the fourth, and the Red Sox pelted him for 11 hits. But Yankee batters clubbed four Red Sox pitchers for 18 hits and 11 runs and Whitey won his 16th, 11–5. Gosger faced Ford again in the fourth and this time, things didn't work out quite as well for the Michigander. He whiffed.

That moment from Gosger's 10-year chaotic run through major-league baseball, a guy who played for seven different organizations, was part of three trades and also part of baseball's expansion draft, all of this gave the Port Huron native an across-the-board look at how the game was played, taught, and studied. And as he looks at things now, he can see how radically it has changed.

"When I played [1963–1974], and I had a chance to play in both leagues," Gosger said, "the big difference between the American League and the National League was in the National League, if you got behind in the count, 99 percent of the time you were going to get a fastball. In the American League, if you got behind in the count, you were going to get a breaking ball.

"If you think about the pitchers in the National League then—[Bob] Gibson, [Tom] Seaver, [Fergie] Jenkins, [Juan] Marichal, they were all hard throwers. If you got up against them, you knew for sure you were going to get a fastball. Even Marichal, he had that big-ass windup, you could look for a fastball off him. Same thing with Gibson. He was a very competitive individual. If you got a hit off him, he'd get upset. Ninety-nine percent of the time, he's trying to throw the fastball by you."

In his vagabond career, Gosger wound up facing 14 different Hall of Fame pitchers with a fair amount of success (35 hits in 126 at-bats, a .278 average, about 50 points higher than his career numbers). "I was a high fastball hitter," he explained. "My dad always told me 'Hit the fastball, Jimmy.' Why, he was on his deathbed, I'd been out of the game for years and he kept saying that to me, 'Hit the fastball, Jimmy.'"

Anomalies at the Plate—Those Matchups

As we've seen in earlier chapters, there are—and always will be—anomalies when it comes to pitcher-hitter matchups.

For example, facing Hall of Fame pitcher Jim Palmer of the Baltimore Orioles, Gosger batted .500 (4-for-8). Against the well-traveled Sonny Siebert, a contemporary of Gosger and Palmer, Gosger was 4-for-35 (.114) with nine strikeouts.

"I came up with Jimmy," Gosger laughed. "He was a high fastball pitcher. That's what I did. I didn't give a shit how hard you threw it. Siebert, he was a sinkerballer. I couldn't get the damn ball off the ground."

Jim Gosger vs. Jim Palmer
Regular Season: 11 PA , .500/.636/.625, 0 HR, 0 K
Playoffs: 0 PA

Jim Gosger vs. Jim Palmer: Batter vs. Pitcher

Jim Gosger vs. Jim Palmer: Year-by-Year Totals   Export Data ▾

Regular Season																			
Rk	Year	PA	AB	H	2B	3B	HR	RBI	BB	SO	BA	OBP	SLG	OPS	SH	SF	IBB	HBP	GIDP
1	1965	2	1	0	0	0	0	0	1	0	.000	.500	.000	.500	0	0	0	0	0
2	1966	8	6	4	1	0	0	1	2	0	.667	.750	.833	1.583	0	0	0	0	0
3	1969	1	1	0	0	0	0	0	0	0	.000	.000	.000	.000	0	0	0	0	0
	Totals	11	8	4	1	0	0	1	3	0	.500	.636	.625	1.261	0	0	0	0	0

Few National League hurlers threw harder than Houston's Don Wilson. But Gosger, a lifetime .226 hitter, swatted Wilson's fiery offerings to the tune of .462 with a double and home run.

"The first time I ever faced him," Gosger recalls, "I had just got traded from Triple-A Norfolk and [someone told him Montreal Expos manager] Gene Mauch wants you in Houston. So I get to Houston, I get in a cab and tell him I've got to go to the ballpark. He says it's a forty-minute ride so I get there and it's about the sixth inning. I get into the clubhouse and change and a coach comes in and tells me 'Get ready, Mauch might need you.'

"Wilson's pitching, out there throwing aspirins. Mauch sends me up to hit. I'm so tired I can't even be nervous and I hit one off the facing of the right field fence, almost for a home run. I'm standing there on second base shaking, I'm so tired. And Mauch tells me you're going to be playing for a few days."

But again, a hard thrower. For Gosger, facing a fireballer generally meant success. Not so against perhaps the hardest thrower he ever faced, Nolan Ryan.

"Only faced Ryan once," he said. "I hadn't played in a few days and we get to about the sixth inning and Mauch says 'Get a bat.' So I said 'Who do you want me to give it to?' I didn't want to go up there against Nolan. And Ryan would show off, you know. He'd throw one up on the screen.

"So I got up there and got in the box and I said to the catcher 'Please don't hit me in the head.'" He didn't but Gosger went back to the dugout, one of Ryan's 5,714 strikeout victims.

One of his later stops was with the San Francisco Giants. When a contract for $17,000 arrived in the mail, Gosger took pen in hand.

"I was traded from the Mets to San Francisco and this contract comes in the mail for $17,000," he said. "I'd been around for a while so I said 'I'm not signing this' and I sat down and wrote a letter to the Giants. 'Dear Mr. Stoneham: I have recently purchased a new Labrador Retriever and he's hungry. So I am returning the contract and would like to sign one for $20,000 and one dollar. The $20,000 is for me and the dollar is so I can feed my dog.' And a few days later, I got a call from Horace

Stoneham, the Giants' owner. He said 'Jim, that was the funniest letter I ever got. You'll be getting a contract for $20,001 and I want to make sure that dog gets that dollar.' He was the nicest man."

Gosger admits it would have been interesting to have all the advantages of modern technology, the breakdowns of what pitches are coming, the modern training methods, the smaller parks, the big money. At the same time, he's so very grateful to have had the opportunities he did *when* he did.

"Being the last guy to face Satchel Paige, what an honor," he said. "We didn't even know he was going to pitch. We got the ballpark and there he is, sitting in right field in a rocking chair. And I led off against him [popout] and made the last out [groundout] and he was throwing damn good. It had to be 85 mph-to 88 mph at that age [59] and nothing was above the belt. Everything was hard and low. I can't imagine what it would have been like to face him when he was young.

"I remember the good stuff," he continued, looking back. "Like the night I hit two home runs off Denny McLain. I run into him every once in a while and we talk about it. He threw right over the top, you know, and everything was straight. Fastballs. It was at Tiger Stadium my second year (1966) and I come up in the third inning. I was strictly looking fastball and I got one. I knew it when it left the bat.

"I come up again in the eighth inning and, you know, the game is tied, 3–3. And he's looking in at me, I know he's going to throw me another fastball, can't believe I got one. He threw it, I got it and it went out. I'm running around the bases and he's giving me the eye. I told him 'I hit the same damn pitch. You know you're not going to throw it by me.'"

That home run, the only time Gosger ever got two in one game, put his Red Sox ahead, 4–3. But an Al Kaline blast in the bottom of the inning tied it and Detroit eventually won the game in extra innings. But it was a night Gosger—and McLain—won't forget.

Like many an old-timer, Gosger is concerned about the future of the game that was such an important part of his life.

"Detroit has some good players coming up," he said, "but you know, it's hit a home run or strike out. That's not the way you play the game.

You need to score runs to win. Not just sit back and wait for one guy to hit a homer because he's swinging from his ass.

"The two best players I ever saw were Roberto Clemente, what an athlete, and Al Kaline. That was a guy I modeled myself after. I watched him all the time and said, you know, I want to play like him."

On the day we chatted, Gosger said he had been in an especially reflective mood.

"I was just sitting out on my porch this morning," he said, wistfully, "thinking about all the hours I spent playing catch with my dad out there on that front lawn. Hours and hours. I was out there for a while, said three rosaries for my mom, dad and my sister. And you know, I hope they're proud of me."

Jim Gosger's career:
Facing Hall of Famers

Don Sutton .273 (3-for-11)

Tom Seaver .300 (3- for-10)

Jim Palmer .500 (4-for-8)

Fergie Jenkins .333 (3-for-9)

Catfish Hunter .429 (3-for-7)

Gaylord Perry .167 (1-for-6)

Jim Bunning .000 (0-for-5)

Whitey Ford .500 (1-for-2), 1 HR

Satchel Paige .000 (0-for-2)

Nolan Ryan .000 (0-for-1), 1 K

Phil Niekro .368 (7-for-19), 1 HR

Juan Marichal .188 (3-for-16)

Hoyt Wilhelm .188 (3-for-16)

Bob Gibson .286 (4-for-14)

TOTALS: .278 (35 for 126)

Other Notable Pitchers

Mel Stottlemyre .350 (14–40), 1 2B, 3 3B, 1 HR, 4 RBIs

Sonny Siebert .114 (4-for-35), 9 Ks

Jim Palmer .500 (4-for-8), 1 2B

Denny McLain .179 (5-for-28), 2 HR, 5 RBIs, 10 BB, 9 K

Fred Talbot .300 (6-for-20), 2 2B, 1 HR

Jim Perry .350 (7-for-20), 1 HR

Luis Tiant .278 (5-for-18), 2 2B, 8 K

Sam McDowell .278 (5-for-18)

Gary Bell .176 (3-for-17), 4 K

Rollie Sheldon .471 (8-for-17), 1 HR

Wally Bunker .500 (6-for-12), 1 HR

Jim Bouton .167 (2-for-12), 1 HR

Don Wilson .462 (6-for-13), 1 3B, 1 HR, 4 RBIs

Afterword: On Writing *Diamond Duels*

Though a reader might think otherwise after reading the entirety of *Diamond Duels*, I'm not really a numbers person. Somehow, baseball numbers, reading box scores, interpreting them, is something else again. At least it is to me.

Maybe it's the romantic in me, but finding that box score moment where the great Honus Wagner connected for a home run—his only home run that year—against the great Christy Mathewson was thrilling. Or finding out that the first time Lefty Grove faced both Babe Ruth and Lou Gehrig was in a 15-inning thriller on July 4 at Yankee Stadium. Or that Harry Heilmann won two—count 'em—*two*—American League batting crowns in the Ty Cobb era on the final day of the season with a six- and then a seven-hit doubleheader performance to snag the batting crowns. Or that Dizzy Dean *did* get to pitch to Babe Ruth. Or that Mel Ott's first home run—at 18 years old—was an inside-the-park shot at the Polo Grounds. And on and on.

Or to begin at the beginning, finding out, thanks to Stathead, that Warren Spahn and Stan Musial actually faced one another 356 times, almost the equivalent of an entire major-league season! Talk about getting to know your opponent.

Hey, I hope reading *Diamond Duels* is as much fun as it was for me to write it. Baseball grabbed me for the first time in seventh grade when I happened to hit a game-winning home run in Mr. Bilodeau's gym class, winning the instant approval of the rest of the class and setting me on a path to learn the game. And I did. Whether it was reading every single sports book in our Fairgrounds Junior High Library or taking a *Sports Illustrated* Teaching Baseball book out to a mound, teaching myself how to throw a curveball, or playing Strat-O-Matic baseball on those wintry New Hampshire nights, or staying up all Christmas Eve reading *Ball Four*, or getting a win throwing one pitch in a high school game (I came in, two out, got a guy to pop up and we scored a bunch of runs to win) or convincing my college journalism teacher—a nun—to let me sit in the lounge of the women's dorm of Rivier College to watch all of Game 6 of the 1975 World Series, including Carlton Fisk's walkoff!, baseball has always seemed a mystical, magical element in my life.

Then to have a son who also took to the game and loved it, who won himself back-to-back Dizzy Dean World Series MVP awards and two titles, set the Cooperstown Dreams Park record, winning two titles there, too, then started as a freshman as a hometown Florida State Seminole, going on to get a hit in the College World Series, going on into professional baseball, climbing all the way to the majors with the St. Louis Cardinals and Pittsburgh Pirates, having his kisser on a banner outside PNC Park, hey, it's not wrong to say we've lived the sport in our house.

So I must offer a special thank you to my wife, Liz, who has become quite the baseball expert over the years and my hard-hitting first baseman son, John Jr., who has given both of us and so many of his and our friends the thrill of a lifetime.

I'd also like to thank the wonderful editor who helped me on both versions of *Last Time Out*, the great Rick Rinehart, and my own crackerjack editor Ken Samelson, who bubbled with just about as much enthusiasm as me on some of our discoveries. Not only was I blessed with a first-class editor, I gained a lifelong friend—even if my son did terrorize his Mets a few years back!

In writing *Diamond Duels*, reliving some of the game's more glorious, historic moments and discovering so many others, you wonder how the game will play into the future. There was a mixed and lively crowd at the Baseball Hall of Fame on a rainy Friday in late August in 2023, neither the Red Sox nor Yankees nor Mets anywhere near close to playoff contention.

Ratings are up, they say; attendance in 2023 was up 9 percent and the two franchises that broke the bank trying to buy themselves a pennant—the Mets and Padres—turned out to be disasters. The mystery of winning, enduring a long, challenging season that runs from spring

to summer to fall, has still not been solved by the financial wizards and slide-rule whiz kids.

True, the characters who used to populate the game seem to have been replaced in large part by temperamental millionaires, many of whom love to watch the majesty of their home runs, instead of modestly running them out, analysts who dissect every pitch and call and replay, enough to take the life out of it, and yak and yak instead of staying in the moment, in the game.

And it seems like the old hunch, like the one Philadelphia A's manager Connie Mack had way back when, deciding to throw long-forgotten Howard Ehmke against the Chicago Cubs in Game 1 of the 1929 World Series, that's probably long gone, too.

Would Red Sox manager Darrell Johnson once again send up Bernie Carbo against Cincinnati's Rawly Eastwick in the eighth inning of Game 6 of the 1975 World Series, not having any idea if the two had ever faced one another, since there was no interleague play then? You wonder. Wouldn't it be great if, once in a while, a manager said "I just had a feeling."

Baseball's unpredictability, a rag-tag bunch of Red Sox like the 2013 club, a bunch of misfits who somehow molded themselves into a world championship team, little known players like Gene Tenace or Stevie Pearce winning World Series MVPs, is its calling card, if you ask me. It's almost as if the endless season—162 games—grinds us down and sets us up for some sort of surprise every October. Or is it November, now?

My hope is that the stories—yes, and the numbers—you'll find in *Diamond Duels* take you where they took me—back to the game of our lives. Baseball.

ACKNOWLEDGMENTS

Writing *Diamond Duels* has been a tremendous amount of fun. The more I wandered through the box scores, the more I wanted to, the more things I turned up. As a pretty serious baseball fan for years and a baseball dad for more than 25 years, there is still so much to learn about the game, stories that were never told or remembered.

Since almost all of the players I've written about have passed on, I had to rely on lots of other source material to assemble these chapters. To do that involved lots and lots of reading, ranging from the *New York Times* archive and the wonderful Arthur Daley to Fay Vincent's trilogy of books about the bygone days of the game to Jane Leavy's book on Sandy Koufax to Roger Angell's masterworks and so many other writers, too many to name them all. All of them documented things in the grand old game and thank goodness they did. YouTube was also a help for videos of Lefty Grove, that great piece on *The Glory of Their Times*, and so many other items were also a help and an inspiration.

The whole project would never have happened without the amazing site Stathead, off of Baseball-Reference.com and their intrepid rep Katie Sharp. If there's such a thing as a font of information, Stathead is a sea.

I truly hope that real baseball fans out there will enjoy *Diamond Duels*, maybe take a turn through Stathead themselves, and perhaps share some of these stories with young people who have otherwise spent idle entertainment hours playing video games or watching less intellectually diverting events like NFL football or get-out-of-my-way-so-I-can-dunk NBA basketball.

Baseball has always honored its past, and I hope the stories here in one way or another add to that glorious history. If I didn't get to write about your favorite team or player, as us Red Sox fans used to say—and may have to again—there's always next year.